MUSIC TO MY EARS

By

Deems Taylor

SIMON AND SCHUSTER

New York · 1949

PUBLISHED BY SIMON AND SCHUSTER, INC.
ROCKEFELLER CENTER, 1230 SIXTH AVENUE
NEW YORK 20, N. Y.

MANUFACTURED IN THE UNITED STATES OF AMERICA
BY AMERICAN BOOK–STRATFORD PRESS, INC., NEW YORK

Table of Contents

PART ONE: PROLOGUE

PART TWO: FIRST THEME

CONTENTS

PART FOUR: DEVELOPMENT SECTION

PART FIVE: RECAPITULATION

PART SIX: CODA

Introduction

LIKE *its predecessors,* Of Men and Music *and* The Well-Tempered Listener, *this book is based upon a series of radio talks that I delivered, over the years, as part of the Columbia Broadcasting System's broadcasts of the Sunday afternoon concerts of the New York Philharmonic-Symphony Orchestra.*

I say "based," because English, to a greater extent than any other language I know anything about, is really two languages: a spoken and a written one. The ancient theatrical adage, "If a play reads too well, it won't play well," applies in reverse to radio. A radio script that is effective when it is spoken doesn't necessarily read well. Consequently, the amount of revision and rewriting that has gone into turning these talks into reading matter entitles the result to be called, for better or worse, a book.

It is divided into six sections, roughly equivalent to the so-called sonata form in which the opening movements of most symphonies are cast. The opening section, "Prologue," is devoted to taking a composer apart to see what makes him tick. A purist might object that it should be called "Introduction"—and quite right, too. But the difference is only one of nomenclature. One introduction is enough. The "First Theme" is devoted largely to discussions of music, especially symphonic music, and the people who make it and listen to it. The "Second Theme" deals exclusively with people—people who created music, played it, conducted it, and wrote about it. The

"Development Section" takes the two themes apart and re-groups them, being devoted to the composer and his problems, music and its troubles, and the opinions of people who listen to it. The "Recapitulation" is concerned with the hand-to-hand struggle that is going on, these days, between music and the composer. The "Coda," in another key, brings everything to a conclusion. If, at times, the analogy shows signs of falling heavily upon its face, be charitable. Pretend that you didn't notice.

DEEMS TAYLOR

New York,
January, 1949

PART ONE

Prologue

I

. . . *Fine Frenzy Rolling*

Of all creative artists, composers seem to be the least understood. Their mental processes and methods of work are apparently a mystery not only to the public at large but even to fellow artists, such as painters and writers. The average imaginative painting of a composer such as Beethoven or Wagner or Chopin generally shows him being kissed delicately on the brow by a highly photogenic girl labeled "Inspiration," and surrounded by a cloud of pictures of moonlit landscapes and volcanoes and swimming female figures, either rising into a cloud of smoke or falling out of one, or various other images that, however alluring, seem more calculated to interfere with his work than to help it. Of the novels concerning composers, only one that I have ever read, Margaret Kennedy's *The Constant Nymph,* showed any particular awareness, on the part of the author, that the hero had any connection with the human race.

The playwrights are the worst offenders. I remember one play whose principal character, a composer, worked on a symphony throughout three whole acts, during which he kept his unfinished manuscript on a table in the middle of a room that was apparently the gathering place of the entire neighborhood. Every five minutes he would interrupt an animated conversation to press his hands to his forehead, rise, go to the table, and write down four notes. I forget exactly what happened at the end; as I remember, the symphony was a success and he died—of surprise, I imagine.

I had a letter on this subject from a teacher in the music department of the Pennsylvania State College, who wrote: "As a teacher of the more technical phases of music, I come upon an attitude of mind on the part of the students that is at times very disheartening. I find my students on the whole extremely reluctant to accept the fact that here and there the composer has done something in his composition which must have been very consciously achieved at the time. In my form and analysis class, where the structural features of music concern us so much, students constantly come back at me with the remark, 'Do you mean to tell us that the composer actually *thought* about that when he did it?' I take pleasure in insisting that the composer's job requires the use of considerable gray matter and that he deserves credit for doing so, but my students won't follow me. They pay excellent lip service to the contention that music, to be really enjoyed, should be followed both emotionally *and* intellectually, but they refuse to believe that this axiom operates in the creative processes."

This fight between technique and inspiration is a very old one, and has been going on in all the arts ever since there were any. In the field of music particularly, there seems to be a great deal of confusion as to how the artist goes to work. The listener hears the finished product—a symphony, a concerto, an opera, what not—and if it's a good one he is moved by it, is carried away emotionally. So he immediately assumes that the composer was equally carried away—sat down and dashed the whole thing off in a white heat of inspiration. According to this romantic conception, the composer's brain and will power have very little to do with his work. He is suddenly overtaken by inspiration, hears angelic voices dictating themes and development and orchestration, then goes to his desk and takes it all down, like a sort of aesthetic stenographer.

If you think it over, I believe you will realize that this ouija-board theory of composition won't hold water. Naturally, no composer can think up a theme by the pure exercise of his mind. In a sense, every composer is inspired, in that his themes, even his bad ones, come into his mind through no exercise of his own will. But once he has captured his themes and written them down, what he achieves with them is a matter partly of instinct and largely of hard intellectual and physical labor. To understand how he goes to work, suppose we take the analogy of an architect who dreams of building a great cathedral. He sees it, in his mind's eye, complete, towering above the houses that surround it, the setting sun gilding its towers and pinnacles, and great streams of worshipers entering its portals. But then to make that dream, that inspiration, a reality, he must sit down and draw plans and figure proportions and areas; he, or his engineers, must cover pages with calculations of stresses and strains, and cover other pages with estimates of building costs; and his draughtsmen must prepare hundreds of blueprints of plans and elevations and full-size detailed drawings. While his first inspiration may dominate all these activities, its actual working out must be done in cold blood.

A composer works like that, too. He may be fired by the ideas for a great symphony. In a vague way his inner ear may hear the thing complete. But there's nothing vague about the hard work he has to put in, in order to get that symphony down on paper. I sometimes think that music, which is the most intangible of all the arts, is also the most laborious. A while ago, just out of curiosity, I counted the number of notes on the last page of the score of Mozart's *Jupiter* symphony. There are 284 of them—and Mozart's orchestration, as you know, is extremely light. A single page of the "battle" section of Richard Strauss's *Ein Heldenleben*—page 60 of the miniature score, if you're curious—contains 714 separate notes. And that is a score of 139 pages. Now, every note on every one of those 139 pages had to be calculated, in its relation to the other notes, and in relation to the tone quality, range, and technique of the instrument that was to play it. Then every one of those notes had to be set down, by hand, and placed accurately on a given line or space. Try copying—not originating, just copying—one page of a full orchestral score sometime, if you want to understand why composers can't afford to spend all of their time in a frenzy of inspiration.

On the other hand, of course, knowing the rules doesn't make a composer. When we speak of someone's writing a first movement of a symphony in strict sonata form, we sound as if we were describing an extremely arbitrary and mechanical process. But what even the teachers forget sometimes is that the forms and the so-called rules of music—of any art, for that matter—were not invented by any one person. They are the result of a process of evolution; they are the thing that, up to now, has worked best. A long line of composers, given two musical themes, has instinctively tended to state them and contrast them and develop their emotional possibilities along certain common lines. And the sum of all these instinctive gropings for logic and balance and effectiveness is what we call sonata form.

When our architect is dreaming of his cathedral, he knows that it will have a nave, a transept, and an apse. In other words, he conforms to a predetermined ground plan. He doesn't find this a handicap. On the contrary, relieved of the necessity of worrying about his fundamental plan, he is all the more free to let his imagination deal with his elevation. And so the composer who writes a piece of music in one of the traditional forms starts out with the knowledge that his ideas, developed within that frame, will reach their most effective expression. Once in a while he may find that the frame doesn't fit. And so, almost unconsciously, he alters it. If the change is a good one, it will tend to become a permanent contribution to the technique of his art, and succeeding generations of composers will find a new rule in the book.

Backstage

SUPPOSE we take an actual example of how a composer goes to work. If the composer whom I cite, with apologies, is myself, it is only because he is the only one with whose mental processes I am completely familiar.

Let us, then, assume that you have decided to write an opera based on a Basque story.* You've read the novel by Pierre Loti, you've read all the books you can find in the public library about the Basques, you have your libretto more or less in shape, and you have sketches for several themes that you think might do. In short, you're ready to go to work. Whereupon, being faced with the age-old crisis that has darkened the lives of so many composers—that is, the necessity of sitting down and actually *going* to work—you decide that in justice to yourself you ought to see the Basques at first hand. So you go to France, catch the blue train from Paris, and eventually reach Saint-Jean-de-Luz, the southwestern port of the Basque country.

It happens that you arrive in Saint-Jean-de-Luz on a Sunday, and that evening your friends take you to the fiesta that is held in the Place Louis XIV every Sunday night. Most of the boys and girls of the town are there, together with their families, strolling about, buying things at the stalls, throwing confetti at one another, and dancing the fandango to the music of a three-piece orchestra consisting of a violin, a clari-

* *Ramuntcho*—produced, without much success, by the Philadelphia Opera Company, February 10, 1942. I still like it.

net, and a drum. The climax of the evening is reached by the arrival of the *toro del fuego*, an artificial bull worked by two of the boys, who chases the dancers, spouting fire from the sparklers and Roman candles that are stuck in his hide.

It suddenly strikes you that the fiesta offers you a wonderful chance for a ballet to open the third act, and what's more, a ballet that, for once, isn't dragged in, that is a perfectly legitimate part of the scene. So you start mapping it out. It should begin, of course, with a fandango, which is the most popular of all dances among the Basques. Then there should be something to follow that contrasts with it, a slow dance of some sort. After that, something very light and lively, not in fandango rhythm, and then a finale of some sort. You begin hunting for authentic Basque tunes. You can't find a fandango that appeals to you, but you do find, in a local bookstore, a little paper-covered edition of Basque folksongs that does contain a lovely slow tune. The words begin, *"Lili bat ikhusi, dut baratze bate an,"* which is impressive but hardly illuminating, inasmuch as your acquaintance with the Basque language is limited to the knowledge that *etche* means "house," *bestitu* means "dressed," and *cetas* means "silk." But from the nature of the tune it must be a love song, so you decide to have it not only danced but sung, to words that you will provide later. You determine to begin serious work and do so for an entire morning, only to discover that the climate of Saint-Jean-de-Luz is not suitable for composition. So you spend a few days acquiring local color and inspiration on the beach, at the pelota games, and on the terrace of the Bar Basque, and then sail for home.

Once settled down in New York, with radio scripts to write and committee meetings to attend and a thousand people to see and the telephone ringing every twelve minutes, you really do get down to serious work. You have the material for your slow dance, and among your sketches you find a scrap of a theme that you scribbled down several months ago. At the time you didn't know just what to do with it, but you see now that, properly developed, it will do very well for the lively dance. In fact, you begin working *that* out right away. It goes quite easily, and in a few days you have it roughed out up to the point where it is to lead into your as yet undecided finale. But still you have no idea for the fandango that is to be the principal number of the ballet.

After wasting a couple of days thinking up themes and trying them over on the piano, with no result beyond a faint touch of seasickness, you abandon the fandango temporarily and start working out the slow dance. This doesn't take long because the tune is a pretty straightforward one and doesn't call for anything resembling symphonic development. So, beyond changing the time signature from waltz time to four-four time, harmonizing it, and roughing in the voice parts, you leave it much as it was.

Now you're stuck. You have all the elements of your ballet except the most important one, that confounded fandango. So you put the whole thing away for a week or so, hoping that your unconscious mind will keep on working, meanwhile, until it presents you with a perfect fandango theme. At the end of ten days you resume work, only to discover that your unconscious has been doing nothing of the sort. It, too, has taken the week off, and you're just where you were when you quit. However, you do manage to keep going. At one time you were vaguely considering the idea of having one of the dances in five-eight time, which is a rather common Basque rhythm, but you abandoned that, because five-eight time is difficult enough for an orchestra to play, without complicating matters by trying to get a troupe of dancers to keep time to it. But you are going to need some music not only to raise the curtain but to run through the first minute or two of the fiesta scene, before the ballet proper begins, so you decide to enhance the

Basque atmosphere by writing *that* in five-eight time. You don't have to wait for the fandango, because although you have no notion of what the theme will be, you do know that it will be in a fast three-eight time. So there's no reason why you shouldn't write your introductory music up to the last eight bars or so, filling those in later when you know what key your fandango is going to be in. So you do write it, finishing your rough draft in three or four days.

Now you really must face that fandango—or, at least, that's what *you* think. But your unconscious, you discover, has other plans. In a sudden burst of co-operation it says to you, in effect, "Look. Wouldn't it make an effective finale if, instead of going into something new, you wound up the ballet by playing both the slow dance and the fandango simultaneously?" You reject this suggestion with considerable violence. In the first place, you demand to know how under the sun anybody who isn't Mozart can ask musicians to play a four-four tune and a three-eight tune at the same time. In the second place, it would be a lot of work.

But the still, small voice insists on arguing the point, and you finally admit, grudgingly, that there might be something in the idea. All you need now is the theme for the fandango, please. At this point your unconscious, exhausted by its attempts to be helpful, washes its hands of the whole business and goes to sleep, leaving you on your own. So you tackle the problem. You decide that if you write the slow dance in a slow two-four time, and with it write the fandango in a fast three-eight time, so that one bar of the fandango equals one beat of the slow tune, the thing can be done. This may sound rather difficult to a layman; to a musician it sounds *very* difficult. And it is, particularly since you haven't the foggiest notion as to what your fandango theme is to be.

Finally you hit on the solution, which, like all solutions, is a basically simple one. You will lay out the slow dance, with its fundamental harmony, and then you will write the fandango as a counterpoint to it—in other words, as a countermelody. Then you will take the two themes apart and play them separately. Then, in the finale, you will triumphantly put them together, to the delighted amazement of the audience, who—you hope—will assume that the juxtaposition of the two themes is a miraculous coincidence.

So, at long last, you write your fandango. It isn't easy, because there's one catch to writing it as a countermelody. When it's played by itself, it mustn't *sound* like a countermelody. It must have a line—personality, so to speak—of its own. This takes a lot of writing and figuring and rewriting and bad language and discouragement, but at length you do evolve something that sounds satisfactory—at least, to you. The back of your work is broken.

But you're not through yet. You must put your ballet together. So you start your second draft. Your introduction starts off in D major and shows signs of ending in F-sharp minor, while your fandango begins in B minor. So you must write a connecting-link passage that *sounds* like the end of the introduction and still prepares the way for the fandango without making the change of key and time signature too obvious. (Does this bore you? It bored me.) Then you write down the fandango in its independent form, treating it rather freely, expanding it here and there, going into different keys in order to put it within the range of different groups of instruments, and still trying to keep its main outlines clear enough for its re-entrance, in the finale, to be unmistakable. Since you decided to have your slow dance sung as well as played, you find that you'll have to write it in F minor instead of E-flat minor, in order to make it vocally effective. Then you have to go back and write a transition passage to lead from the fandango to your slow dance, both to get the listeners in the mood for the slow tempo and to give the dancers a chance to get their breath. The fast dance that follows doesn't offer any particular problem, except that you have a feeling that it may be a little too long.

But you don't have to settle that now. It can be pruned at rehearsal. The finale goes rather easily, because you had already worked it out pretty completely. You put both tunes in the key of E minor, so that the chorus can sing the slow tune in unison; otherwise, you have little to do. In structure and outline, your ballet is finished. You look at the scrawled and smudged and scratched-out sheets, and say to yourself, "Well. There it is it. I wonder if it's any good."

Guaranteed Handmade

NOW THAT you have sketched the ballet we discussed in the last chapter, what happens then? That question has been asked by a great many people, generally in about these terms: When a composer, they ask, sets out to write a piece of music, does he actually write it out for the orchestra itself, or does he write a piano part and have someone else make the orchestral arrangement? Did a composer like Wagner, for example, actually write out all the notes of every instrumental part in his operas?

I suppose the confusion of thought arises from the fact that in the field of popular music, precisely that does happen—that composers do just write a piano version of their songs and turn the actual job of orchestration over to someone else. As a matter of fact, I doubt whether more than half a dozen of our composers of songs and musical-comedy scores would be able to make their own orchestrations even if they wanted to. Many of them, I know, can't even write a piano part. They write the melody out for the arranger, or even just hum it to him, and let it go at that. In radio circles, of course, orchestration is practically a separate art. Every name band and orchestra of any pretensions has its own repertory of special arrangements of the popular songs. Some of them, I am pained to state, have their own special arrangements of serious music as well. Some of the popular arrangements really deserve the adjective "brilliant," so successful are the arrangers in making silk purses out of the traditional material.

Now, there's no harm in this procedure, because the writing of popular songs is largely an industry rather than an art. The average popular song is designed for entertainment alone, is manufactured as a seasonal and highly perishable product, and makes no pretensions to being a work of art. Aesthetic considerations enter into its manufacture very little more than they enter into the making of a radio set. But when you get into the other field of music, when you ask of a composer of serious music, "Does he do his own orchestration?," you might as well ask of a painter, "Does he draw the outlines of his picture and have someone else fill in the colors?"

You can't separate the orchestration and the music in a work of symphonic pretensions. No two composers work exactly alike, but I'm positive that every composer who sits down to write a serious work has a more or less definite conception of the quality of the sound of his music as he composes it—in other words, imagines not only the themes but their instrumental coloring. He thinks instrumentally and vocally. If he's writing a violin concerto, for instance, he conceives his music in terms of the violin, and for that reason it is going to differ in many ways from the music that he would write for a piano concerto. If he's writing for a string quartet, he isn't going to write the same music that he would write for a full orchestra.

As a matter of fact, it's sometimes a handicap for a composer to be too good a pianist. Grieg and Schumann were both piano virtuosos, and their orchestral works occasionally contain passages that don't "sound," that don't come off, because when they wrote them they were obviously thinking too much in terms of the piano. Any artist who works through interpreters, like the composer, the architect, or the playwright, has to think not only of what is on the paper before him but what his work is going to sound or look like when it comes *off* the paper. The composer must think, as I say, of the sound of the instruments, and dictate those sounds; the architect has to think of the materials of which his building is going to be made, and so specify them; the playwright must think of the differences in gesture and pose, the tricks of speech, that make his characters come alive. If any one of these three delegates any part of his work to somebody else, the finished product is going to lack the very thing that is assumed to make it a work of art—that is, the artistic personality of the man who supposedly created it.

However, that still doesn't definitely answer that question: Assuming that you have made a rough draft of your piece, what do you do next? What you will probably do is start writing a second draft, an orchestral sketch. Some composers skip this intermediate step, but most of them do not; for, while it takes time *at* the time, it's a great timesaver when the work reaches its final stages.

Your orchestral sketch is exactly what its name implies: a sort of compressed version of the orchestral score, written on two, three, or four staves, depending on how complex the scoring is likely to be at any given point. In this sketch you work out the progression of the various orchestral voices, even though you may not yet have decided just what instruments are to play them. At some points, of course, where you have definite ideas as to what the instrumentation is to be, you *do* indicate instruments or groups of instruments. If there is an important harp part, you'll probably work that out as you go along, so as to get it out of the way. Most composers loathe writing harp parts, because they mean writing out so many notes. Not only that, but as the harp isn't chromatic, the player has to sharp or flat the notes by pressing down on a series of pedals. Not being a centipede, he can't change more than two notes at a time, so that his part, if it's to be playable, entails a lot of advance figuring and simplifying, in order to give him time to make important changes in key. But let's not get ahead of our story.

Your sketch done, you're ready for the actual work of scoring. The first thing you'll do, if you're wise, is to go over your piece very carefully and see what instruments you can eliminate, particularly the less common instruments. Must you have *two* harps? Are there passages that absolutely *must* be played by a bass clarinet? Can you possibly do without a contrabassoon? Do you have to have two oboes *and* an English horn, or can the second oboe also play the English-horn solos? Do you need three trumpets, or can you get along with two? And how about that fourth trombone you've been dreaming about?

Now, there are two reasons for this process of elimination. One is purely aesthetic. One of the commonest faults of inexperienced composers is over-orchestration. The best-sounding scores are generally those that are the most economical, that call for the smallest possible combination of instruments that will properly convey the music. This minimum number of players may go as high as ninety or a hundred, as in the case of a work like Strauss's *Ein Heldenleben.* On the other hand, many a score that calls for ninety players would sound as well, or better, if it called for seventy. One of the most exquisitely scored works in the orchestral repertoire, Debussy's *The Afternoon of a Faun,* can be performed satisfactorily by an orchestra of sixty players. But, as I said, the tendency of the young composer is to call for an orchestra about the size of a state legislature, and then fill his score with heavily orchestrated passages that are the result less of artistic necessity than of a desire to give the boys something to do. That is why I think that the best way for a beginner to begin the study of orchestration is to study string quartets. When he sees what a man like Beethoven or Brahms or Debussy can do with four string players, he can begin to realize what any military man can tell you: that sheer numbers don't necessarily win battles.

There's another reason why your orchestration should be as economical as possible. It's a purely practical one. Naturally, the aim of any composer is to have his music played as widely as possible, and the merits of his music are not the only factors that contribute to getting him performances. There is also the simple economic fact that communities capable of maintaining orchestras of ninety and a hundred men are very few in number. It is the average, sixty-man orchestra that is the most promising outlet for any comparatively unknown composer, because it has less at stake, both artistically and financially. It can afford to experiment a bit. The composer who turns out a score so massive that it can be played only by the New York Philharmonic-Symphony, or the equivalent in size, is, whether consciously or not, definitely limiting the demand for his work.

I remember—it must have been twenty years ago—being on the jury of an important contest for orchestral works by American composers. One of the prize winners, a symphonic poem lasting about ten minutes, was an exceptionally grateful and interesting work, one that would be likely to appeal to an average audience even more than those that we placed ahead of it in sheer merit. And I thought to myself, "Now, here's a piece that's going to be played all over the country." Then I took a second look at the score, and knew that it was *not* going to be played all over the country. Among other things, the composer called for eight horns. Now, horn players don't grow on trees. Any orchestra that has four good ones can count itself lucky. Even the Philharmonic-Symphony, big as it is, has a regular horn section of only five. Also, he called for a bass flute, an instrument so rare that it's almost a curiosity. Yet here was a composer asking the average orchestra to go out and hire—probably import—four extra horn players and an instrument that is practically a museum piece, all to play a work that lasted ten minutes, that would be new to the audience, and wouldn't draw five cents at the box office. Is it any wonder that the average conductor, faced with such a score, throws up his hands and says, "Oh, let's put on the overture to *William Tell*"? I doubt whether that particular piece, good as it is, has had twenty performances in the past twenty years.

"But," our young composer may argue, "look at men like Strauss and Stravinsky. Most of their most popular works are written for an enormous orchestra. But they get plenty of performances. Why should *I* be handicapped?" There are two answers to that, of course. One is that you're not Strauss and Stravinsky. Even if your new symphony is better than anything either of them ever wrote, the fact remains that they are box-office attractions and you aren't. The second is that the composers, even the famous ones, who call for gigantic orchestral forces don't get nearly as many performances as you might think. The fact that they are played by our major symphony orchestras gets a lot of space in the newspapers; but the fact that they're very seldom played, if at all, by a vast number of our minor symphony orchestras who can't afford to hire extra players gets no space at all. But there, just the same, is the fact.

Now the Grease Paint

YOU HAVE now composed your ballet, made the orchestral sketch, and determined the smallest possible instrumental combination that will do your work justice. Where do you go from there?

Good instrumentation is mainly a matter, first, of what the composer hears in his mental ear, and, second, of how much of it he gets down on paper. And the "what" and "how much" are purely a matter of how his mind and imagination work. The question people ask most frequently about orchestration is, in substance: Does a composer hear the orchestration of his work as he writes his sketch, or does he make his sketch and then orchestrate it? Well, while in degree that's up to the individual composer, I should say that no composer does either of those things exclusively. Any composer does think in terms of his medium. To take a very simple instance, if he's writing a piano piece, he will instinctively avoid passages containing sustained notes that are held over three or four measures, for the simple reason that the piano can't sustain notes that long. On the other hand, if he's writing a piece for orchestra, he won't write elaborate, unsupported arpeggio passages in the bass—such as you find in many of Chopin's nocturnes—simply because they sound thin and ineffective when played by stringed or wind instruments.

In other words, he does compose in orchestral terms, even when he hasn't consciously worked out the actual orchestration. Any composer undoubtedly does *hear* the orchestra when he's composing. But what he hears in his mind is likely to be pretty vague. He'll come to a given passage and hear it in terms of brass instruments. Another he hears in terms of strings, and still another in terms of woodwinds. Certain solo passages may strike him as needing to be played by certain definite instruments. Others, on the other hand, he may write down as pure music, leaving the "casting," so to speak, for a later decision. To maintain, as I have heard composers insist, that they hear the actual orchestration, from start to finish, as they sketch a piece is to maintain something that I don't believe. In the first place, there are countless practical problems to be solved before a work is effectively orchestrated, and I don't believe that any human mind has the imaginative power and intuitive practical mastery to solve all those problems on the wing, except in the case of an extremely short and simple piece.

People will tell you that a composer hears the precise instrument that is to play a given theme while he is conceiving it. I agree that he may very well hear the instrument that *announces* the theme, but what about subsequent repetitions? Is that theme always to be played by the same instrument, and if it is, isn't it going to become monotonous? There again, it's a matter of the individual composer and the specific theme. Listen to the passage for solo bassoon that opens Stravinsky's *The Rite of Spring*, and you will hear something that was, without a shadow of a doubt, conceived in terms of that instrument. The hollow, despairing quality of a bassoon playing in its extreme upper register fits that theme like a glove. It wouldn't sound the same played on any other instrument, and as I recall, Stravinsky doesn't assign it, in its original form, to any instrument *except* the bassoon. On the other hand, listen to the section called "Mystic Circles of the Adolescents" that begins about four minutes after the introduction to the second part of the suite. As first heard, the main theme is played by six solo violas. Later, it recurs played by horns, flutes, clarinets, and strings; almost immediately afterward it is played by three oboes and three solo cellos. Now obviously, except in the vaguest terms, that theme didn't occur to Stravinsky as being played by any one combination of instruments, and I would wager a large sum that he did not hear the orchestration of those three versions in detail as he was sketching the music.

What a composer does, in starting to score a work of any length and pretensions, is to lay his orchestration out in general before he goes at it in detail. He must decide where he's going to call for heavy orchestration and where for light; he must plan his climax, and scale the weight of his scoring so as to work up to it and not anticipate it; he must decide what passages he wants to be prominent and what others he wants to be subordinate. And while doing this he must consider his orchestration in the light of its appropriateness to its subject matter. In other words, he works out his general structure in much the way an architect does, deciding what materials are appropriate to his design, and where and in what proportion those materials are to be used.

Having done that, he begins at last to put notes on paper. And that putting notes on paper makes heavy demands upon both his powers of imagination and his technical knowledge. The four elements of good orchestration, as I see them, are appropriateness, color, balance, and proportion. The first I just discussed. Your orchestration must be neither too colorless nor too rich for the kind of music you have written. Incidentally, *The Rite of Spring* is a magnificent example of orchestration that is utterly and inevitably appropriate to the music that it transmits. If you want to hear good examples of *in*appropriate orchestration, listen to almost any so-called "special arrangement" of a popular song as played on the air, where, nine times out of ten, you'll hear a simple dance tune scored in terms of the Immolation scene from *Götterdämmerung.*

In creating so-called orchestral color, a composer works very much like a fresco painter. Just as the latter must work with wet plaster whose final colors don't show until it has dried out, so the composer must write down combinations of instruments to produce certain qualities of tone that he won't hear until it's too late to correct them if they're wrong. In devising these combinations, he must rely on his memory of how they sounded in other scores, on his ability to analyze sounds, on his theoretical knowledge of how they *ought* to sound, and on a generous helping of guesswork and hope. And I mean guesswork and hope. Listen to any composer who tells you that every note and every bar of an orchestral work of his sounds *exactly* as he planned it to sound, and you're listening to a direct descendant of Ananias.

The question of orchestral balance is largely a question of experience and technical knowledge. Here, the composer's problem is to keep the accompaniment of a solo passage audible and still subordinate, or to keep one section of the orchestra from swamping another. He must know the dynamic scope of his instruments, at what point in their range they sound the loudest—an oboe, for instance, is weaker at the top of its scale than at the bottom, and a flute is just the reverse. Also, he must know that the *quality* of one sound can obliterate another sound. A single stroke of a triangle can ruin a passage for muted strings more effectively, sometimes, than a quartet of trombones.

The all-important *technical* element in orchestration is, of course, a knowledge of the instruments. The composer must know not only what they can do but what is difficult and impossible for them to do. He mustn't write low F sharps for the violins or too many high C's for the horns. He must know the seven positions of the trombone, and avoid writing fast passages that make the trombone player look like a sword swallower. He must remember, too, that his wind instruments are blown with human lungs, and see to it that he allows the players time to breathe. These and a hundred other purely technical considerations are what make it hard for me to believe that any composer can orchestrate simultaneously with his composing. Then comes the problem of proportion. He must avoid allowing a given orchestral effect to last so long that it becomes monotonous. On the other hand, he mustn't call for so many changes of orchestral color that his score sounds scrappy.

Somehow or other he solves these problems as best he can. The score is finished and goes off to the copyist. For twenty-four hours the composer walks about in a daze of self-admiration. Not only is the music a flawless gem, but the score is a masterpiece of orchestration. But the ensuing thirteen days, until the parts come back from the copyist, are spent in wondering why he was ever such a fool as to take up composition, and how he could ever have been such an idiot as to try to write for an orchestra.

Eventually, the parts come back. The day comes for the first reading rehearsal. He has set his alarm the night before, and spent the ensuing hours lying awake for fear he might not hear it in the morning. He makes his way to the concert hall. There on the platform sit seventy, eighty, or ninety men—whatever the number is, it's too large—staring at their parts with what looks to him like cynical amusement. He bows obsequiously to one or two players whom he knows, and then sits back in the darkest part of the hall. The conductor mounts the podium. He raises his baton.

And then—well, the subsequent rehearsals may be torture, the concert performance may be bad, the audience may be indifferent, and the critics murderous. But he has had his moment, and no power on earth can take it from him: the moment when those thousands of little black spots came off the paper and for the first time were turned into sounds.

PART TWO

First Theme

I

On Getting Acquainted

IF YOU were to ask me, "What is this book about?," I'm afraid that the answer, after a few worried moments of cogitation, would be, "That's a little hard to say. Would you mind very much if I tried to tell you what it is *not* about?" Assuming that you do *not* mind very much, let me begin by quoting a letter that reached me in the early forties, while I was serving time as intermission commentator on the New York Philharmonic-Symphony broadcasts. It came from a listener in Spokane, Washington, who was disturbed. He began by saying that he had been trying to listen to my weekly remarks with an open mind and to be tolerant. But he had lost patience at last, because he was trying to understand good music and to appreciate it, and these talks of mine were no help. He cited a concert in which the principal numbers on the program were the second symphony of Jan Sibelius and Glazunoff's violin concerto. And what did I talk about?

First [he wrote], I'll tell you what we expected to hear. We wanted to know something about the program. If it is true that the second symphony shows the break from Tchaikovsky's influence, that Sibelius has launched forth with a new musical philosophy of his own, then what we want to know is the relative place this new step holds in the world of music today. How does Sibelius compare with Tchaikovsky, whom he formerly imitated? How does he compare with his former self? Where in the composition can we recognize these fragments of life which he supposedly wove into a final, full pattern? What did Sibelius attempt to portray? What is his main theme, and how did he broaden and expand it? What about his instrumentation and mood? What accounts for his popularity today, and will it endure? But the well-known Deems Taylor did not answer any of these questions. He did not so much as approach the subject. In fact, he seemed to be unconscious that, preceding and following his comments, there was a symphonic performance going on. I wondered, as I always do, why vaudeville was injected into serious symphony. For Deems Taylor talked first and foremost about Deems Taylor, and that is an everlasting habit of Mr. Taylor. In fact, we are beginning to suspect that this is the major reason he is "well known" to the American public. First he tells us about "my" little talk last Sunday, or a year ago this Sunday; about "my" commercial plug given unwittingly and "my" telegram that came in answer, and "my" reply to the telegram, and "my" opinion on commercial plugs in general.

Next, he launches into—not a brilliant interpretation of Glazunoff or modern music trends or even biographical or historical facts about the composer in question, but we are given amazing information regarding the number of high-school bands in the United States and what Deems Taylor thinks about it; and he is off to another race with Deems Taylor and vacuity. Take the first-person pronoun out of Mr. Taylor's comments, and there isn't a great deal left. Really, we are growing extremely tired of having a beautiful performance interrupted with comments that are remote from the program. It is cheap and it is meaningless. Please, for the sake of your vast audience, for the sake of the composer, the symphony, for the sake of music itself, please talk about the program or else sit down.

If I reprint that old love letter, I do so not from any impulse to stride into the forum and exhibit my wounds to the populace. If a gentleman in Spokane heard my remarks with something less than passionate admiration, that would seem, at first blush, to be our own private tragedy. But there is more to it than that. Here was someone obviously in earnest about music, who wanted to know more about it and more about how to listen to it. Furthermore, irate as he was, he was evidently someone of education and intelligence. He, and others like him, deserve an answer—several answers.

My first answer would be that, at the time he wrote his letter, he could have received in advance, for a small yearly sum, the official printed program notes of the concerts, wherein he would have found the discussions of the music, the structural analyses, and the biographical material that he craved. Furthermore, the station announcer, Mr. Frank Gallup, offered additional factual material during the pauses between numbers. Presumably there was no point in the commentator's going over this same ground.

As for my possibly excessive preoccupation with that most fascinating of subjects, myself: I think he misunderstood the purpose of that. I do use the first person singular a good deal, I suppose. But when a commentator (at least, this commentator) does that, he is assuming that his thoughts and reactions are those of the average person. He may be a professional musician and, as such, he may admire, for technical reasons, certain works that you don't. He may loathe certain works of which you are very fond. Nevertheless he does assume that his attitude toward music in general, when he listens to it, is that of any other listener. So he passes on to you the experiences and opinions of the one listener whom he knows at firsthand. And if he passes them on in the first person singular, perhaps it is to remind you that they are only the opinions of one man.

The main reason why I answer the letter in such detail is that I think the writer of it is on the wrong track. He says, "I am trying to understand good music and I desire to appreciate it," and proceeds to list a number of topics that he wants discussed. Now, virtually none of those topics is going to help him to understand and appreciate music. Any intelligent discussion of them is rather the result than the cause of appreciation. They are the trimmings, the extra pleasure you get from discussing the fine points of music that has already given you pleasure and with which you are thoroughly familiar. If a group of musicians and veteran concertgoers should be sitting around a fire after dinner, I can imagine that they might pass a very pleasant evening discussing whether or not Sibelius's second symphony shows a break from Tchaikovsky's influence, and what accounts for his popularity today, and what changes have taken place in his musical personality, the characteristics of his instrumentation, and so on. But don't try to discuss those same topics with a group of people to whom the second symphony is still a comparatively unfamiliar experience. In the first place, it wouldn't be a discussion; it would be a monologue. In the second place, I doubt very much whether you would enhance their appreciation of the music at all; I think you would merely put them to sleep.

If I were a gambling man, I'm sure I could win enormous sums by betting that every person who talks or writes to me about my profession will begin his conversation or his letter with the sentence "Of course I have absolutely no technical knowledge of music." I might not win every time, but the odds would be about fifty to one in my favor.

I've often wondered why people find it necessary to make that apologetic statement. Persons who obviously know nothing technically about painting have not the slightest hesitation in telling me all about pictures. I know dozens of people who hold, and express, the most positive opinions about the merits of contemporary novels without finding it necessary to explain that they know nothing about how fiction is written. I've had poetry discussed for me with great fluency by people who would have a hard time remembering whether a sonnet has twelve or sixteen lines. If I want to know whether or not some contemporary play is worth going to see, I know a score of people who will tell me all about it without ever dreaming of saying, "Of course I know absolutely nothing about the technique of the drama." In fact, I know several dramatic critics in good standing who neglect to put that line at the top of their daily columns. But when it comes to discussing music, an extraordinary modesty seems to descend upon the shoulders of every listener who doesn't happen to be a professional musician.

I've often wondered why this should be so, and I think I have at least a plausible explanation. In the other arts the average listener, reader, or beholder has something definite to hang on to, something by which he can defend his opinion for or against. If it's a picture he's commenting upon, he can at least approve or quarrel with its representational merits, or its design and color. He can say, "That right leg is too long," or, "What a beautiful color that sky is." If it's a novel he's discussing, he can praise or criticize the plot, even if he isn't an expert on style or character drawing. Discussing a poem, he can say, "That doesn't sound like poetry to me," and nobody can argue with him. And of course anybody who steps inside a theater immediately becomes a seasoned dramatic critic.

But when it comes to music, the lay listener is strangely timid about having any opinion at all. There's nothing about it that he can lay his hands on, so to speak. Program music undertakes to tell a story, true enough; but the story has no bearing on the essential quality of the music itself. So-called absolute music has no plot at all. Nor has it any real pictorial quality. Aside from occasional frank imitations of natural sounds, such as the sheep music in Strauss's *Don Quixote,* which are hardly discussible as music, it represents nothing but emotions, which are essentially intangible. And so he develops a mild inferiority complex in the presence of serious music and serious musicians. He humbly assumes that all symphonic music is of equal excellence; that if some given work doesn't appeal to him, the fault must be his own; and he gets the idea that music is a terrifically mysterious art, which only the initiated can appreciate, and that he can't possibly understand it unless he has gone through a course of technical training.

I suspect that there is a fundamental confusion of thought at the bottom of most of our attempts to teach people how to appreciate various forms of art; that in our educational endeavors we draw no distinction between the patron, audience, appreciator—or whatever you want to call him—and the practitioner. We teach everything the way we teach English. Now, when we study English we study to be writers as well as readers. We must do so, if we are to communicate with our fellow beings. So we study spelling and grammar and rhetoric and composition as well as reading. Unfortunately, even there, we are taught as if we were all planning to be writers, not of letters but of books. We are set to analyzing Keats's *Ode to a Nightingale,* without anyone's asking us whether or not we enjoy reading it. We are asked to draw little charts tracing the three plots of *The Merchant of Venice* without ever having seen a performance of the play. That is unfortunate but not necessarily fatal, for we all do so much reading that eventually we develop some sort of appreciation of literature on our own hook, so to speak, in spite of those early attempts to make us cultured. But this sort of cart-before-the-horse approach is dangerous in the other arts. We tend to teach musical appreciation to the would-be concert-goer by handing him a mass of factual information and technical comment that should be the climax, not the beginning, of his musical education. Let me illustrate:

The entire mass, striking a chord both loud and short, discovers an oboe during the silence which succeeds. The entrance of this oboe, hidden by the orchestral attack, had not been previously perceived; and it now states the opening melody in *sostenuto*. The amplitude of this subject is at once very striking, the progression upon which it is founded plainly suggesting a subsequent busier employment of the time occupied by its broad pulsations. This is all the more the case [are you listening, friend from Spokane?] as the subject is purely a rhythmical one; that is to say, the gist of it lies in the weight of the pulsations and not in any actual melody further than is implied by two descending intervals followed by a rise.

Now, that is part of an analysis of Beethoven's seventh symphony, from a book by an eminent British musical authority. I won't tell you the title of the book because I consider it a menace. An advanced student of composition might make head or tail of it; but suppose his autopsy fell into the hands of an earnest layman who wanted to learn how to "appreciate" Beethoven?

As a matter of fact, I have an idea that music is the one art that can be enjoyed by someone who has no technical training whatsoever. We hardly realize, I think, how much technical training we do bring to our appreciation of the other arts. Before enjoying a novel or a poem, you must have learned to read. That's technique, even though you take it for granted. To enjoy a play you must at least understand the language in which it is being spoken; and the fact that we all learn to speak at least one language by unconscious absorption doesn't alter the fact that speaking it is a technical achievement. The person who looks at a picture with interest, no matter how ignorant he may be of its technical subtleties, is, more than he thinks, an expert. To a child, a dog, or a savage, a painting is a meaningless arrangement of colors and lines. In order to recognize the image that the painter tries to convey, one must first accept and comprehend the painter's convention of representing a three-dimensional object in terms of two. Sculpture is easier to understand than painting, in that it is a more or less faithful reproduction of an existing object. But even sculpture can be puzzling if the object that it represents is an unfamiliar one, or a familiar one oversimplified. What gives music its universal appeal is the very fact that it is at the same time the most subtle and intangible and the most primitive of all arts. It makes its primary appeal through the ear, directly to the nerve centers. It doesn't have to be translated, and it doesn't have to be understood to make its impression. It can make a dog howl, and silence a crying baby. Its intellectual appeal is secondary, and is the result, and not the cause, of its emotional appeal.

In other words, a person who knows nothing about its technique or history, who cannot define a phrase or a bar or a sonata or a symphony, can derive genuine pleasure from listening to music—provided only that he isn't tone deaf. And such a listener has no need to apologize to anyone for his technical ignorance. This is not to say that if you appreciate the structure and the finer points of a given composition, you won't enjoy it more than the completely ignorant listener. But the enjoyment must come first, if the technical knowledge is to do you any good.

So-called symphonic music differs in two fundamental respects from so-called popular music. The latter is built on a series of balanced, recurrent four- and eight-bar phrases, which are easily recognizable, whereas the former deals with themes —melodies, if you like—that do not, necessarily, have any such regular bar structure, and which, when they recur, may do so in various aspects; in other words, in what we call "thematic development." The first movement of Brahms' second symphony, for example, begins with a *one*-bar phrase. Then follows a phrase of eight bars; then one of ten; then one of twelve; then three of four bars each.

Now, that is why symphonic music is difficult for the layman who is familiar only with the comparatively rigid structure of the popular tune. The only way for him to grasp such music is not to read about it nor be told about it, but to listen to it, over and over and over, until he is able to retain in his mind some coherent impression of the piece as a whole. When he can do that, he is on his way toward understanding and appreciating serious music. It is then that he will have the right to say whether he likes it or not. And it is then, when he begins to have some defensible opinions of his own, that other people's opinions will begin to be of some use to him. For never forget: no pronunciamento, no comment on music—no, not even mine—is anything but somebody's opinion. There are no abstract truths in art; and that is why opinions are worthless if they are merely handed down. To have any value, they must be exchanged.

All of which is why this book is no treatise on music appreciation.

Hearing's Not Enough

Did it ever strike you that there are several different kinds of music? I don't mean just different forms—such as songs, dances, waltzes, marches—but different actual *varieties* of music, varieties that call for different kinds of listening.

Let me show you what I mean. First of all, there's absolute music—music that makes sense by itself, independent of any program or accompanying action, music that is presented to you as itself, to be taken or left, according as it does or doesn't impress you. That's the music that composers write in the form of symphonies, quartets, sonatas, suites, formal ballets, songs, and operatic arias. Listening to a program made up exclusively of that sort of music, we sit and listen to it for what it is, probably unconscious that there's any other form of listening. But as music has increased in explicitness and articulateness, it has tended to divide itself into specialized groups. And if you can't bring to each of those groups the *kind* of music that it needs, you're likely to find yourself not enjoying a lot of music, simply because you're asking it to be something that it isn't.

Now, "specialized listening" sounds very complicated and formal, but as a matter of fact, we've been doing it all our lives, more or less unconsciously. Take an opera by Mozart. That's fairly uncomplicated music. Yet even that demands two kinds of listening. We listen to the overture, the solos and duets and trios and choruses, solely as music. But what about the recitatives? We hear them, to be sure, but not with the same ear. Heard in connection with the story and the movements of the singers on the stage, they're very agreeable. Yet if we transferred them to the concert hall, had them played by an orchestra, or even had them sung as they are in the opera, we'd find them pretty uninteresting.

This is true of all operas up to the middle of the nineteenth century. When we come to Wagner, we find him abolishing the aria almost entirely, and thus demanding more and more listening that is *not* purely musical. Not that we notice that fact, particularly. We're accustomed to hearing symphonic excerpts from his music dramas—things like the "Ride of the Valkyries," the "Good Friday" spell, the preludes to *Tristan and Isolde* and *The Mastersingers,* extended symphonic arrangements of passages like the "Garden" scene from *Tristan.* We're so accustomed to hearing these that we tend, subconsciously, to assume that we're hearing all of the music. Yet I should say that at least one half of the score of any of his music dramas is music whose structure is so completely dictated by dramatic rather than musical considerations that we would find it rather dull if we had to listen to it away from the theater.

After Wagner came Richard Strauss, who in some of his tone poems demands two kinds of listening in the course of a single work. In *Don Quixote,* for instance, much of the score can be enjoyed as pure music. On the other hand, in the flight section, which introduces the wind machine, and in the famous sheep passage, unless you have been told that the music does represent a flight in the air and a flock of sheep, it is virtually meaningless.

The great ballet impresario Diaghileff was also an innovater. The ballet music of composers such as Adam, Delibes, and Tchaikovsky, while it accompanies a dramatic story, is written as a series of dance movements that tend to conform to a fundamental balanced, formal pattern. Under his direction, several composers, Stravinsky in particular, wrote ballets that were not only called into being by dramatic scenarios but whose music was frequently cast in forms that were not in themselves musical. It was music that the Hollywood picture scorers call "Micky Mouse" music—music that not only followed the movements of the dancers but faithfully mirrored their every gesture. When we hear a symphony orchestra play the *Firebird* or *Petrouchka* suites, we are not hearing the ballets in their entirety. We are hearing suites *based* upon those ballets, in which a great deal of music has been omitted that would sound incoherent and meaningless, divorced from the stage action.

I bring this up because I receive letters, from time to time, from people who want to know why our symphony orchestras don't play some of the music from our more serious motion pictures. They point out that composers like Aaron Copland, Bernard Herrmann, William Walton, and Erich Korngold have written excellent music for the films, and that it seems a pity to have the life of the music for a picture limited by the life of the picture itself because in many cases the music is better than the picture.

That's all true, but it doesn't change my belief that if these listeners could have the privilege they crave, nine times out of ten they would be in for a great disappointment. There may be occasional exceptions, of course. Not long ago there was a concert in New York at which the audience heard extracts from two of Aaron Copland's picture scores. I didn't hear them, but I understand that they were successful. On the other hand, I've heard the sound tracks of several pictures played separately, and without exception they sounded scrappy and meaningless. They all had some fine material, but it wasn't developed; it had no continuity, no structure. I don't think that any contemporary picture could get along without music. On the other hand, there are very few moments when the music is allowed to be heard for itself. Most of the time it is reduced to furnishing bridges between scenes, or acting as a background for spoken dialogue. There's no denying its effectiveness in this connection; in fact, it often creates the illusion that we're hearing much more of it than there actually is. But transferred bodily to the concert stage, it isn't likely to sound particularly important.

This is not to say that if the composers would rewrite their picture scores, use them as raw material for symphonic music, we wouldn't hear some highly interesting works. As a matter of fact, Copland has done just that. So has Bernard Herrmann. So, too, has Virgil Thomson, whose music based upon his *The Plow That Broke the Plains* has been particularly successful. Their colleagues would do well to follow their example. If they will take their music out of the theater, translate it in terms of the concert stage, they can hope for success. If they refuse to do that, they must not be disappointed if we hearers are not impressed. Scene designing can be a great art, but a scene designer who insists upon hanging his scene sketches in an exhibition of paintings is asking for trouble.

Name-Calling

YOU DON'T have to be told, of course, that Beethoven's third symphony is called the *Eroica,* and his ninth is called the *Ninth;* that Tchaikovsky's second is the *Little Russian,* his third is the *Polish,* and his sixth is the *Pathétique,* while the other three merely have numbers, as do all four of Brahms'. Now comes a correspondent who objects to this inconsistency. He wants all musical works, long and short, to have names, and offers several arguments to support his proposal.

"Any composition," he writes, "must have personality, to last. Therefore it deserves a name, just as people and books are named. Employees have social-security numbers and soldiers have serial numbers, but they all have names, too, because they are persons. To music lovers, musical compositions are friends, and are therefore in the class of things that deserve names, in addition to their numbers."

He goes on to point out that some compositions suggest their own names—works like the *Surprise* and *Unfinished* symphonies. But since a great many others weren't named by their composers, and haven't acquired any, during the years, he suggests that they be officially named by a competent musical board, with outside suggestions from the non-professionals. Compositions so abstract that they suggest no names at all, he thinks, could be given names worked out in some way to honor the composer or his birthplace or some historical event with which he was connected. Well, of course all that has been done, on various occasions. There's Tchaikovsky's "1812" overture, for instance, which commemorates a historical event; and Bach's *Brandenburg* concertos and Beethoven's *Razoumoffsky* quartets, while they don't honor the composers' names, do honor the names of the patrons who commissioned them.

But to get back to my correspondent. He wants to make it clear that he isn't arguing that all musical works be given *descriptive* names, but simply that every composition ought to have a name for its own dignity, to honor the composer, and for ease of identification. "Operas and swing compositions," he writes, "are all named, and are thus easier to remember. Why should the *Beer Barrel Polka* be given the advantage of a name over Chopin's polonaises, which have no identification other than opus numbers? [He forgets the *Military* polonaise.] The popularity of so-called 'popular' music over classical music may be due in very considerable part to the names of the former and the lack of names of the latter." (I don't know. If I were a trial lawyer, I think I'd register an objection at that point.)

"Isn't it easier and more natural," he asks, "to remember the music of Beethoven's *Emperor* concerto than to remember 'Number Five in E-Flat Major, Opus 73'?" (I think he has something there.)

He doesn't want these names for the use of professional musicians, or, as he writes, "for those in the large group that have to do with dispensing music to the public and are probably well content with numbers. So is a manufacturer content with numbers for his machinery or goods, while he is processing it in his factory; but when he offers it to his customers he gives it a registered trade name, so that the public may more readily speak of it. By the same reasoning, the purveyor of classical music might find sales resistance lessened if he would give the prospective customers music with names, instead of mere filing numbers. Football players have numbers for identification, but let a football announcer call out the players' numbers instead of their names and he wouldn't last through a quarter."

He concedes that older music lovers might protest that they could never learn to know a work like Beethoven's fifth symphony by any name. Well, he's willing to let them go on thinking of it as the *Fifth,* and would put the number in parentheses beside the new name. The latter would be for the annual crop of new listeners. "You, no doubt," he suggests, "could make a list of good names for Brahms' first symphony, submit them to the public, and ask for a mail vote." He concludes on a rather gloomy note, to the effect that the publishers would probably object to any change, since it would entail a lot of reprinting. He thinks they shouldn't, because, as he says, "would not that in itself give the public a new appeal? An opportunity to dress one's goods in a new and different package is always welcomed by progressive merchants."

Now, there is a plan that has at least the virtue of being entirely logical, although I must say I sense certain difficulties in putting it into effect. Who would appoint that board, for instance? How large would it be, who would be the members, and who would abide by its decisions? And would it ever arrive at any decisions? After all, the name you would give to a piece of music would be determined, at least in part, by what you thought of the work. For example, many of my correspondents have written to suggest names for some of the modern works that the orchestras have been playing lately; but they're not all as short as they might be, and some of them are decidedly not for the kiddies. You put a board of twenty or thirty people to work thinking up a name for, say, Shostakovich's first symphony, and you're going to get some wildly divergent ideas as to what it ought to be called. What would they evolve as the name for even a comparatively uncomplicated work such as the Brahms double concerto? *Mr. and Mrs.? Boy Meets Girl? Argument in E Flat? Two for the Price of One?* It's a difficult problem.

Besides, my correspondent overlooks the fact that some of those numbers he so dislikes have become names in their own right. You say "the Beethoven Fourth" or "the Brahms Fourth" or "the Tchaikovsky Fourth," and you instantly evoke three separate and very definite musical associations in the minds of the people who hear you. A title doesn't even have to be a name. Hail a New York taxicab and say "Twenty-one" to the driver, and with no further questions he'll take you to a famous restaurant that has no name other than its street number.

I think it is not without significance that my correspondent is an engineer. You know how engineers loathe disorder and illogic and inconsistency. His plan is orderly, perfectly logical, and utterly consistent, but there is one thing which, I'm afraid, is going to block his path. And that is the fact that man is a disorderly, illogical, and inconsistent animal. Certain compositions have been given names, and certain others haven't. Why? I don't know, and I doubt if any of you know. Point out to us that if Beethoven's third symphony has a name, his fourth should have one too, and we agree with you instantly and heartily—and do nothing about it. I wish my correspondent all the luck in the world with his plan. But if it succeeds, I'm afraid it will do so in spite of the fact that it's logical.

4

In the Order Named

HERE is an idea that was tossed into the arena by a correspondent who wrote: "If you haven't already done so, and I missed it, would you remark on the sequence of the symphony? I can put my records on the record changer in *any* sequence and enjoy the music. Just now I have Beethoven's Fifth ending with the *first* movement and I like it. Anything wrong with that?"

My first reaction to that suggestion was the same as yours. I was scandalized. I thought to myself, "But you can't *do* that!" But then I thought, "Well, if it's as unthinkable as all that, it ought to be very easy to prove that it's unthinkable."

So I started to prove it. Why can't the four movements of a symphony be played in any order you choose, without spoiling its effect? Well, first of all, it does violence to the structure of the work. And just there it occurred to me that it might be a good idea to *define* a symphony. So I got down Grove's *Dictionary of Music and Musicians,* and turned to the article on the symphony, expecting to find the whole thing cleared up in the first paragraph. It wasn't. I went through all the forty-two pages of that article, and in no place was I able to pin the author, the late Richard Aldrich, down to a definite statement of just what a symphony is. I've looked through every other reference book that I own, and have come to the conclusion that although we're all very positive that we know a symphony when we hear one, there is no simple definition of it that can't be shot to pieces in ten seconds. So far as I can determine, the rough definition is this: A symphony is an orchestral work in four movements. The first is based on two alternating themes, one slow and one fast. Sometimes it has an introduction, and sometimes it hasn't. The second is generally a fast movement, except when it's a slow one. The third is a slow one, except when it's fast. The last movement is a rondo, except when it's in sonata form like the first.

Now, vague as that definition is, it has plenty of exceptions. A symphony is not always a purely orchestral work. Beethoven and Mahler add a chorus. Nor does it necessarily have four movements. César Franck's famous D-minor symphony has only three. The Beethoven Fifth, to which my correspondent alludes, has four, but only on paper, because the third telescopes into the fourth without a break. Lalo's *Spanish Symphony* has *five* movements, of which we generally hear only four; and besides, it isn't a symphony, anyhow, but a violin concerto. Beethoven's *Pastoral* has five, *all* of which we hear. The Brahms Fourth has a slow movement at the end, which is neither a rondo nor a sonata formula; it's a passacaglia, except that half the critics refer to it as a chaconne.

In other words, nobody can convict you of violating any set of inflexible rules if you choose to upset the composer's order of events in presenting or hearing his symphony. On the other hand there are reasons against doing that, reasons that are all the stronger for being intangible. The traditional order of the movements in a symphony has a very sound psychological basis. The first movement of the classic symphony is the most complicated. Therefore the listener wants relief from complication. So the second movement is comparatively simple. Whether it's a fast or slow one depends on which tempo offers the best *contrast* to the one that went before it. The third movement ought, again, to offer a change in mood from the second. The finale is generally more complicated than the preceding two for the same reason: contrast.

Also, particularly in the symphonies since Beethoven, there's a dramatic element to be considered. Take Tchaikovsky's familiar *Pathétique* as an example. The first movement, lyric as much of it is, is definitely dramatic, and one of its two main themes is rather elaborately developed. The second movement is—and properly, I think—simply a smooth, uncomplicated pattern of sound, with its unusual five-four time to save it from monotony. The third is martial in feeling and—for Tchaikovsky—pretty cheerful. It offers a mood that hasn't hitherto been developed in the work. The last is a dirge, one that strikes a note of complete pessimism.

Now upset that order. Start off with the martial scherzo, then play the dirge, then the elaborate first movement (it's seventeen minutes long, by the way), then finish with the uneventful five-four movement. Now that, to my ears, offers too violent a set of contrasts, tires your attention with too long a stretch toward the end, and ends in an anticlimax. A well-written symphony, aside from the merit of its actual music, offers you an added kind of enjoyment, a sense of what you might call dramatic satisfaction that results not only from the intrinsic quality of its movement but also from the order in which they are played. Break up that order, and you're very likely to damage the effect of the symphony as a whole.

However, if you really like to change the order of the movements, there's no law against enjoying yourself. But don't try to frighten me by saying, "Why *shouldn't* I do this?" I think the answer to that is the obvious one: "Why should you?"

Ancestor Worship

THERE came this cry for help from a student at the University of California: "I may be built in reverse of the ordinary pattern of things, but I don't think I'm alone in my plight. I like Richard Strauss, Shostakovich, and Stravinsky, and have liked them for a long time. But it has been less than a year since Beethoven and Brahms have first entered the limits of my field of appreciation. Haydn, Bach, Handel, Mozart, and others of the 'old boys' are still beyond me. I know I'm missing something, because so many other people enjoy the works of these masters. You commentators often try cautiously to lead the older generation into a more broad-minded attitude toward the modern composers, but had you ever thought that a few of us of the younger generation might wish to be led back toward the old masters? Perhaps it isn't worth the effort. Then, again, I may have to grow up, to mature, in order to appreciate Papa Haydn and Mozart and their too, too polite little compositions. I listen to them frequently, even have some of their symphonies on recordings, but I always come back to the moderns for relief."

My young correspondent is by no means alone in what he calls his plight. Furthermore, I venture to state that I am in a better position than most to understand exactly how he feels, because at the beginning of my own career as a listener I felt precisely as he does today. True, that was a generation back, and the ultra-moderns for whom I had a low hankering have by now either disappeared or have become safely classic. But my cycle of appreciation, like his, ran backward. Bach, Mozart, Haydn, and Beethoven were the last people I appreciated, not the first. That may have been my fault, as it may be his. On the other hand, there are several possible reasons why we may have failed to grasp the classics at first hearing. Apropos of one reason, let me quote another letter, from the American composer and pianist Abram Chasins, who unburdens himself as follows: "The so-called 'Haydn' concerto in D major which is so popular among cellists has fairly recently been published in its original version with a preface by Dr. Hans Volkmann, the musical philologist, proving conclusively that this work is not by Haydn but by Haydn's pupil, Anton Kraft." Concerning this discovery, Mr. Chasins then quotes a comment by Sir Donald Francis Tovey, professor of music at the University of Edinburgh, who writes as follows:

> I personally find it easy to give Kraft credit for a beautiful piece of work in a form in which Haydn never achieved his full stature. It belongs to a period when his forms were sufficiently imitable to tempt publishers to secure a market for other composers by ascribing their works to a master whose early popularity was so remarkable. My former analysis [of the cello concerto, that is] will not be found to contain anything committing me to uphold this charming concerto as a great work.

"This kind of thing," writes Mr. Chasins, "makes me see red. Heaven knows that everything that Haydn did was not a stroke of genius. But the viciousness of the halo of a name comes forth here. No sooner is it found that Haydn did *not* write this work than an apology—or more properly, a protestation—is forthcoming from Sir Francis Tovey, to the effect that 'nothing in my analysis contains anything suggesting that this is a great work.' One rather expects this sort of thing from the musical snob or the musically deaf. But not from Tovey."

I must say I share Mr. Chasins' feelings on the subject. Among the following of any artist, whether he be composer, painter, sculptor, or writer, you will find a large number of persons who tend to put the emphasis on the artist rather than on his work. Within reason, that's perfectly fair. You hear half a dozen works by some composer, and those works convince you that he's a great artist. So when the seventh comes along you are ready to find his particular genius in it even before you've heard it. And even if it's unworthy of him at his best, you are going to do your best to find it worthy of him.

Now, that's all very human and would harm nobody, except that after the man is dead and established as a classic, his admirers, through subsequent generations, acquire a habit of indulging in the most idolatrous praise of everything that he ever wrote. Not only that, but they show a deplorable tendency to assume that a given work of his is good, not because it's good in itself, but because he wrote it. I venture to predict, for example, that when the real authorship of that alleged Haydn concerto is more widely known, the prevalent critical enthusiasm for it will cool perceptibly.

This cult of the composer for his own sake is all right for the experts, who discriminate almost unconsciously between his best and his far from best. But it's likely to be disconcerting and discouraging for the inexperienced listener. From anything he can read or is ever told, he will never know that there is any difference, in artistic intention or in musical weight, between Mozart's Symphony No. 25 in G minor and his Symphony No. 40 in G minor. I've heard a lot of Beethoven and I believe that I can appreciate his best work; and so I find the courage to say that one or two of his piano sonatas put me to sleep, and that his *King Stephen* overture is a dull and perfunctory piece of work, which would long ago have died if it had been written by some unknown contemporary of his, and that *Wellington's Victory* is trash. But the beginning listener has neither the experience nor the self-confidence to make such distinctions. He hears a work by some classic master, a work that he never would like, no matter how much he knew about music. But he doesn't realize that. All he knows is that it's a work by a great master and therefore must be good. So, if he doesn't like it, that master is beyond his sphere of appreciation. Another Beethovenite or Mozartist fallen by the wayside.

But there are other factors, and still more important ones, that tend to make the classics rather unexciting hearing for a certain type of listener. For one thing, when we're not yet in the veteran stage of appreciating the arts, we tend to respond most readily to the idiom of our own time. If one has been brought up on a diet of Hemingway and Steinbeck and O'Hara, it is not easy to arrive at a just estimate of the worth of Edgar Allan Poe and James Fenimore Cooper. And whatever Mozart may have to say, he certainly doesn't say it in the language of Shostakovich.

Another barrier is the revolution wrought in orchestration during the past hundred years; Mozart's G minor symphony No. 40 is scored for pairs of flutes, oboes, clarinets, bassoons, horns, and strings. No trumpets, no trombones, no tuba, no English horn, no bass clarinet, no harps, no celeste—to name a few of the gaps. Naturally, his orchestration sounds a little naïve when you compare it with the brilliant coloring of the masters who succeeded him. Beethoven was about the first symphonic composer to practice what a present-day arranger would call real orchestration; and Beethoven is elementary compared with Strauss or Stravinsky—or even Brahms.

But in the case of my present correspondent, I think that his disappointment with Haydn, Mozart, and the rest has its source in the fact that he is listening for something that he will not hear. Notice the list of composers whom he does like:

Beethoven, Brahms, Strauss, Stravinsky, Shostakovich. Notice that every one of these men has one of two characteristics. He is either intensely pictorial and dramatic (dramatic in the emotional, not the theatrical sense) or intensely subjective. And dramatic and subjective are precisely what the eighteenth-century classicists, in their symphonic works, were not. Not only were they not temperamentally so inclined, but the musical vocabulary and the orchestral resources at their command were not sufficiently developed to enable them to give satisfactory expression to highly colorful or subtly introspective ideas. Beethoven was the first symphonist to make his work a deliberate expression of intensely personal feelings and reactions. Where Mozart achieves emotional heights, as he does in the great G minor symphony, it is almost in spite of the form in which he writes, not because of it. To these men of the eighteenth century the task of the composer was, in its essence, to compose as beautiful themes as they could, and to arrange and develop them in accordance with a fixed form. True, they made changes in the forms as they went along, but nevertheless they wrote according to *a* form, if only a personal one.

Ever since Beethoven's time, composers have tended to employ the various forms of musical composition as vehicles, rather than as ends in themselves, until today we tend to think of music almost wholly in terms of emotional or dramatic impact. A composer can't write a piano concerto today without having a lot of commentators poking around in it to discover its message—as if he were a spy, writing in invisible ink. The classicists weren't particularly worried about messages. In the main their concern was the working out of a beautiful, balanced pattern of sound.

The exception, to me, is Bach. I'm a little worried that my correspondent doesn't care for Bach. It may be that he has heard the wrong people talk about Bach, or that somebody has tried to teach him how to listen to Bach. The usual method of teaching appreciation of Bach is to make the would-be appreciator take a short course in counterpoint and fugue, which is about as sensible as taking a short course in anatomy and perspective in order to appreciate Michelangelo. The fact that Bach was a consummate master of a hideously difficult and complicated musical form doesn't alter the fact that working in that form he produced music that was emotionally a good century ahead of its time. He may have done so unconsciously. Nevertheless he did it. The best way to listen to Bach is to eliminate the word "counterpoint" from your vocabulary and listen to the music.

As for the others, don't expect from them the apocalyptic thunderings of Beethoven and Brahms and Strauss and Wagner. That isn't what they were striving to create. Listen to them as patterns of lovely sound. That's all you *may* hear at first, but it isn't all there is in them. In the statuary pavilion of New York's Metropolitan Museum of Art you will find the work of many of the great sculptors, from the Greeks on down, either in originals or casts. But when I have been there, after I have looked at the Donatellos and the Michelangelos and the Rodins, I like to visit the Egyptian wing and go to a certain case in which is a head of a goddess, carved in low relief. It dates from the twenty-sixth dynasty, about 650 B.C. It isn't any particular goddess; it's just a small head, done in the conventional Egyptian style, with the face in profile and the eye in full face. It was intended as a model, a pattern to be followed by stone cutters in carving temple decorations. No one knows the name of the sculptor or the girl who posed for him. She's a little thing; you could hold her in the palm of your hand. But there is something in her exquisite, meaningless, timeless perfection that I have found more moving than many a monumental group a thousand times her size.

And you will find the same timeless, serene beauty in the

music of so many of those eighteenth-century composers—Haydn, Mozart, Lulli, Corelli, Rameau—and in the lesser works of later composers—Delius's *Cuckoo*, Tchaikovsky's *Nutcracker*, Stravinsky's *Firebird* lullaby. It is not music that undertakes to stun, or transport, or scale any alpine heights. But it has its own quality of greatness. Listen to it, and recall the words of the shepherd Amos in Heywood Broun's lovely Christmas story:

"To my heart there came a whisper."

6

Grandpa Talks Too Much

ANOTHER correspondent, discussing the same topic, is a bit more truculent about it.

"I should like," he writes, "to ask one question and, I suppose, carry a chip on my shoulder, musically speaking. I seem to be out of step, musically. Dare I say that I do *not* enjoy the music of the old masters up to Tchaikovsky? I hasten to admit that I have no musical education, and that my work is not even remotely connected with music. But I do find that listening to music is a paramount thing in my life.

"Now, is the following illustration of my point of view unreasonable? An automobile of, say, the vintage of 1925 has a motor, seats, lights, a horn, runs forward and backward, and turns corners. Yet when the annual auto shows come around, we don't haul out one of these old-timers, set it beside a sleek present-day model, and claim that it's just as good. But when it comes to programming symphonies for a present-day audience, nine times out of ten the program offers none but these 1925 models—or, rather, *1825* models. It is true that the old works also have melody, harmony, rhythm, structure, and the like, but compare them with the brilliant, full-bodied numbers that our modern composers turn out. A conductor might haul out a Haydn or Mozart symphony once in a while as we occasionally exhibit a 1925 model car, as a curiosity. But we who love modern music practically have to go down on our knees to get a hearing of Tchaikovsky or Bruckner, not to mention a little Ravel or Schönberg."

If I might interrupt my correspondent for a moment, I have an idea that his use of the term "modern" is likely to cause considerable bewilderment to Constant Reader. Any music lover who can group together Tchaikovsky, Bruckner, Ravel, and Schönberg, and call them all "modern," is certainly not using the word in any contemporary sense. He's probably using it, broadly, to include all composers who do not belong to what we call, almost as broadly, the "classic" school. But he has more to say:

"To those who dislike the modern works," he continues, "the critics say, 'Listen to them over and over, until you know them thoroughly, and you'll find that you like them.' Well, if that's true, I ought to love the classic masters, for heaven knows we certainly have plenty of opportunities to hear the old boys. What really happens is that when the placid ramblings of Mozart's one hundred and somethingth symphony are finally over, I sit and whisper to myself, 'Why, oh why, couldn't he have been struck down at page fourteen, instead of going on for fifty-five pages more?' In New York there is, I suppose, a good deal of modern music played. But consider the one hundred-odd million country fellows like myself who for years have munched steadily away on a diet of Mozart, Bach, and Beethoven. Sometimes, as a novelty, they give us Beethoven, Bach, and Mozart; and then, as a *complete* surprise, Bach, Beethoven, and Handel! Just check any of the network programs during the months past, and see how much Schönberg or Howard Hanson we Westerners ever get to hear."

You know, I enjoyed receiving that letter. Such a huge proportion of my incoming mail is devoted to lambasting the orchestras and conductors for playing so much modern music that, just for the sheer novelty of the thing, it's a rather invigorating change to hear from somebody who's annoyed because they play the classics. I think I'm safe in assuming, from the general tone of his letter, that he doesn't care for Bach, Beethoven, and Mozart; and I would even go so far as to guess that he doesn't care much more for Berlioz, Schumann, and Brahms. If you won't be too horrified, I'll confess that, to a certain extent, I sympathize with his point of view. I do think that some conductors tend to overplay the classics, particularly the conductors of our smaller orchestras. There are several reasons for this, not all of them aesthetic ones. For one thing, the classics are the cheapest music to play. In the case of an orchestra with a limited budget, the fact that you can buy the score and parts of a Mozart symphony for a fifth of what you'd pay for a modern work—to say nothing of the fact that you don't have to pay Mozart a performance fee—is necessarily an important factor in making up the season's programs. Furthermore, the classics are comparatively easy to play. The orchestras of Mozart's and Beethoven's day were relatively primitive aggregations, and wise composers made no very heavy demands on their skill. But the technical demands of Strauss or Ravel or Debussy or Stravinsky are simply staggering, compared with those of the classic masters. The big major symphony orchestras have no trouble with their works. After all, there probably isn't a member of the first or second violin section of a major symphony orchestra who couldn't step out on the platform and play Tchaikovsky's violin concerto, a work that only half a century ago was supposed to be impossibly difficult. But the small-town or small-city orchestras, that can't afford to pay the salaries that attract the top-ranking players, have to take the question of average technique very seriously. Even if the conductor of one of them could afford the expense of producing a work such as Stravinsky's *The Rite of Spring,* he might need a dozen rehearsals before his men could even get through it. On the other hand, they can play the notes of the average Mozart or Beethoven symphony practically at sight. Then, too, the music-loving group in any small city, the group that goes out and raises the money to support its local orchestra, is likely to be made up of people who have grown up on the classics, or to whom the classics are still an exciting novelty. In either case, the classics are what they want their orchestra to play.

My correspondent obviously belongs to neither group, and probably doesn't realize of what an extremely small minority he's a member. There's no point in arguing with him. I defy anyone to convict him, successfully, of being wrong in not liking the classics. In the last analysis, your arguments will all boil down to the assertion that since millions of other people do like the classics, he ought to like them also. That's the argument that my mother used to bring to bear in my youth, when she was trying to prove to me that I ought to like stewed turnips. My answer was that those other people could have my share. And I still think it's a good answer. And I still don't like stewed turnips, and my writing friend still won't like Beethoven. And both of us are entitled to our opinions.

On the other hand, I do quarrel with his reasoning. I think his analogy between music and automobiles is way off. It does hold good in the case of mechanical devices. Any machine made today is likely to be an improvement over one made ten years ago. But once you get out of the field of machinery, that doesn't necessarily hold true, even of material objects. I remember Harpo Marx's telling me of the time he took his brother Groucho to hear a violin recital by Jascha Heifetz. It was Groucho's first recital, and he was inclined to be critical. First he criticized Heifetz's stance. He thought the show would be more interesting if, instead of holding the violin under his chin all the time, Heifetz would play it over his head or behind his back, or lie down and play it looking into a mirror. And when Harpo incautiously volunteered the information that Heifetz's violin was two hundred and fifty years old, Groucho was horrified. He said that he would have thought that a man of Heifetz's reputation would have saved up enough money, by this time, to be able to buy a new violin. That's what's the matter with my friend's analogy. If it were sound, then a brand-new violin would be immeasurably better than an old, tired Strad, made in 1690.

When you get into the field of art, and especially of music, the analogy falls down completely. For there you begin to deal with abstractions that can't possibly be evaluated in terms of timeliness, appropriateness, or utility. It isn't the date attached to a piece of music that makes it valuable or worthless; it's what went on in the composer's brain when he wrote it, whether it was yesterday or a century ago; how significant his ideas were, regardless of the language in which he clothed them. I think that what probably bothers my correspondent is the difference in idiom between the classics and the moderns. The music of the latter is so highly colored, harmonically and instrumentally, that the classics may sound colorless and uninteresting by comparison.But that's listening to the outside of the music. Harmony and instrumentation are the sauce on the dish. The meat of any composition, what makes it live or die, lies in its ideas—that is, its themes—and how they are put together—in other words, the structure of the piece. No two pieces of music could sound further apart than a symphony by Beethoven and a symphony by Shostakovich. Yet the creators of both have a common goal: to deliver a message—one that can't be expressed in words, but that is a real one nevertheless. And if Beethoven sometimes sounds a little drab and Shostakovich sometimes sounds a little noisy, that is not important. In music, it's not the sound that beats upon the ear that matters; what matters is the music *behind* the sound, the music that passes through the ear, that goes beyond, into the mind and the heart.

The First Hundred Years

THE New York Philharmonic-Symphony Orchestra is not only the oldest permanent orchestra in America but the third oldest orchestra in the world. Its only seniors are the Vienna Philharmonic, founded in 1841, and the Royal Philharmonic of London, founded in 1813—which, come to think of it, was the year of the birth of Verdi and Wagner.

The orchestra began almost by accident, its formation being the outgrowth of a casual meeting of a congenial group of music lovers at a coffee house in Park Row, just below City Hall Park, one evening a bit over a century ago. Over their presumable cups of coffee they discussed the possibility of forming some sort of society of professional musicians—or, as they were known then, "professors of music." The leader in the discussion was a man who, despite his New England ancestry, rejoiced in the rather gaudy name of Urelli Corelli Hill. He worked indefatigably at the idea, called several subsequent meetings at his own house, went about among the professors, enlisting their co-operation, and finally saw his labors crowned by a formal organization meeting held in the Apollo Rooms, at No. 410 Broadway, where he and his colleagues founded a society that should have for its object "the study and rendering of symphonies, overtures, and other classical music in such manner as to cultivate a more general knowledge and a more correct public taste. The orchestral personnel was limited to seventy members; and every prospective member who was not a founder had to pass an entrance examination and pay an initiation fee of twenty-five dollars. The orchestra was strictly co-operative. That is, members received no regular salary, but at the close of the season, after deducting expenses, shared alike in the profits, if any. Incidentally, the orchestra remained on that basis until the early nineteen-hundreds.

Suppose we take a look at the world into which the infant orchestra was born. John Tyler was President of the United States, with Daniel Webster as his Secretary of State. New York was a city of less than half a million inhabitants. Chicago had been a city for just five years. On the Pacific coast, the little village of Yerba Buena, with eight hundred inhabitants, would still wait five years before it changed its name to San Francisco. In England, Queen Victoria, a bride of two years, had attended the christening of her first-born, Edward, and had just had her first ride in a railway train, while in France, Alexandre Dumas was just putting the finishing touches to *The Count of Monte Cristo.*

In the musical world, Mozart had been dead for half a century; Beethoven had died fifteen years before, and Schubert fourteen. A popular young pianist and composer named Frédéric Chopin had just given a tremendously successful recital in Paris and was nearing the end of his romance with the novelist George Sand. Over in Russia a mining engineer named Tchaikovsky was wondering about the future of his two-year-old son, whom he had named Piotr Ilich. In Hamburg a nine-year-old boy named Johannes Brahms had just started piano lessons with Herr Friedrich Cossel. Robert Schumann, who was later to hear of the boy, had just begun his first symphony.

Five days after the founders of the Philharmonic Society had met, a twenty-nine-year-old German composer named Richard Wagner would be leaving his wretched little lodging at No. 14, Rue Jacob, in Paris, to take the stagecoach to

Dresden, where, he hoped, rehearsals of his new grand opera, *Rienzi,* had already begun. Twenty-four days *before* the founders met, at La Scala, in Milan, a young Italian composer named Giuseppe Verdi, likewise twenty-nine years old, had seen his opera *Nabucco* produced with a success that had not been equaled since the palmy days of Gioachino Rossini. In Paris, not two months before, that same Rossini, after a silence of thirteen years, had come forward with a *Stabat Mater* that his contemporaries had hailed as a masterpiece.

In America, however, music occupied a very minor place in the affections of the public. An occasional traveling grand-opera company eked out a precarious existence, and once in a while a European violinist or pianist would venture to these shores, only to return with tales of the barbarism of American taste. The most successful of these seems to have been a pianist named Hatton, who electrified his audience by playing the piano with an obbligato of sleighbells that he shook with his right leg. The favorite concert piece in New York was an orchestral work entitled *The Firemen's Quadrille,* in the course of which a company of firemen in full uniform came out on the stage and danced. Louis Moreau Gottschalk, the first distinguished pianist that America produced, was then only twelve years old. He was to make his debut two years later, but that would be in Paris.

Such was the hardly fertile ground that the founders of this orchestra undertook to cultivate, and it is no wonder that for several years they gave only four concerts a season. The wonder is that they had the courage to give any at all. Even their own subscribers must have given them trouble, for as late as 1857 a New York clergyman preached an entire sermon on the bad manners of the Philharmonic audiences, deploring their habit of carrying on loud conversations while the music was being played. Also, one of the striking features of New York life was what we now delicately allude to as the

"Department of Sanitation." At that time it was administered entirely by droves of pigs, who ranged up and down Broadway, happily devouring the by-products of New York cookery in the daytime, and repairing to their various places of residence at sundown. When you attended a Philharmonic concert in those days, you sometimes arrived in strange company.

The first rehearsal was held in May, 1842, and thereafter the members rehearsed every other Saturday through the summer and fall. Whatever the shortcomings of its early programs, they could hardly be accused of having been thrown together on the spur of the moment. The first concert of the orchestra of the Philharmonic Society of New York took place in the Apollo Rooms on the evening of December 7, 1842. Mr. Hill, who had been elected president of the society and its first conductor, conducted the opening number, the "grand symphony in C minor of Beethoven"—in other words, his Fifth. This was the first performance of the work in America. It was the only one, by the way, that Mr. Hill conducted at that concert.

I'd be curious to see what impression that first Philharmonic program would make on a present-day audience. Not that it was bad, but it was hardly what we would consider a "symphonic" program. Of the eight numbers, only three were for orchestra alone. It opened, as I say, with the Beethoven Fifth. Then followed a scene from Weber's *Oberon,* sung by a Madame Otto and conducted by a Mr. H. C. Timm, who, in his spare moments, also played the trombone. Then came a number programmed as "Quintet in D minor for strings and piano, by Hummel." This was probably Johann Nepomuk Hummel, an early nineteenth-century pianist and improviser, who had been a protégé of Mozart in his youth and whose music was greatly admired at the time.

That ended part one of the program. The second half

opened with the overture to *Oberon,* conducted by D. G. Etienne, who doubled on the French horn. Then came a duet from Rossini's opera *Armida,* sung by Madame Otto and a Mr. C. E. Horn. Madame Otto having already had a solo, it was time to give Mr. Horn one, so he then sang a scene from Beethoven's *Fidelio.* But Madame Otto was not to be deprived of the last word, and accordingly offered an air from *Belmont and Constantia* (*The Abduction from the Seraglio* to you). The concert ended with an overture in D by Wenzel Kalliwoda, a Czech musician who was then taken very seriously as a composer. There were sixty-three playing members at that first concert, some in white tie and tails, most of them in frock coats. They were seated between numbers, but, like a chorus, rose to perform—with the exception of the incorrigibly sedentary players of the cello. According to Mr. Howard Taubman of the New York *Times,* from whom I have stolen several other facts, the gross receipts for the opening season amounted to $1,854.50, of which the members themselves contributed six hundred dollars. One certainly can't call them money-mad. Just what the expenses amounted to, I don't know, although obviously they must have been pretty modest.

In 1867 the Philharmonic celebrated its twenty-fifth anniversary. Andrew Johnson was President of the United States. We had just purchased Alaska from Russia, and the newly laid Atlantic cable was a subject of wide discussion. An obscure foreign correspondent of the New York *Herald,* named Karl Marx, had just finished the first volume of a book entitled *Das Kapital,* Piotr Ilich Tchaikovsky had just finished his first symphony, Johannes Brahms had heard the first performance of his *German Requiem,* and the Russian composer Modeste Moussorgsky was working on an opera based on the life of the Tsar Boris Godunoff.

The conductor of the Philharmonic was Carl Bergman,

who opened the season with a program that included a Mozart piano concerto, Mendelssohn's violin concerto, and Beethoven's *Pastoral* symphony. The orchestra had eighty-six playing members. There was only one other major symphony orchestra in the country, and that, too, was in New York. It had been founded three years before by a German-born violinist and conductor named Theodore Thomas. In that year of 1867 he began giving his concerts in the Central Park Garden, a hall that had been built for him at Seventh Avenue and Fifty-ninth Street, at the lower edge of Central Park. In the days of my youth it was famous as Durland's Riding Academy.

I have a copy of the annual report of the Philharmonic Society for the season of 1867–68. It was in that year that the society for the first time elected a president who did not play an instrument. This was Dr. R. Ogden Doremus, a famous chemist, who for many years, up to the time of his death, in 1906, was professor of chemistry at the College of the City of New York. The founder, Urelli Corelli Hill, had retired to the comparative obscurity of vice-president. In its early days it was the custom of the Society annually to elect some eminent musician to honorary membership, and by 1867 it had an imposing list, one that included Henri Vieuxtemps and Ole Bull, the violinists, Mendelssohn, Bottesini, the great double-bass player, Louis Gottschalk, the composer-pianist, and Jenny Lind.

According to the treasurer's report for that year, the total receipts, including gifts and gate receipts, amounted to $14,508.88. Of this sum, something over five thousand dollars went to the members. Rent amounted to a little under three thousand, and miscellaneous salaries took fourteen hundred. Ten soloists appeared with the orchestra during the season, their total fees amounting to $827.70. When you consider that among those who cut this melon were the famous French violinist Camilla Urso, an equally famous pianist, Richard Hoffman, the distinguished opera singer Madame Parepa Rosa, and (as violin soloist) Theodore Thomas, you can imagine what an artist of lesser rank earned in those days. The highest fee went to Madame Rosa, who got three hundred dollars. Some of the others, including Theodore Thomas, seem to have played for nothing. All in all, after deducting all expenses, the Society's budget for 1867–68 showed a triumphant balance of $106.88. In recent years the annual budget of the Society has averaged around a million dollars, and as I think of the tears that must be rolling down the cheeks of the Board of Directors if they read this book, I am almost sorry I brought up that old report.

In 1892 the Philharmonic was fifty years old. Benjamin Harrison was president of the United States, and Victoria was in her fifty-fifth year on the British throne, with William Ewart Gladstone as her prime minister. A young German composer named Richard Strauss was finishing his opera *Guntram*, Anton Bruckner had just finished his ninth symphony, the *Strand Magazine* was printing a series of stories relating the exploits of a detective named Sherlock Holmes, and the French composer Claude Debussy had the experience of hearing an audience hiss the first performance of a piece of his called *The Afternoon of a Faun.*

By this time there were five major symphony orchestras in the United States. There was one in Boston and one in St. Louis. Theodore Thomas, who had been conductor of the Philharmonic since 1877, had gone to head the Chicago Symphony Orchestra, and was opening his second season. In New York there were still two rival orchestras, the New York Symphony, under the direction of Walter Damrosch, and the Philharmonic, under Anton Seidl.

1917. The Philharmonic was seventy-five years old. Josef Stransky was its conductor. The list of major symphony orchestras had been augmented by five more—Cincinnati, Philadelphia, Minneapolis, San Francisco, and Pittsburgh. In 1909 the Philharmonic had been reorganized, and was no longer a co-operative organization, but a regularly subsidized orchestra, with a list of guarantors. We were at war with Germany. The New York Board of Education had ruled that German operas were not to be discussed at its educational lectures, prominent concert artists amused themselves by publicly smashing German phonograph records, and the Board of Directors of the Philharmonic Orchestra issued a statement to the effect that no music by any living German composer would be included in its programs.

1942. In its hundredth year the Philharmonic-Symphony was going its way in a country that can boast sixteen major orchestras (i.e., organizations whose annual budgets range between one and eight hundred thousand dollars), two hundred and fifty professional orchestras of more modest pretensions, and upward of thirty thousand school, college, and conservatory orchestras. Once more we were at war with Germany—and Japan and Italy. But despite Pearl Harbor, despite everything, the Metropolitan continued to produce *Tristan and Isolde, Der Rosenkavalier, La Traviata,* and *La Bohème*. The orchestras still played Strauss and Respighi—any music, in fact, by no matter what composer, living or dead, of no matter what nationality. At last we had arrived at the point of distinguishing the work of art from the artist. America had outlived its adolescence in the arts. America had grown up.

Seven Score and Spry

SPEAKING of the centennial of the Philharmonic-Symphony, it is described, quite accurately, as the oldest symphony orchestra in America. In that connection, of course, the term "professional" is understood. And it's important that it *be* understood. For there is in active existence a non-professional orchestra that is thirty-four years older than the Philharmonic-Symphony, namely, the Pierian Sodality of Harvard University.

The year was 1808. John Marshall had just been appointed Chief Justice of the United States Supreme Court, Congress had just passed legislation forbidding the further importation of slaves into this country, and Thomas Jefferson was finishing his second term as President of the United States. On March 6th of that year, a group of students in Harvard College, as it was then called, met and established a society to be known as the Pierian Sodality (in other words, a fellowship of the Muses), for "mutual improvement in instrumental music." We would call it an ensemble rather than an orchestra, for its structure was extremely sketchy, and for a good many years the size and personnel of the combination were determined by whatever instruments happened to be played by whatever undergraduates happened to belong. Its early aims were as much social as they were musical, and its members were amateurs in the true sense of the word, in that they met primarily for the pleasure of playing together, without being too fussy about the quality of the performance.

They were, however, conscientious about keeping the minutes of their meetings, and the archives of Harvard contain a complete set from 1808 to 1821, and from 1832 to the present day. The early records are a bit vague as to just what instruments were used, and what music they played. Apparently some of it was in manuscript, for the minutes of June 15, 1808, record the passing of a motion to the effect that "If any member neglect to copy into his book the tunes which shall be noted on the list, he shall be fined twenty-five cents for each tune." Two years later there was a mention of a definite piece of music, when the members voted to "receive" a piece called Handel's *Air*. Just what air isn't specified, but my guess is that it was the dear old *Largo*.

In 1814 the Sodality comprised seven playing members and several honorary members. Then a decline apparently set in, until, in 1832, it was reduced to just one member, Henry Gasset, of the class of '34. However, Mr. Gasset carried on bravely. He used to meet with himself once a week, play the flute, and keep the minutes of the meetings. He finally initiated two more members, and the Sodality was saved. It was not only saved, but made a revolutionary proposal. The minutes for September of that same year recorded that "Last term a subject of great importance to the Pierians (meaning the intrepid Gasset and his two friends) was agitated among the higher powers; that is, the establishment of a musical Professor in the college. President Quincy intimated to the Sodality that such a plan was agreeable, and that he would endeavor to procure one from the faculty." Nothing came of the idea, though, as the faculty decided that it was too expensive. However, the seed was planted, and twenty years later bore fruit; because in 1855 Harvard established its first professorship of music, which was the first in America.

The literary quality of the minutes was frequently rather on the purple side. For example, in the record of December

15, 1839, we find the following bit of rich prose: "Sodality met at seven o'clock and played in a most delectable manner. Music has charms doubly delightful; it calls forth the deepest emotions of the soul; it purifies the heart; it cleanses one of the infirmities which the flesh is heir to." However, leaving aside the merits of the music, the quality of the performance apparently left, upon occasion, something to be desired. Whoever recorded the meeting of May 31, 1841, reports that "Few of us who assembled on that night will forget the pathetic strains of the bassoon, which appeared to come from the proboscis rather than the mouth of Brother Ladd, and which sounded like an old lady of ninety attempting to sing *Old Hundredth*. No one will forget the complaining notes of the squeaking flutes, interrupted as they were by the sobs of the performers or the dolorous snorts of the horn, poured forth as they were, with unusual strength, by Brother Smith."

Things went from bad to worse. Take the meeting of October 6, 1845: "It is with inexpressible pain that the Secretary records the transactions of this meeting. No one of the members seems to have come with a desire to play, and all the instruments acted as if possessed with an evil spirit. Even the cello seemed determined to flatten the tone of the other instruments; it persisted in being obstinate and unruly for nearly an hour. Altogether it was a shameful meeting, for nothing was done of any consequence, and many beautiful pieces were actually murdered by the horrid discords."

Six years later the secretary was equally gloomy. "September 18, 1851. Met and played abominably. September 26. Met and played like thunder."

The playing personnel varied, as I said, from term to term; and some of the effects achieved by the various combinations must have been rather peculiar. For example, in 1850 the instrumentation consisted of five violins; one each of clarinet, cello, cornet, French horn, and trombone; and seven flutes.

In 1859 the combination was four violins, one cello, two flutes, one cornet, and two pianists. This the secretary called "the best selected orchestra the Pierians have ever had." Incidentally, in 1856 the society had had another crisis when its membership sank to two playing members. What they played, the record doesn't say.

Matters began to improve, however. The year 1860 seems to have been a landmark in the history of the society, for the minutes of October 16th of that year report a series of rehearsals under the leadership of Mr. Wulf Fries, who "impressed on this society the necessity of minding the pianos and fortes, which have always been treated with more or less contempt in this society."

The next ten years marked a tremendous improvement in the size and balance of the playing membership. By 1871 the society had a complete symphony orchestra with the exception, of all things, of the percussion instruments. By 1886 the orchestra numbered forty players, all amateurs in good standing. Today, as the Harvard University Orchestra, it is a well-balanced symphonic group averaging about fifty players, and is technically equipped to play anything except the more elaborate modern augmented orchestral scores. It is a completely undergraduate organization, maintained by its members and functioning entirely on its own, with no financial help from the University. Since it really found itself, artistically, in the eighties, it has had many distinguished names on its roster of conductors, including Professor Philip Greely Clapp, Chalmers Clifton, Walter Piston, and its present conductor, Malcolm H. Holmes, who took over in 1932.

It has probably lost some of the happy-go-lucky characteristics that distinguished it in the early eighteen-hundreds; it looks no longer with contempt upon the pianos and the fortes. In short, the Pierian Sodality has grown up. It is older and wiser. But after all, who wouldn't be, at the age of seven score?

9

Reducing Diet

A GROUP of us were discussing symphony orchestras and the struggle they have in keeping going. Of the two hundred-odd orchestras, of all sizes and shapes, that we have here today, I doubt if there are half a dozen whose income equals their expenses; the larger the orchestra, the larger the deficit. The biggest item of expense is, of course, the payroll. In general, I should say that the salaries of the players make up very nearly two-thirds of the budget of any orchestra.

These things so, we were discussing whether it would be possible either to reduce the salaries of the players or cut done the size of the orchestra. Now, the first alternative is, under present conditions, very difficult, if not impossible. The skill and the necessary preliminary training of orchestral musicians have increased so incredibly since the middle of the nineteenth century that the average first-desk player in any major symphony orchestra today would have been considered a concert virtuoso a hundred years ago. He is probably a conservatory graduate; in any case, he has had to put in years of study and practice, not only in the technique of his instrument but in composition and orchestration. He knows the scores of the works that he plays, and could probably conduct a respectable performance of any work in the classic repertoire. Whatever the instrument he plays, he is, in his field, technically and artistically the equivalent of a Heifetz, a Liszt, or a Rubinstein.

Such a man is in demand, and deservedly commands a

high salary. Considering his skill, he is not overpaid. On the other hand, that salary is not necessarily the minimum that he would accept under certain conditions. If the continental orchestras were able, in past years, to operate at less expense than ours, the whole reason does not lie in the higher purchasing power of money or a less expensive standard of living. As a rule, the European orchestral musician is employed the year round. Here he is not. Even with a major symphony orchestra he has no guarantee of employment beyond a season of from twenty to twenty-eight weeks. He must be prepared to live for a year on what he can make in seven months. Any additional income is dependent upon what jobs he can get playing single concerts, recording, or broadcasting. No wonder his salary is high. There have been attempts, here, to put orchestras on a year-round basis, but so far they have failed, resulting merely in bigger deficits. Until we can solve that economic problem, we can't expect orchestral musicians to play for less money than they are now getting.

Well, then [someone said at that discussion], how about reducing the size of the orchestra? Instead of a hundred men, why not sixty, or even fifty? After all, the classic masters got along with comparatively small orchestras.

As a matter of fact, the orchestras for which the classic masters wrote weren't quite as small as we assume them to be. The earliest orchestras were pretty haphazard affairs. In their infant days, at the beginning of the seventeenth century, an orchestral score consisted of four, or possibly five, vocal parts, and the orchestra consisted of whatever instruments happened to be lying loose, each one playing the part that happened to suit it best. In the earliest operas, the singers sometimes doubled as orchestra players when they didn't happen to have anything to do on stage. They could do this because the orchestra always played behind the scenes. One famous orchestra was the one that Monteverdi assembled for the wedding festival of his patron, the Duke of Mantua. Here's their idea of an orchestra in those days: twelve viols (the immediate ancestor of the violin), two violins, two double basses, three viole da gamba (that is, undersized cellos), two harpsichords, two lutes (they looked something like mandolins), two pipe organs, one portable organ, a piccolo, a sort of clarinet, two cornets (which were made of bone), three trumpets, and four trombones.

Even that weird combination numbered thirty-seven players.

When we come to Bach, a century later, we find him writing for a much smaller combination, from eighteen to twenty players. But remember that his scoring was very simple, and that his more ambitious choral works were performed in a church, and not a very large church, so that he didn't need a large orchestra. Handel's orchestra varied in size, depending on where it was supposed to play. For his oratorios he used from thirty-four to thirty-six men. His *Fireworks* music, on the other hand, which was to be played outdoors, called for a wind band of fifty-one, including six trumpets and twenty-four oboes.

Haydn wrote for a fairly small orchestra, never more than thirty. He did that, first, because he had to, since he was writing for a private orchestra, and second, because he could, since he employed very little brass. Mozart can also be played by a comparatively small group, since, except in his operas, he, too, was rather sparing with the brass.

Beethoven is a different story. His symphonic works were intended for what is still the average small-city orchestra, this is, between forty and fifty-five men. The specially augmented orchestra that played the first performance of his Ninth symphony numbered seventy-two players. Then Berlioz and Wagner, between them, began to make instrumental demands for their music that swelled the orchestra way beyond its former proportions. Berlioz loved size and volume, apparently, for their own sake. Where the average large orchestra today employs one bass clarinet, Berlioz thought nothing of writing for four or five.

Wagner called for an average orchestra of about ninety players. However, there is this to be said in explanation of his apparent extravagance. Remember that all of his music dramas after *Lohengrin* were composed with the aim of having them produced in a specially designed theater, in which the orchestra pit was to be sunk well below stage level, and screened over so that it would be invisible to the audience. That made it easy to maintain a proper balance between the singers and the orchestra. On the other hand, if the orchestra was to preserve its proper sonority, and not sound thin and muffled, it would have to be a big one. So he wrote for triple wood winds, eight horns, and thirty-two violins instead of the traditional twenty-four. I don't think he would have done this if he had been planning to have his works produced in an ordinary opera house. When we hear a performance of a Wagner music drama today, with the orchestra playing in an open pit, we are not hearing it playing under the conditions that Wagner planned for it.

However, the triumph of Wagner's music, and the demand to hear performances of his works, resulted in orchestras all over Europe being expanded accordingly, whereupon other composers began to write for that orchestra. Richard Strauss was the first. All of his tone poems demand an orchestra of at least ninety players, and in at least one of his works, *Elektra*, he goes Wagner one better, calling for an orchestra of one hundred and sixteen. Gustav Mahler followed suit, using an enormously swollen orchestra, until he broke the record with his so-called "symphony of a thousand," which calls for an orchestra of one hundred to a hundred and twenty players and a chorus of nearly nine hundred. Then composers outside

Germany took to writing for these super-orchestras. Debussy's *Pelléas and Mélisande* employs an orchestra fully as large as Wagner's, as do most of the works that Stravinsky wrote for the Diaghileff ballet.

In recent years there has been a reaction against these huge instrumental combinations. Composers have discovered that they can get more performances of their works if they call for something less than the full roster of a major symphony orchestra. However, there are dozens of works in the standard repertoire, works that audiences emphatically want to hear, that make it necessary for our big orchestras to stay big. The major symphony orchestra of today, with its average membership of a hundred and six players, is none too large if it is to continue to play Wagner, Strauss, Berlioz, Debussy, and Stravinsky.

Smaller and Louder

Just the same, isn't there some way of reducing the size of even our major symphony orchestras—say, from one hundred players to sixty-five—and still have them sound adequate? Suppose we scrutinize the average symphony orchestra, group by group, to see what reductions in personnel we might make.

Well, let's see. First of all, you can't do much about the wind and percussion sections. Occasionally the clarinets are all playing the same notes, or the horns, or the trumpets, and so on—but as a rule all the wind and percussion players have separate and dissimilar parts to play. In order to perform the classic and modern orchestral repertoire as it was written, a symphony orchestra must employ a minimum of three flutes, two oboes, an English horn, two clarinets, a bass clarinet, two bassoons, a contra-bassoon, four French horns, three trumpets, three trombones, a bass tuba, one timpani player and two other percussion players, and a harp; a total of twenty-seven players.

This, as I say, is a minimum. For many modern scores, from Wagner on, that combination would have to be augmented by extra clarinets, extra horns, trumpets, and trombones, extra percussion players, another harp, and a couple of extra tubas. To be equipped to play every orchestral work written to date, a modern orchestra really should have a wind and percussion section of about forty players.

What about the strings, then? The string section alone of

many a symphony orchestra often numbers sixty-five players. Can't we swing the ax there? How did it get to be so large during the past century, and why does it have to be?

It has to be large, for one thing, because of the complexity of modern orchestration, which necessitates far greater numbers of wind players than did the scores of the classic masters. Beethoven's *Eroica* symphony calls for no trombones or tuba. Mozart's E-flat symphony is written for a wind section consisting of two each of flutes, oboes, clarinets, bassoons, horns, and trumpets—twelve players altogether. Contrast this with Richard Strauss's *A Hero's Life,* which calls for a wind section of thirty-four. Naturally, the strings in a modern orchestra have had to be more numerous in order to hold their own.

And not just to avoid being drowned out. Even when wind instruments are playing softly, certain combinations of them, playing in certain registers, tend to smother the strings, to render them not so much inaudible as incoherent. The human voice suffers the same disadvantage. Any operatic soprano can easily make herself heard over trumpets and trombones, if they're not playing *too* loudly. But make her sing against flutes and clarinets playing in her own register, and she's likely to be blotted out. You can still hear her, but you can't hear any of her words. That's why singers are sometimes blamed for bad enunciation when the real person to blame is the composer. The same thing happens to strings sometimes, when there aren't enough of them to balance the wind instruments. You know they're playing, but you can't quite make out *what* they're playing.

Even so, suppose a way could be found to increase the volume and sonority of the stringed instruments. Couldn't the orchestra get along with fewer of them? That brings me to a letter that propounds the problem and then sets about solving it.

"The question in my mind," my correspondent writes, "is whether we can bring the orchestra payroll in line with the potential ticket income, make the orchestra self-supporting, by reducing the traditional number of instruments in each section where the full orchestra now uses more than one instrument of the same *kind* on the same *note*. Is it a fair assumption that the only reason for using six cellos, for example, instead of one cello is to produce six times the volume of sound from the cello section? Is there any other reason for more than one cello, or for playing more than one instrument of any kind in any other section when all are playing exactly the same notes?"

He continues: "With the recent marvelous advance in the controlled amplification of sound, it would seem to be possible to take the best of those six cellos, amplify it to the volume of the original six, and actually produce better music, besides cutting the cello-section payroll to one star player. There seems to be no question of the practicability of amplifying the volume of a single instrument up to the volume of six—or sixty, for that matter. There is no question that the finest performer in a given section can produce truer notes than can possibly be produced by a large section, with all the possibilities of being a trifle out of tune or a shade off in timing. It would be an interesting experiment to have symphonic music produced by a small group of outstanding artists, only one instrument for each part in each section, with each amplified to standard symphony volume by skilled control engineers."

That's a tempting thought, and it sounds practicable, but there are several things the matter with it. I've already pointed out that the wind section of the orchestra, aside from occasional unisons, are all playing different parts, so that there's no chance of cutting there. But the strings by no means necessarily play identical parts. My correspondent's idea seems to be that, granted you could amplify the tone of the strings sufficiently, the string section of the orchestra would consist of only five players—a first violin, a second violin, a viola, a cello, and a bass viol. But it's not so simple as that. In the garden scene of *Tristan and Isolde,* Wagner's score calls for first violins playing four different parts; second violins playing three different parts; violas playing three parts; the cellos playing two; and the basses playing two. Take another example, the section entitled "Perfumes of the Night" from Debussy's *Iberia* suite. At one point he divides the first violins into seven different parts; at another he divides the violas into two parts and the cellos into three; at still another, he divides the first fiddles into six parts, the second violins into two, the violas into two, and the cellos into three. In other words, to play just these two examples, with only one player to a part, you would need not one but seven first violins, three seconds, three violas, three cellos, and two basses—eighteen string players in all. That isn't sixty-five, to be sure, but it's considerably more than five. And the two examples that I've cited are two of dozens of modern scores that call for elaborately divided strings. Strauss, on occasion, divides even the double basses into four parts.

However, for the moment let's assume that an orchestra is playing a symphonic work in which the strings are *not* divided. We reduce the string section to five solo players, and then contrive to step up the volume of all five until they are just as loud as the traditional full string section. Would we get the effect of a large symphony orchestra? As a matter of fact, we would not. And if you want proof of that assertion, just listen to any violin concerto—the Brahms concerto, for instance. Now, there's a work in which the solo instrument is treated almost as a part of the orchestra. The latter isn't just an accompaniment. The part it plays in the musical proceedings is just as important as that of the soloist. Sometimes one takes up the thread of the music, sometimes the other; sometimes they take it up together. Yet the solo violin is always audible. Why? Because a single violin doesn't in the least sound like sixteen, any more than sixteen tenors sound like Jan Peerce. A large symphony orchestra doesn't have sixteen first violinists only because they're sixteen times louder than one. As a matter of fact, they're little more than twice as loud. But the quality of the sound they produce is a different matter. No two single violins have exactly the same tone quality. If they did, you couldn't tell Elman from Heifetz, or Heifetz from Milstein. Also, as my correspondent points out, they may not all play equally in tune; their intonation may differ by four or five vibrations a second. One may play a minute fraction of a second slower or faster than another. But when you combine a number of violinists into a group of eight or ten or more, all those differences combine to form a new tone, the one that we recognize as an orchestral tone. It's broader than the tone of a single instrument; it's a little less sharp on the edges; and it's what, for want of a better word, I call a *larger* tone. Sixteen violins, playing with their mutes on, as softly as they can, are a larger sound than a single violin playing as loudly as he can. If you take a string quintet and amplify its sound ten times, you don't get a string orchestra; you just get a very loud string quintet.

On the other hand, it's not beyond the range of possibility that someday we can find a way to reduce the string section of an orchestra by one half, say, and by amplification give it the power of a full-sized section. But it won't be simple. The men can't play into microphones, for the microphones tend to "leak"—to pick up other sections of the orchestra—and that spoils the balance. We could do it by placing the various sections in soundproof compartments. That would be fine for broadcasting, but no good for live concerts. Even then, the loudspeakers couldn't be on the stage. If they were, they'd "play back," as they call it, and would produce an echo; you'd get double talk from the orchestra. But if the loudspeakers were placed away from the orchestra, in a fixed position, we'd begin to lose the effect of the sounds coming from various directions that is so characteristic of a big orchestra. Any workable amplification device would have to be placed in the instruments themselves.

I don't say it couldn't be done, or that it won't be done someday. But meanwhile I think we'd better risk the deficits and keep our orchestras what they are.

Place aux Dames . . . Bitte

As a rule, any time a man begins a sentence with "Now, the trouble with women is . . ." you can safely stop listening, because he undoubtedly doesn't know what he's talking about. However, admitting that fundamental truth, I am about to take a little space in which to discuss women. Not women in general—I still have a little sense—but women in connection with one branch of music. What started me on the subject was a letter that came from a young woman who was studying at a famous conservatory, and who wrote as follows:

"I'm a music student. I study conducting. Also, I'm a woman, the only one at present in the conducting course at school. If I had stuck to the violin I might, after becoming five times better than any man, procure a back chair in a major symphony orchestra." (I think she's a little unnecessarily bitter on that point. She wouldn't have to be five times as good as a man to get a job like that. Three times as good would be ample.)

"However," she continues, "I preferred greater odds. I want to be an example. There is no reason why a man and a woman with equal talent shouldn't be judged by their ability rather than by their sex. Yet in Chicago, although they have got so far as to have a women's orchestra, a man conducts it. Perhaps you would have a suggestion as to a 'follow up' after the conservatory. I think my best bet would be to start with a string orchestra in the Middle West. Most musicians pat me on the head, so to speak, and say, 'Of course, *study* conducting all you like, but of course a woman conducting an orchestra looks—well, just silly.' Please, don't you say that, too!"

All right, I won't. Some of them do, just the same. Still, some men do, too, so that's not the trouble.

What *is* the trouble? I must confess that I haven't any ready or particularly conclusive answer to that question. I can only speculate. So here are my guesses as to the reasons that contribute, at least, to the fact that we have so few women conductors.

One reason might be a physical one. I doubt whether people realize that conducting entails a lot of hard manual labor. I should say that the energy expended in conducting a symphony program, in continuous motion for approximately an hour and fifteen minutes, is the equivalent of at least three hard sets of tennis. I have seen tennis championship matches played in less time. Moreover, a conductor is under not only a physical strain but an intense nervous one as well. If you want a taste of what it's like, next time you hear your favorite symphony over the air, try standing up and beating time to the first movement. I can guarantee that at the end of it you'll know that you have been exercising. On second thought, perhaps you'd better *not* try it if you have a weak heart and want to enjoy the music. It's not enough for a conductor to be an artist; he must be an athlete as well. I think it would take a woman of exceptional physique to survive the strain of a season's rehearsals and concerts.

There is another minor physical aspect to the case, too. I have heard athletic trainers say that a woman's shoulder muscles are not attached the same as a man's. That, they say, is why so few women can play baseball: because as a rule they can't master an accurate overhand throw. Also, they point out, a woman tennis player, no matter how severe her ground strokes may be, never serves or smashes as hard as a man of equal ability, because those strokes entail the use of the shoulder muscles. Whether this is true or not, I don't know; I'm no anatomist. But if it should be true, it would interfere with a woman's conducting technique.

Well, there is one guess. My second guess is that there's a possible psychological barrier in the way. I wonder whether women tend to have the particular quality of leadership that a conductor must possess. Granted that a conductor is equal to the physical demands of conducting, granted that he is an artist, that he knows exactly how he wants every bar of the music to sound, he still has to face the job of making the musicians play it the way he wants it. Tchaikovsky's fifth symphony was more or less of a failure at its first performance in St. Petersburg. Why? Because Tchaikovsky conducted it. He was simply not a conductor. He was too timid, too much of an introvert, to be able to discipline a group of orchestra players. Great musician as he was, he was not a leader. In his entire career as guest conductor, his only entirely successful performances of his works were occasions upon which someone else had rehearsed the orchestra for him, so that he had little to do beyond beating time at the performance. His own rehearsal consisted in little more than running through the score.

There are two kinds of leadership: the kind that is based on authority, imposed from without, and leadership that comes from within. The former is generally exercised over large bodies of people, such as armies or even nations, and it doesn't necessarily entail coming into close personal contact with the bodies that are being led. There have been many women rulers in history, from Cleopatra to Marie of Rumania. They ruled through law and through subordinates. They were great administrators. But the ability to run a country or a nationwide organization isn't necessarily the ability to run an orchestra. That latter kind of leadership is the ability to impose your will, backed by no authority but your own personality, upon a comparatively small group of persons, and make them carry out, and *want* to carry out, not only your literal orders but your intentions. The qualities of a great conductor are not those of a great general; they are rather the qualities of a great top sergeant. And while women might make great generals, I'm not sure that many of them would make good top sergeants. I have an idea that the combination of alternate bullying and persuasion that is the necessary tactics of a conductor at rehearsal doesn't come altogether natural to them.

And then, of course, any woman who tries to conduct an orchestra runs up against a fearful barrier of male prejudice. Don't ask me why, but as a rule men bitterly resent taking orders from a woman—unless, of course, they happen to be married to her.

Well, there you have my three guesses. And I might as well make a fourth guess, which is that probably none of those guesses is correct. Most of the objections that I have raised apply to men as well as women. After all, comparatively few men have the physical stamina to conduct, and even fewer have the quality of personal leadership that successful conducting involves. I think my statement at the end of the third guess is the nearest to being accurate: that men generally resent taking orders from a woman. In other words, it's a matter of age-long prejudice, a prejudice that will eventually break down. After all, it's only a few years, in the history of the race, since women have been allowed to engage in *any* sort of professional activity. As recently as Shakespeare's day they weren't allowed on the stage. Only since World War I have they been allowed to vote. Already they are making their way into our symphony orchestras; it is, I think, only a matter of time until some of them make their way to the conductor's stand. You may hear again from that girl whose letter I have quoted.

Music in Your Eye

THERE is one very comforting feature about arguing questions of art and literature and music: nobody ever wins the argument. Nothing is ever settled because nobody can *prove* that he's right, and so the argument can continue on through the ages. Seeing the announcement of Tchaikovsky's *Romeo and Juliet* overture as part of a concert program made me think of that, because it brought to mind a question that I've often discussed, and which still seems to have an endless fascination for many of my correspondents; that is, the old battle between program music and absolute music. Is the one inferior to the other? Is it wrong to make up stories about music that has no story, or to see pictures that the composer doesn't paint? Is the third *Leonore* overture worse than the *Eroica* symphony because it has a plot? And is the *Eroica* worse than the Fifth because it was concerned with Napoleon? Only a short time ago a correspondent wrote to say, "Am I wrong in thinking that program music is of a lower order than that of pattern and structure? Am I wrong in finding it better to be completely carried out of myself into a wordless realm than to weigh careful conclusions of accurate meanings?" The answer to both those questions is, of course, "Certainly not." On the other hand, that doesn't mean that my correspondent has all the right on her side.

The meaning, or the message or whatever you want to call it, of any given piece of music is determined not so much by who the composer is as by who the listener is. I think people overlook that fact. Some persons, for example, are strongly eye-minded. They think visually. I know I do. Any thought or idea, no matter how abstract, converts itself into a picture in my mind. I *see* dates, for instance. You say "1492" to me, and instantly I see a little cube with "1492" painted on it, resting on a landing of an endless flight of steps that go down into infinite space. Now, you ask a person with a mind like that *not* to experience some sort of visual reaction when he hears music, and you're asking the impossible. On the other hand, there are many persons to whom an abstract idea, an abstract sound, *is* abstract. They don't think in pictures at all. Ask that type of person to look for Friar Lawrence and the two lovers in the *Romeo and Juliet* overture, and you merely irritate him.

Fundamentally, I don't think that any of that is important. What matters, and what makes any piece of good music worth hearing, is that it speaks to every listener in his own terms, conveys something that is valuable to him, whether it's a picture, a story, or an abstract spiritual uplift. I think the people who frown upon any sort of dramatization or visualization of music overlook one thing, which is that persons who are not experienced listeners, who are comparatively unfamiliar with symphonic music, find its form very difficult to grasp at first. You take someone who has been brought up on an exclusive diet of popular songs, whose conception of musical form is a sixteen-bar verse and a thirty-two-bar chorus, broken up into easily swallowed four-bar mouthfuls, and suddenly require him to retain in his mind the structure of, say, first movement of Beethoven's Fifth symphony, and you're confronting him with a problem that he isn't yet equipped to solve. But let him make up a story or imagine a series of pictures to go with that first movement and you've given him an invaluable prop, a framework on which to hang the music in his mind. I know that that sounds like desecration, to some, but I must admit that I don't feel guilty about saying it. You offer food to a hungry man. I don't think it matters much whether you offer him the correct fork—or any fork at all. The important thing is that you feed him.

Besides, the program, or lack of it, of any piece of music is much more the composer's business than the listener's. Some composers think abstractly, like other people, and some think visually or dramatically. The first variety don't need a definite springboard for their music; the second do. But the pretext for the music doesn't affect its quality. Wagner is a great composer, even though he did always conceive his music in dramatic or pictorial terms. So is Beethoven a great composer, even though most of his music is abstract.

But doesn't all this story telling and picture painting give the inexperienced listener a wrong conception of the music? Doesn't it prevent his hearing and enjoying the music for its own sake? I think not. I know my own experience in listening even to frankly descriptive music is always the same. In the early stages of hearing it, while the piece is comparatively unfamiliar, I *am* conscious of the program, and find myself trying to follow it. I remember that the first few times I heard the *Romeo and Juliet* overture I enjoyed picking out the Friar Lawrence theme and the passage that depicts the row between the Capulets and the Montagues, and recognizing the balcony scene when it arrived, and the death of the lovers, and all that. But with repeated hearings of the music, the program began to fade into unimportance. When I hear *Romeo and Juliet* today, I don't think of Romeo and Juliet at all. I don't care whether that certain theme represents Friar Lawrence or General Grant. All that I'm conscious of is that I'm listening to a familiar piece of what, to me, is good music. And that, I believe, is the eventual experience of every listener, to any piece of music. Music survives by reason of its own vitality, and *not* because of the title its composer happened to give to it.

Those of you who are amateur gardeners may have run across something that its makers call a "pattern" garden. It consists of a long roll of tough paper in which holes about an inch in diameter have been punched to form a regular pattern, the pattern of a flower bed. You spade and rake the ground, and take out the stones. Then you peg down the paper pattern. The holes are numbered to correspond with the packages of flower seeds that came with it, and you just drop the seeds into the proper holes, brush a little earth over them, water them lightly, and let Nature take her course. The paper, where it isn't punched, keeps the weeds out, and the holes give the flower seeds a chance to sprout. In due time they come up—and you have a flower garden. If the seeds were well selected, it's a pretty garden; if they weren't, it isn't. In either case, by the time the flower plants have bloomed, the paper pattern has rotted away and vanished. By midsummer, looking at your garden, you would never know that there had ever been a paper pattern. Of course, if you're the kind of gardener who doesn't want a paper pattern, you can drop the seeds where you please and do your own weeding. By midsummer, both gardens may look alike.

I have often thought that music is like that. In a symphony or a tone poem, a sonata, or a ballet, as in a garden, what matters, in the long run, is not what the pattern was or where it came from, but what ideas went into it and how they were tended and how they grew.

Experts Can Stub Their Toes

IN THE preceding chapter I ventured the suggestion that the "message" of a given piece of music depends more upon the listener than upon the composer. I might amplify that a bit, taking for my text a letter from a plaintive correspondent who found himself out of step with current musical conceptions. "My trouble," he wrote, "is that notwithstanding many years of intent listening to the best that radio and my own local symphony have to offer, I seldom or never can co-ordinate what I hear with what I'm told it represents. If it is stated that such and such a movement depicts man's struggle against unyielding fate, it is quite likely to seem to me a delightful suggestion of a quiet afternoon in a forest. In fact, Beethoven's symphonies evoke different emotions every time I hear them. Does this mean that I'm hopelessly unappreciative of established musical idiom, and congenitally unable to translate it properly? Is there anything to be done about it now? I know that experts frequently differ in their interpretations of the musical meaning of symphonic masterworks, but they always seem so cocksure of themselves. Once they have decided on the meaning of any given composition, they stick to their interpretations. I wish I could be as sure of my own."

I can assure that particular listener that he is not alone in his trouble. Even the critics stub their toes once in a while. I remember two instances out of my own experience. About twenty years ago a promising young American conductor was invited to conduct the Pasdeloup Orchestra of Paris in two programs of music by American composers. He called me up and offered to include a piece of mine on one of the programs, the particular number that he wanted being a pantomime ballet that I had written as part of the incidental music to the play *Beggar on Horseback*. It had been written for two pianos and had never been orchestrated, and what he wanted to know was whether I could score it for orchestra in time for the concert. Naturally, the prospect of having stuff of mine played in Paris by a famous French orchestra was very exciting, and of course I agreed.

Well, one thing led to another, as frequently happens with lazy people, and about a month before the concert I realized that I wasn't going to get that score done in time. I finally had to cable him to put somebody else's music in that spot. This he did, substituting for the ballet a suite in five movements, entitled *Stevensoniana*, by Edward Burlingame Hill.

Let me be parenthetical long enough to explain that there is—or was—a little weekly magazine published in Paris that printed, among other things, advance programs of opera performances, recitals, and orchestral concerts. This enjoyed rather a wide circulation, and was sent free of charge to all dramatic and music critics. It was called, I believe, *La Semaine à Paris*. Let me also explain that theater and concert programs in France are sold, not given away.

What happened, then, was as follows: The notice of the substitution arrived too late for correction in the columns of *La Semaine à Paris*, which, accordingly, went out to the critics with my number wrongly included in the program of the concert. The correction *was* made in the house program, which carried the name of Mr. Hill's suite. But the critics frugally didn't bother to buy a house program. They just brought along the one that was printed in *La Semaine à Paris*. As a consequence, most of the Paris newspapers, the following morning, carried rather extensive and deeply thoughtful criticisms of my ballet from *Beggar on Horseback*. Just how a suite in five movements could manage to sound like a pantomime in one movement, I wouldn't venture to say. Nevertheless, apparently it did. I recall particularly that Alfred Bruneau, who was a well-known composer as well as critic, wrote that while not knowing the plot of the pantomime, it was difficult to decide how appropriate the music was, nevertheless the work did show considerable grasp of the technique of the theater.

The other disaster happened to me some years ago, when I was music critic of the old New York *World*. There was a matinée concert of chamber music whose program included a new suite by a well-known British composer which I was anxious to hear. Having another concert to cover that afternoon, I got to the hall a bit late, arriving as the suite got under way. The title was, I believe, *Impressions of a Holiday*. After all these years I can't remember the exact titles of the five movements, but they went approximately like this: No. 1, *The Old Mill;* No. 2, *Deep Forest;* No. 3, *By the River;* No. 4, *Sunrise in the Fields;* No. 5, *Village Dance*.

The first movement was appropriately smooth and serene and a little melancholy—a very good suggestion of the old mill. The second had a swelling, murmurous quality that did suggest a forest of the English oaks. The third had a broad sweep to it that brought to mind the quiet, irresistible flow of a river. The fourth did have the buoyancy and triumphant quality of a gorgeous sunrise. The fifth—but there wasn't any fifth. The audience applauded, the musicians got up and bowed, and that was that. I hadn't arrived in time to hear the first movement. I had been sitting there attributing to every movement of the suite the title and the mood of the movement that preceded it.

There is not just one moral attached to those stories, but two. The first is that if a composer attaches a definite title or description to a given piece of music, the average listener, even the professional listener, will accept his program without question and will strain his imagination to the breaking point in the effort to find justification for it in music. Alfred Bruneau worked hard and conscientiously to find some traces of ballet in a suite that was pure concert music, just as I worked hard trying to fit the wrong titles to the music of another suite. We were both of us doing our intellectually dishonest best to help the composer mean something he hadn't meant to mean. That subconscious impulse, on the part of the hearer, to co-operate is a great help to any composer in putting over a piece of descriptive music.

Of course, that same impulse may backfire. If the composer chooses a program that is too explicit or too grandiose, he may find the listener pulling against him instead of for him. If, for example, he describes his music as—I quote from an actual program note—"designed to convey a sense of cosmic futility," his audience is likely to look for the futility and forget the cosmic part. Richard Strauss ran a much greater risk in composing *Death and Transfiguration* than he did in writing *Till Eulenspiegel*. In order to be acceptable, the former had to be great music almost *in spite* of its program. I remember the first time I heard Liadoff's *The Apocalypse*. It struck me that to interpret the Book of Revelation in terms of music was a pretty ambitious assignment for any composer, including Bach, Beethoven, and Wagner; and I was all too ready to find that Liadoff fell short of his mark. If it weren't for his program, I might today think that his *Apocalypse* is a lot better music than I do think it is—if you follow me.

The second moral of those unfortunate incidents is that granted that a composer has the right to attach any meaning to his music that he chooses, the listener who attaches the wrong meaning to it has a certain amount of right on his side, too. If I listen to a village dance and find that it also fits the description of a sunrise, or hear a piece called *The River* and find that it sounds like a forest, a sunrise and a forest they *are*, so far as I am concerned. That's my privilege and yours, and don't let any composer bully you out of it. Every once in a while a composer unconsciously admits that even *he* isn't positive of the exact significance of his music. One of the world's favorite pieces is the overture to Rossini's *The Barber of Seville,* and there are plenty of music lovers who will tell you that they can trace the whole course of the comedy and even identify the character of Figaro in that overture. As a matter of fact, the work began as the overture to a serious opera of Rossini's called *Aurelian in Palmyra,* dealing with the Emperor Aurelian of Rome and Queen Zenobia of Persia. It was a failure; whereupon the composer promptly transferred the overture to another opera, *Elizabeth, Queen of England.* That was a failure, too. So when it came time to deliver the score of *The Barber,* and there was no time to write an overture for it, Rossini calmly took Elizabeth's overture away from her and gave it to Figaro.

The point is—and I have made it before and shall probably make it many times again—that music, while it is a language, is a wordless language, and fundamentally does not precisely express anything that words can convey. You can put words to it, but they aren't the only possible words. The tune that we know as *America* has three sets of words to go with it—American, British, and German—and they all sound appropriate. Of all the arts music is the most fluid and, like any other fluid, it takes the shape of its container. Naturally, the container mustn't be too inappropriate. You don't drink champagne out of a beer mug, and you don't drink Burgundy out of a teacup. But wine glasses can be of many shapes and sizes and still be appropriate to wine. The same principle holds good in regard to the "container" of a musical composition—that is, its title or program. The fact that that title or program is appropriate doesn't make it exclusive. Appropriate it must be, of course. A composer who writes a serenade and then changes the title to *The Battle of Lexington* is likely to cause a certain amount of bewilderment in the minds of his hearers. But he might call his piece a morning song or a lullaby or a nocturne instead of a serenade—and I doubt if you would know which had been the original title.

And if he calls it a serenade and it sounds to you like a nocturne—go ahead; think of it as a nocturne. If a spring song sounds like summer, let it be summer. What any given piece of music means to you is strictly your affair, provided only that it means *something* to you. If that is so, no composer in his senses would have any quarrel with you. And certainly the music doesn't mind.

The Tongue Without Words

SPEAKING of music's being a wordless language, I had a complaint—or, rather, a challenge—from a correspondent who objects to my insisting that music cannot convey definite ideas, and at the same time discussing what music "says" or what a given composer "has to say." Why the apparent inconsistency?

Well, first let me point out that our vocabulary of aesthetic discussion is painfully limited. If you start discussing one of the arts, sooner or later you're likely to find yourself talking about it in terms of some other art. You can get along pretty well discussing architecture and sculpture, but even so you'll probably find yourself referring to the *rhythm* of a building or a statue. Literature, yes. Words, after all, are a symbol for ideas, and so there are plenty of them with which to discuss an art that is mainly concerned with ideas. But talk about painting or music, and you find yourself interchanging terms half the time. We discuss the rhythm and composition of a painting; we talk of harmony; we say the colors sing. When we get to music, we use a dialect borrowed from painting, sculpture, and literature. We talk about the massive structure of a Beethoven symphony, the long line of a passage, the feminine ending of a phrase, the color of the harmony, or the orchestration. We discuss the value of a composer's ideas, and whether or not he has something to say.

All that is not as inconsistent as it sounds. It's easy enough to describe an object or to discuss the logic of an argument or to express an intellectual idea. It is in that field of the intelligence that words are most useful, and most exact in their meaning. But the fundamental appeal of a great work of art is not primarily intellectual. It is what we call—for want of a better term—emotional. And when we start discussing those moods that art arouses in us, those emotional reactions, we're using words to describe abstractions that are not capable of being conveyed precisely in words. When I say that the color of a Brahms symphony reminds me of the coloring of a Rembrandt painting, I can only *hope* that you will know what I am talking about. What I am trying to say, in a figure of speech, is that the harmony and orchestration of Brahms produce, through my ear, an emotional—or, if you prefer, spiritual—response very much like the response that Rembrandt's coloring produces through my eye. In other words, I'm using the word "color" to describe an effect, not a cause. There ought to be one word to cover both effects, but since there isn't, I borrow one from painting.

Similarly, when I remark that a composer has something to say, I'm trying, very imperfectly, to describe an impression of significance—of emotional importance, so to speak—that his music conveys to me. The reason why music is so difficult to discuss in terms of language is that, as I said before, music *is* a language, and a language that expresses precisely things that lie outside the language of words and ideas. When I say that the ideas of the average student of composition are not likely to be as important as those of, say, Mozart, I'm not really saying "ideas" in any intellectual sense of the word. I'm trying to convey my opinion that Mozart's themes and phrases sound the more capable of expansion and development for my emotional satisfaction, just as the ideas of an essayist sound capable of expansion for my intellectual satisfaction.

The same with the word "say." When I tell you that I think Bach has more to say than Chaminade, I'm not comparing two philosophers. I can, however, hope that I'm expressing a difference between the—I don't like the word, but I know of no better one—between the *emotional* importance of the music of the two. Not that I don't like Chaminade's music, because I do. I think much of it is charming. I wouldn't mind hearing both composers on the same program. But when I need something more from music than charm, something more than just being pleasantly entertained, then I must turn to Bach, whose music says things which, however little I may be able to define them in words, nevertheless bring me a message that is important to me. And it is that quality of eloquence in music that makes it live. If Mozart and Bach and Beethoven and Brahms and Wagner and all the rest have survived, it is because they had something to say, something that spoke, wordlessly, not to the minds but to the spirits of successive generations of listeners.

PART THREE

Second Theme

Phenomenon

SOONER or later, any discussion of violinists and violin playing is almost certain to evoke the name of one of the most fantastic geniuses in the history of music, the legendary Nicolo Paganini.

He was born in Genoa on the 18th of February, 1784, and from the beginning showed signs of possessing extraordinary talent. When he was five years old he could play the mandolin. At seven, his father taught him the elements of violin playing, with such success that in a few months he could play almost anything at sight. Paganini, Senior, then turned him over to two other masters, Giovanni Cervetto and Giacomo Costa. At eight he was playing solos in church. At eleven, he made his first public appearance, and at twelve he gave a concert in Genoa that was so successful that his father took him to Parma and put him under the famous Paer, who taught him theory and composition as well as the violin. At thirteen he made his first concert tour, through Northern Italy, then came back to Genoa to study and practice.

His career as a finished violin virtuoso began in 1801, with another triumphal tour of Northern Italy, this time without his father. The unaccustomed freedom, along with the tremendous adulation that he got from everybody, were a little too much for the seventeen-year-old youngster, and he began sowing one of the largest and most flourishing crops of wild oats in musical history. Among other things, he fancied himself a gambler, with the result that he lost everything he had earned, including his violin. Luckily for him, a wealthy amateur lent him a superb Guarnerius, and was so carried away by his playing that he gave it to him. Paganini eventually bequeathed it to the city of Genoa, where you can see it in the museum there today.

Then follows a gap in Paganini's life that his biographers have not yet completely filled. We find him next, with any certainty, in 1805, when, at the age of twenty-one, he was court violinist of the so-called republic of Lucca. Here he stayed until about 1808 or '09, after which comes another gap, which has been plentifully filled in with legends, one of them being that he spent four years in jail for murder, during which time he learned to play the violin on one string. As a matter of fact, he was probably recovering from one of the attacks of ill health that hounded him all his life. In 1813 he made his debut at La Scala, in Milan, where he gave ten concerts in six weeks. He was now, at the age of twenty-nine, acknowledged to be the greatest violinist in Europe, and his career from that time on is little more than a chronicle of wildly successful concert tours. He played in Bologna, Rome, and Venice; in 1815 he toured Rumania; then back to Italy for several years. In 1828, Vienna, for a long stay; then Prague; then Vienna once more. In 1830 he visited all the principal cities of Germany. In 1831, at the age of forty-seven, he made his first appearance in Paris, which promptly went mad over him. That same year, he went to London, which went equally mad. Then back to Paris, which he made his headquarters thereafter. In '37 he left Paris and went to the Midi, hoping to regain his health in a warmer climate, and during the next two years visited most of the famous watering places in the Pyrenees. He died in Nice, on the 27th of May, 1840, at the age of fifty-six.

As I say, he has become an almost legendary figure, all the more so since the numerous periods in his life that are unaccounted for allow the Paganini legends to flourish without being blighted by facts. But what we do know of his life and his career is enough to show that he was an extraordinary genius. In his day he was a celebrated composer, and even Berlioz praised his orchestration. In public he played virtually nothing except his own compositions, and many of them still survive in the violin repertoire. He was a good orchestral conductor and an exceptional linguist. At the age of seven he spoke Italian, French, and German with equal fluency. He was supposed to be very avaricious, but could be equally generous on occasion. In 1837 he attended a concert in Paris where Berlioz conducted his own *Harold in Italy*. At the close of the performance he rushed up, knelt at the feet of the startled Berlioz, and pronounced him a genius. The next day he sent him an enthusiastic letter and a present of twenty thousand francs. Any composer who will give another composer four thousand dollars as a gift cannot be completely avaricious!

His appearance seems to have been as extraordinary as his playing. Several people, including Goethe and Heinrich Heine, have attempted to describe him. Heine said of him, "He wore a dark gray frock coat which came down to his heels and made him look very tall. His dark hair came down to his shoulders in disorderly locks and formed a black frame around his livid and ghastly face on which melancholy, genius, and torment had marked their ineffaceable stigmata." As a matter of fact, Paganini was only five feet five.

One of his biographers says of him, "He is as thin as any human being could be, with a sallow complexion, a beak of a nose, and long, bony fingers. He looks as if he could hardly bear the weight of his clothes, and when he bows his body doubles up in such a singular way that one is almost afraid to see his legs come loose from his body and the whole man collapse into a heap of bones. He plays with his right foot forward, and in fast movements keeps time with it with almost comic vicacity, his face, meantime, never losing its deathlike impassivity. It does light up with a faint smile when he hears the thunders of applause. At such moments he pouts his lips, while his eyes, profound but cold, glance about on all sides. During waits his body bends so as to form an extraordinary sort of triangle, with his head and his right foot thrust forward."

Just how great a violinist was he? That, of course, we shall never know exactly. A German *Kapellmeister* named Guhr studied his playing for several months, and has left an analysis of it that is rather interesting. Paganini differed from other violinists, he concluded, in six ways: First, by his system of tuning his violin; second, by a method of bowing that was all his own; third, by an alternation and combination of sounds produced by the bow with sounds produced by left-hand pizzicato playing; fourth, by his extensive use of single and double harmonics; fifth, by his G-string technique (he could get a range of three octaves out of the G string alone, as compared with the octave and a half of the average violinist); and sixth, by his incredible technical agility.

Paganini's playing, he said, demanded very thin and weak strings, for several reasons. One, that he played many more extreme high notes than other violinists. Another because harmonics come out better on weak strings than on strong ones. Again, because his left-hand pizzicato wouldn't be effective on heavy strings; and lastly, because he frequently tuned his violin up a half tone, with the G string a whole third higher, and heavy strings couldn't stand the strain and wouldn't stay in tune. What impressed Guhr particularly about Paganini's bowing was his wonderful use of what we call *saltando* bowing; that is, playing by letting the bow literally bounce off the strings. Any contemporary violinist can do it, but Paganini seems to have got much more volume out of the strings than that method of bowing usually produces. The alternation of bowing and left-hand pizzicato playing is likewise no mystery to any violinist today, but seems to have been unusual in Paganini's time. As for his harmonics, Guhr says that he could play ascending and descending chromatic scales, passages in thirds and sixths, and single and double trills, all in harmonics. If Guhr is not a liar, Paganini in that respect must have been miraculous. Also, as Guhr remarks, Paganini had a phenomenal control of the lowest string on the violin, the G string. He would tune it up a minor or a major third, and play an entire sonata on that one string. Incidentally, he was not above showing off this accomplishment by allowing the other three strings to break at a concert, apparently by accident, and then finishing on the remaining G string.

All in all, he was probably one of the greatest technicians that the violin world has ever known; in some respects, notably in the playing of harmonics, he was probably *the* greatest. As to how great an artist he was—well, that's more debatable. Certainly his audiences went to hear him out of curiosity and remained to hear him do stunts—and he did do stunts; and he did play only his own stuff, which he wrote for the express purpose of showing off his technique; and his music, while agreeable and frequently dazzling, is hardly profound. Liszt, who admired him tremendously, could, nevertheless, write of him, after his death:

"Let the artist of the future, then, willingly renounce the vain and egotistical role of which Paganini was, I believe, a final and illustrious example. May he fix his goal not in himself but beyond himself; may virtuosity be for him a means, not an end. And may he always remember that if *noblesse oblige*—that is, if nobility has obligations—all the more does genius have obligations."

We are on safer ground if we approach him simply as a supreme master of his chosen instrument. Many of the marvels that he accomplished are parts of the technical equipment of almost any first-rate orchestral violinist today. To realize how far violin technique has progressed in the past century, consider the fact that in the spring of 1940, at a concert by the New York Philharmonic-Symphony Orchestra, one number on the program was the third movement (*La Campanella*) of Paganini's second violin concerto, with the solo part played by *the entire first violin section* of the orchestra. Paganini wrote that concerto as a show piece for himself. If he had not lived, it is doubtful whether such orchestral virtuosity would yet be possible. He revolutionized violin technique, and in so doing has proved over again that once a man has accomplished the impossible, it was not so impossible after all.

Swan Song

THE story of the Requiem Mass of Wolfgang Amadeus Mozart—how it came to be written and its tragic connection with his own death—has been told many times before; yet I think it will still bear repetition. It was commissioned by a certain Count Franz von Walsegg, an Austrian nobleman who rather fancied himself as a musician and who seems to have been a curious mixture of vanity and humility, for he was fond of ordering works by professional composers, buying them outright, and then having them played in public as his own compositions. His wife had died a few months before, and, wishing to play something in her memory, he sent his secretary, Leutgab, to visit Mozart and order a Requiem Mass, which he was then going to have performed—which, as a matter of fact, he *did* have performed—as his own. Mozart, of course, knew nothing of this plan of Walsegg's—in fact, didn't even know his name.

To describe what happened, we must go back to a July evening in the year 1791, to an uncomfortable little flat in the suburbs of Vienna, near the estate of Prince Starhemberg, where a young man was toiling over some sheets of music paper, working on a piece for the theater which, he hoped, would bring him some money. The actor-manager Schikaneder had approached Mozart earlier in the month, suggesting that he write the music for a libretto that he himself had concocted, called *The Magic Flute*. Mozart was only too glad to get the order, for two reasons: one, that the plot contained numerous allusions to the Masonic ritual, and he was an ardent Freemason; the other, that he was even more desperately hard up than usual. His wife, Constanze, had to go to the country for her health, and in June he had borrowed enough to send her there from a friend of his named Puchberg. The latter was a Viennese businessman of whom we know nothing except that he was devoted to music and a great admirer of Mozart's, and had often come to his rescue before.

Mozart stayed on in Vienna. In order to keep his eye on him, Schikaneder had found him lodgings in a house near the theater, which was on the Starhemberg estate. The house had a garden with a summerhouse, and here Mozart worked during the day. At night he worked in his room. Toward the end of July he was both delighted and depressed to hear that on the 26th, in the little town where she was staying, his wife had borne him a son. This was their sixth child, four of whom had not survived infancy. Although Mozart was a good father, the prospect of another mouth to feed was a rather frightening one.

On this particular July night there was a knock at his door. He opened it to admit a tall, bony stranger, dressed, as he afterward described him, "from head to foot in gray." The man had come, he explained, on behalf of an anonymous patron, to commission a work by Mozart, a Requiem Mass. For this he was willing to pay one hundred ducats. "Who is this patron?" the composer asked. That, the stranger told him, he was not at liberty to reveal. Mozart, even then, was a little disturbed, both by the mysterious atmosphere of the whole transaction and the sinister implications of the title of the proposed work. But the price was tempting. A hundred ducats at that time had a face value, in our money, of about two hundred and twenty-five dollars; in purchasing power today it would mean well over a thousand dollars. That meant at least temporary relief and a chance to pay some of his most pressing debts. He accepted, promising to start work at once.

Since *The Magic Flute* was about finished, he probably would have done so, except for another unexpected commission that was offered him a few days later. This was nothing less than an invitation to write a serious opera for production at Prague during the coronation ceremonies of Leopold II. The libretto would be provided for him. Naturally he accepted this commission as well, and immediately set to work on the music, as he had less than a month in which to finish the piece.

Late in August he started out for Prague by stage coach, with his wife and his pupil, Süssmayr. The latter (who was destined to complete the Requiem Mass after his master's death) went along, both as copyist and to write the chord accompaniments for the recitative passages. At the very moment of Mozart's departure the mysterious stranger appeared at the coach window, reminding him that the new Mass had not yet been received. Much disturbed, the composer promised to finish it just as soon as he got back to Vienna.

The new opera, *La Clemenza di Tito—The Clemency of Titus*—was produced in Prague on September 6th. Partly because it was not Mozart's best work, and partly because of a stilted and uninspired libretto, it met with a very lukewarm reception and was obviously a failure. Greatly depressed, he came back to Vienna to put the finishing touches on *The Magic Flute* and to start work in earnest on the Requiem Mass. He was temporarily cheered up by the reception of *The Magic Flute*, which was produced on September 30th and was an immediate success.

Toward the end of October his health began to fail with alarming rapidity. Doctors today believe that in view of his symptoms—rapid loss of weight, difficulty in breathing, fainting spells, swelling of the extremities, and, toward the end, delirium—he was probably dying of Bright's disease. In any case, he became obsessed with the idea that he might have been poisoned, and that the new Requiem Mass was going to be his own. In November he was a little better, wrote a short cantata for a Masonic festival, and continued to work on the Requiem. Late in the month he took to his bed—for the last time, as it turned out—but continued to work on the music.

On the afternoon of December 4th three friends came to see him, and the four of them read through the vocal parts of the unfinished Mass, with Mozart taking the alto. When they came to the *Lacrimosa* section he broke down and put the score aside. Early that evening his sister-in-law arrived. "I'm glad you're here," said Mozart. "Stay with me tonight and see me die." She tried to cheer him, but he stopped her. "I have the flavor of death on my tongue," he said. Late in the evening he became unconscious, and then lapsed into a delirium. Toward midnight he suddenly sat up in bed, then sank back, and lay with his face turned toward the wall. At five minutes before one o'clock, on the morning of December 5, 1791, he died at the age of thirty-five years, ten months, and eight days.

Since Constanze was completely prostrated, a certain Baron van Swieten, a wealthy admirer of Mozart's who had always given him everything except money, offered to take charge of the arrangements and expenses of the funeral. There were three grades of funerals available in Vienna in those days. Baron van Swieten ordered the third-grade funeral—price $21.50, with $7.50 extra for the hearse. The funeral services were held in St. Stefan's Church. There were five people present: Salieri, the court conductor; van Swieten; Süssmayr; a friend named Roser; and a cellist named Orsler. It was raining torrents. The weather was much too dreadful, they agreed, to allow anyone to go to the grave. So little Mozart, in his seven-fifty hearse, went to the cemetery alone. The Baron had forgotten to order a private grave, so Mozart's coffin, along with eighteen or twenty others, was slid into a common trench reserved for paupers. About a week later, when Constanze came to the cemetery to look for her husband's grave, she found a new gravedigger who knew nothing about the matter and was not interested. She never did discover where her husband was buried. No one knows, to this day. Not that it matters. We have had, and always shall have, all of him that is important to us.

3

Masterpiece

MOZART'S Requiem is estimated to have been his 626th composition. But it is not the size of his output that makes him a musical giant. Sheer bulk is no guarantee of the value of any composer's contribution. For consider another master who, in proportion to his importance in the world of music, has the smallest active repertoire on record: one symphony, two orchestral suites, and one opera.

His name was Alexandre César Léopold Bizet—at least that is the name given him at his birth in Paris on the 25th of October, 1838. For some unknown reason his grandfather insisted on calling him Georges, and as grandfathers are important people in French households, Grandpa was allowed to have his way, so much so that his family, and eventually the public, knew him and still know him only as Georges Bizet.

His father, who was a music teacher, saw from the beginning that the youngster had unusual musical talent, and enrolled him at the Paris Conservatoire when he was only nine years old. In a very short time he was recognized as one of the most promising students in the school, studying the piano under the famous Marmontel—who was later to be Claude Debussy's piano teacher also—and theory under Zimmerman, who was Gounod's father-in-law. As a matter of fact, Gounod occasionally came to the conservatory and taught young Bizet himself. He studied, too, with Halévy, the opera composer, whose daughter he later married.

He stayed at the Conservatoire nearly ten years; and it was during that period, in his seventeenth year, that he composed his enchanting C major symphony. He made one attempt to try for the Grand Prix de Rome, but was not allowed to compete because the judges thought him too young. At this time he was considered a brilliant pianist, and many of his teachers thought it was a tossup as to whether he would make a career as a composer or as a concert artist.

In 1857, when he was nineteen, he entered a prize competition for an operetta, to be written to a libretto called *Doctor Miracle*. Charles Lecoq, who already had somewhat of a reputation as a composer of operettas, was also one of the contestants. The judges were unable to decide between the two, and finally gave the prize to both of them and produced both of their versions of the same story, as two halves of an evening, at the Bouffes Parisiens. That same year he made another try at the Prix de Rome, and won it, with a cantata called *Clovis and Clothilde*. What became of it, we don't know. At all events, he was assured of three years of freedom to study and compose in Rome, at the expense of the French government.

He had a wonderful time in Italy, for he was a great admirer of Italian opera, particularly Italian light opera, and spent most of his time studying the scores of Rossini, Cimarosa, and Mozart (Mozart, at that time, was still considered more of an Italian composer than an Austrian one). The conditions under which a young composer accepts the Prix de Rome provide that he must send back a certain amount of finished work; Bizet, accordingly, sent back as his principal offering a comic opera called *Don Procopio*, set to an Italian libretto. Incidentally, the score was lost for many years, and wasn't found until long after Bizet's death. It was finally produced, without much success, at Monte Carlo in 1906. Toward the end of his Italian visit he spent three months in Naples—from August to October, 1859—and it was there that he first began to suffer from the throat trouble that pursued him all his life and finally killed him.

When he returned to Paris, he found it comparatively easy to get a hearing, as he already had established a reputation as a highly promising young composer. An orchestral suite of his was performed at the Institute. Thus encouraged, he wrote another, which he called *Souvenirs de Rome,* based on his stay in Italy. In fact, he found it easy to do everything except make a living. For a time he lived the life that so many composers have to live—teaching, accompanying, coaching, copying, and making piano transcriptions of other people's orchestral scores. He got his first big chance through a man who was to be one of his greatest benefactors and one of his greatest handicaps, a man named Léon Carvalho.

At that time, Carvalho was the director of the Théâtre Lyrique, Paris, and some now forgotten music patron had just presented him with a subsidy of a hundred thousand francs to produce an opera based on a libretto called *The Pearl Fishers.* Carvalho commissioned Bizet to write the music—and you can imagine how eagerly the twenty-five-year-old composer jumped at the chance. The opera was produced on the 29th of September, 1863. Since this is not entirely a success story, I regret to report that it lasted eighteen performances, and was then taken off. Parts of it were produced at the Metropolitan Opera House in 1893, and the whole opera was presented as the opening offering of the season at the Metropolitan on November 13, 1916. Even with Caruso singing the leading tenor role, it lasted only three performances. I saw one of those three, and, if memory serves, I know why it didn't last longer.

However, much to his credit, Carvalho had great faith in Bizet. He got him started on another opera, *Ivan the Terrible.* Apparently it *was* terrible, for Bizet didn't finish the score, and burned what he had written. Then Carvalho commissioned another, *La Jolie Fille de Perth.* He produced it in December, 1867; still no luck. It managed to survive twenty-one performances, and then closed. Bizet, rather discouraged, turned to other forms of music. He wrote a quantity of songs and piano pieces, none of which are taken very seriously today, and finally heard a performance, by the Pasdeloup Orchestra, of his *Souvenirs de Rome*.

But Carvalho still had faith. He commissioned a third opera, *Djamileh,* which had its first performance on May 22, 1872. It was the same old story. This one lasted only ten performances. One might think that almost any impresario would give up after producing three successive failures by the same composer. But not Carvalho. That same year, 1872, he left the Théâtre Lyrique to take over the management of the so-called Vaudeville Theater. This was a dramatic house, and his first production was a play by Alphonse Daudet called *L'Arlésienne*. It needed some music, and Carvalho commissioned Bizet to write it. He composed, altogether, twenty-seven pieces of incidental music to go with Daudet's drama. It was produced in Paris on the 1st of October, 1872. The plot of the play concerned a young peasant, Fredri, who falls in love with a girl from Arles, meets with violent opposition from his parents because she isn't exactly a nice girl, gets ready to marry another girl, realizes that he is still enamored of his former love, and jumps out of the window. Paris supported this cheery little number for just fifteen performances. So far as I know, it has never been revived. However, at least five of Bizet's incidental numbers, the *Prelude, Minuet, Adagietto, Provençal Dance,* and *Carillon,* are still world-famous as the first *L'Arlésienne* suite. They became immensely popular almost at once, and Bizet at last knew the taste of success.

A night three years later, the 3rd of March, 1875, saw the production of his masterpiece, *Carmen*. There are two current legends concerning that first performance of *Carmen*. One is that it was a failure; the other is that Bizet died of a broken heart three months later. Neither is true. It's perfectly true that the critics didn't like it, but critics have been known to make occasional mistakes. And the public did like it. Considering the difficulties under which it was produced, the wonder is that they liked it as well as they did. Eyewitnesses of that historic performance have left testimony to the effect that the orchestra was bad and the chorus was worse. For example, in one passage when Madame Galli-Marié, the original Carmen, was singing pianissimo, the bass drum player, having counted his bars wrongly, came in with a couple of fortissimo crashes that didn't do her performance any good. The chorus, of course, being accustomed to the good old style of operatic choral singing, in which the chorister marched in, stood and faced the conductor, raised the right arm, raised the left arm, and marched out, were horrified to find that they were supposed to run about, fight, smoke cigarettes, pull hair, and generally raise Cain around the place. Not being used to singing and acting at the same time, they gave up singing whenever it was more convenient.

There was the usual division of the house, with Society and money downstairs and the musicians and other intellectuals upstairs. The upstairs loved it, loved its color and its realism. The downstairs were horrified. They considered it low and immoral, first, because Madame Galli-Marié apparently played the title role in the style of Mérimée's Carmen, who was not as refined as some Carmens that have been seen since; second, and worse, because she smoked cigarettes.

It is true that Bizet, soon after the opening of the first act, went straight to the director's office and sat there throughout the evening, in despair at having, as he thought, another failure on his hands. But he was soon to learn differently. One of the finest ways to get free publicity for a play or an opera is to complain about its immorality. As the rumors concerning Carmen's morals began to float about, the *Carmen* audience began to grow, and *Carmen* performances became more and more frequent. The opera ran steadily until June, was taken off for the summer season, and was put back into the repertory in September.

Bizet, meanwhile, went to his country home at Bougival, on the Seine not far from Paris, where he died three months later. Whatever he died of, it was certainly not a broken heart. One story is that he went downstairs in his dressing gown to pay the laundress her bill, caught cold, and contracted pneumonia. Another, slightly less fanciful, is that he died of heart disease, aggravated by an abscess in the throat. He died on June 3, 1875, in his thirty-seventh year.

But if *Carmen* was not a failure, why was it left out of the repertoire of the Opéra-Comique for a period of seven years? The answer is comparatively simple. The Opéra-Comique closed in February, 1876, because of financial troubles, and remained closed for eight months. When it reopened, Carvalho had come back from the Vaudeville Theater to take up his old post. Curiously enough, *Carmen* was the one opera of Bizet's that he didn't care much for. Furthermore, his wife, Madame Miolan-Carvalho, was the principal soprano at the Opéra-Comique, under his management, and as the role of Carmen was too low for her and the role of Micaela was too unimportant for her, she simply decided not to have it performed. Meanwhile, during those seven years, *Carmen* had gone all over the world, with tremendous success everywhere; so that when public opinion in Paris finally compelled the management of the Opéra-Comique to revive it, in 1883, it was already world famous. As originally written, *Carmen,* in conformity with the rules of the Opéra-Comique, had many passages of spoken dialogue. It is still performed that way in France. But when it began its world tour, the spoken scenes were turned into recitative, the accompaniments to which were composed, oddly enough, by an American. He was Ernest Guiraud, who was born in New Orleans in 1837 and died in Paris in 1892. The recitative passages were first used for the Vienna production, and, outside France, are still in use everywhere. *Carmen* is a masterpiece, and a success, first, because it has one of the best librettos ever written, and second, like so many of Verdi's operas, it manages to carry on the dramatic action of the story in terms that the man in the street can whistle. No other opera, with the possible exception of *Aïda,* contains so many song hits. And in no opera of its kind does the composer succeed so completely in creating an illusion of continuous action through the medium of a series of set, formal numbers. In writing it, Bizet was obviously getting into his stride. No one will ever know what other masterpieces of his we lost by his dying before his fortieth year. At least we can be grateful to him for the one perfect thing that he did give us.

The Dumb Genius

If Bizet died too young, so did one of his contemporaries, a composer just a year his junior. The untimely death of Modeste Petrovich Moussorgsky was probably as great a loss to music as was that of Bizet, Schubert, or even Mozart. Few people, I think, realize just how comparatively young he was when he died. The best-known portrait of him is a painting by the Russian artist Repin. Looking at it, you get the impression of a bleary, bloated, bewhiskered muzhik about sixty-five years old. And that is probably how Moussorgsky looked. The fact remains that he was forty-two years old when he died. That was the age at which Brahms was just finishing his first symphony. If Wagner had died at that age, we would not have *Siegfried, Götterdämmerung, Tristan, Die Meistersinger,* and *Parsifal.*

Of his early life we know very little, outside of what information is contained in an autobiography that he wrote shortly before his death—and much of that has turned out to be more the product of a lively imagination than an accurate memory. We do know, contrary to the legends concerning his alleged poverty-stricken youth, that he was the son of a rather well-to-do landowner who owned an estate in the district of Pskoff. Outside of that, and the fact that he was music-mad, we know nothing of his father. Of his mother we know only that she, too, came of a landowning family, had a romantic disposition, liked to write poetry, had no poetic talent, and played the piano.

However, one fact concerning his family that is probably significant is that one of his grandmothers had been a serf—in other words, a slave to the land—and I imagine that admixture of peasant blood had something to do with his instinctive feeling for Russian folk music and his great sympathy with the minds and hearts of the Russian common people.

According to his autobiography, he started piano lessons, with his mother, when he was about six years old, and by the time he was ten was able to play a concerto by John Field, an Irish pianist and composer who was highly popular in Russia. That same year he was sent, with his brother, to St. Petersburg, to prep school, where he continued his piano lessons. A couple of years later the two boys entered the school of the Cadets of the Guards. Outside of our private military schools we have no equivalent to the school of the Cadets. It corresponded roughly to our West Point Military Academy, but West Point doesn't admit thirteen-year-old boys—and that is what Moussorgsky was when he began his military studies.

The school differed in another respect from West Point. According to a singer named Kompaneisky, who entered about four years after Moussorgsky had left and who wrote a description of the place, the primary requisites of an officer and a gentleman, in those days, were that he be a good drinker and a good gambler. The general in charge was quite proud of his boys if they came in late at night dead drunk on champagne. Vodka, no; but champagne—that was a gentleman's drink. On one occasion, when he caught Moussorgsky reading, he said to him, "My dear boy, what kind of an officer are *you* going to make?" This sort of training might possibly explain the spectacularly negative record of the Russian armies under the Tsarist regime. You can imagine what it did to a thirteen-year-old boy, fresh from the country. By the time he left the school the poor youngster was a confirmed dipsomaniac, with a hectic craving for alcohol that pursued him all his life, that finally killed him, and for which he was no more to blame than if he had been a victim of infantile paralysis. When he left the school, in 1856, at the age of seventeen, he joined the regiment of the Preobrazhensky Guards as a lieutenant, but not for long. For in that same year he met Borodin and Balakireff. The latter, particularly, exerted a profound influence upon his career, and was his only teacher.

There has always been a great deal of talk about Moussorgsky's lack of musical training. To read some commentators, you might think that he was as musically illiterate as the average Broadway songwriter. Not only is that not true, but if he was illiterate, so were his contemporaries. So far as concerned musical education, Russia, in the forties and fifties, was as complete a desert as this country was during the same period. There were no professional schools of music, and no professional teachers. The St. Petersburg Conservatory, the first one to be founded in Russia, didn't open its doors until 1862. If a young Russian of Moussorgsky's day wanted a formal musical education, he had his choice of going to Germany, France, or Italy. He couldn't get one in Russia. Balakireff, Moussorgsky's teacher, was wholly self-taught. Borodin was a chemistry professor—and a famous one; César Cui was an engineering officer in an artillery school. Rimsky-Korsakoff, in his own memoirs, admits that he had only a vague knowledge of harmony and counterpoint when he accepted the professorship of composition and orchestration at the St. Petersburg school. As regards strict technical training, they were all in the same boat.

"They" were a group of five who banded together in a more or less deliberate effort to establish a nationalist school of Russian music, basing their material on Russian folk music, with Glinka as their inspiration, and determined to offset the so-called "German" influence of composers such as Tchaikovsky. The five were Balakireff, Borodin, Moussorgsky, César Cui, and Rimsky-Korsakoff. They were six, really, for a prominent member of the group was the music critic Vladimir Stassoff. Viewed in the softening perspective of elapsed years, the Five are often cited as an example of perfect mutual faith and understanding. As a matter of fact, they all rather looked down on Moussorgsky, whom they seem to have regarded as talented but dumb. Even Balakireff considered his pupil rather stupid. The only one of the lot who had any early realization of his genius was Stassoff. Rimsky came to appraise him at his true value, but much later.

In 1858, at nineteen, he resigned from the army in order to devote himself entirely to music, and for a few years worked under Balakireff without accomplishing anything very important. In '61, Tsar Alexander II proclaimed the liberation of the serfs—which had much the same effect as Lincoln's Emancipation Proclamation in '63: it freed a vast multitude from slavery, and ruined their former masters. Moussorgsky, with no more income, was thrown on his own resources. In 1863 he got a job as a government clerk. In '65, following the death of his mother, he took to drink, collapsed with delirium tremens, and was eventually dismissed in '67. He was given another post in 1868, lost that, was reinstated, and finally left the service for good in 1879, a little over a year before his death.

His career as a composer began in earnest in 1864, when he composed two songs, *Kallistrat* and *Night*. These were the first of a series that established his right to a place among the world's great song composers. Songs such as *Death, the Commander; Trepak; Death's Lullaby;* and *At the Ball* are as fine as anything that Schubert or Schumann or Hugo Wolf ever wrote, and the fact that they are seldom heard in concert is no compliment to the musical discrimination of singers—or their audiences. In '67 he wrote the first draft of the orchestral piece that we know now as *Night on Bald Mount*—about the only purely orchestral work that he ever wrote, and one that was never performed during his lifetime.

In 1868, at the age of twenty-nine, he began work on his masterpiece, the operatic version of Pushkin's tragedy *Boris Godunoff*. In December of the following year it was finished and submitted to the management of the Imperial Opera. After taking a year to make up their minds, the management rejected it, in February, 1871. They couldn't make head or tail out of a so-called opera whose hero was a basso, that had no first tenor, no prima donna, no ballet, no arias—nothing but recitatives, scenes, and choral numbers. So he rewrote it, cutting certain other scenes and adding a whole act in which the tenor and soprano could do their stuff. Again it was turned down, in May, 1872, by which time he was busy with another opera, *Khovanshchina*. In February of the following year, however, the Imperial Opera did produce three scenes from *Boris*, which were a success; and in January, 1874, thanks to the insistence of one of the singers, Julia Platonova, the whole opera finally had a production. Of the famous "Five," only the sixth, Stassoff, realized the greatness of the work. Balakireff criticized it in public, Cui wrote a nasty article about it, Borodin was silent, and Rimsky-Korsakoff disapproved of what he called its "illiteracy." The work was repeated from time to time, with generous cuts, and managed twenty-six performances between 1874 and 1881. After that it was withdrawn, and was forgotten for many years.

That same year (1874) he started work on a third opera, *The Fair at Sorochintsk,* and worked on it at irregular intervals until he lost his government post in 1876. Then he worked for a while as accompanist and musical adviser to a singer named Daria Leonova. The following year a group of his friends made him a monthly allowance to finish *Khovanshchina,* and a little later another group made him another allowance to finish *The Fair at Sorochintsk*. He was trying desperately to work on both operas simultaneously when his final illness overtook him and he died on March 16, 1881, just a week after his forty-second birthday.

So passed, untimely, a great man, the greatest composer that Russia has given us. It is not altogether easy to say why his contemporaries were so slow to recognize him for what he was. I think it was because he belongs to that group of master artists who say their say so simply, so directly, that hearing it we say, "Of course, I always knew that." It takes time for us to realize that no one had ever said it in quite that way before.

Innovator

GIUSEPPE VERDI enjoys one rather melancholy distinction. While his is one of the most celebrated names in musical history, and while his music gets worldwide performances, it is only on the rarest of occasions that anything of his finds its way to the programs of a major symphony orchestra.

There are two reasons for this neglect of Verdi in concert circles, one of them perfectly obvious, and the other, while apparently trivial, equally strong. To name the second one first, opera and operatic music have never been taken as seriously by the music-loving public as so-called symphonic music. Your real, dyed-in-the-wool symphony subscriber, while he may condescend to attend operatic performances, is just a little inclined to turn up his nose at them. He admits that great composers have written operas, but he is very reluctant to admit that it was their operas that made them great. Of course there is one exception—Wagner. But he's a special case. I'll come to him a little later.

The other and the obvious reason why we don't hear Verdi at symphony concerts is that in all of his operas—and there are twenty-six of them—there is very little that lends itself to performance outside the opera house. He was, first and last, a man of the lyric theater. And in the theater I'm not sure that he isn't a greater man than Wagner.

That, of course, sounds like utter heresy. But before you light the faggots under the stake, let me explain that statement. Suppose we discuss Wagner for a minute. His crowning achievement was the creation of the music drama. His first successful opera, *Rienzi,* was an opera in the strict Meyerbeerian sense—a succession of solos, duets, choruses, trios, and processions that existed as much for their own, musical sakes as for the development of the story. In *The Flying Dutchman,* while he still relies upon set numbers for the main structure of his drama, we find him tending to break away from this rigid form, to find some more authentically dramatic means of expression. In *Tannhäuser* he moves still further away from the conventional opera form. In *Lohengrin* he throws over the old form entirely and emerges with a brand-new one, in which he combines dramatic continuity with musical coherence through his employment of a series of short, recurrent themes that he calls leading motives. From then on, through *Tristan, Die Meistersinger,* the *Ring,* and *Parsifal,* his stage works are, literally, music dramas—that is, plays unfolded through the medium of music.

Now, this was a magnificent achievement, and a revolution in the lyric theater. But it was not brought about without paying a price, which was that he managed to invent a form of writing opera that only a Wagner could handle successfully. If there are people who scorn every other kind of opera and yet flock to hear Wagner—and there are thousands and thousands of them—it is because Wagner, who thought of himself as a writer for the theater, happened to be one of the greatest symphonic composers that ever lived. If he abolished the set vocal numbers in favor of the leitmotiv system, it was, whether he was conscious of it or not, because he thought primarily in terms of the orchestra rather than the voice. The most significant feature of his leading-motive system is that the leading motives are invariably first heard in the orchestra and are developed in the orchestra. Study the vocal line of almost any scene in one of his later dramas, and you will find that the voice part is much more of an obbligato than a real solo part. But it is rarely a true *vocal* melody, in that it would make musical sense without its orchestral support.

Now, Wagner got away with it. First, because of his uncanny skill in so blending an independent voice part with the orchestra as to create the illusion that the voice and the orchestra are one; and second, for the simple reason that the overwhelming articulateness and emotional drive of his orchestral writing are alone sufficient to sustain the dramatic interest of his story. The singer is a help, but he is not essential. These are hard words, and annoying ones; but I think they are true. Think a minute. When you hear the "Good Friday" spell from *Parsifal* played by an orchestra, are you, honestly, distressed by the absence of the voice part? From hearing the music alone, would you ever guess that Gurnemanz is singing through a large part of that scene? One of the favorite pieces in the orchestral repertoire is the one that combines the prelude and the finale of *Tristan and Isolde*. The former is purely instrumental, and the latter, theoretically, is Isolde's big scene. Do you really notice the absence of Isolde's part when the work is played in concert? I think the answer is no. We're delighted to have Isolde come along, but if she is absent we can and do get along without her.

That's all very well for a composer like Wagner, who, as I've said, and believe, would still be a titanic figure in the orchestral world if he had never had a stage production of one of his works. But there has been only one Wagner, and composers who have since attempted to write according to his formula have learned, painfully, that an audience tends to listen only to what it sees. In other words, it looks to the singer, rather than the orchestra, as the source of the music. Normally it expects that singer to give it recognizable melodies, and if it doesn't hear them and the orchestral writing isn't up to the standard of Wagner, it loses interest. Of all the operas written according to the Wagnerian formula during the past sixty years—and there are scores of them—not half a dozen have been even partially successful. The Wagnerian formula demands Wagner's genius.

Verdi, on the other hand, brought about his reforms—and they were very real ones—through the medium that distinguishes—musically, at least—opera from symphony: the human voice. Wagner once said that he never thought of a theme without hearing its appropriate instrumental setting. Verdi did exactly the opposite. From the beginning to the end, his important musical ideas are vocal.

He began his career in a country where operatic forms were much more rigid and conventional than they were in Germany. He was born in the same year as Wagner—1813—but there had been no Weber in Italy to accustom audiences to dramatic sincerity and the growing importance of the orchestra. His first opera, *Oberto, Conte di San Bonifacio,* was cut to the same pattern as those of Bellini, Rossini, and Donizetti. It was enough of a success to establish him as an accepted newcomer at the age of twenty-six. During the ensuing ten years he wrote thirteen operas, which made him immensely popular, but which had nothing in particular to distinguish them beyond melodic spontaneity and vocal effectiveness. *Ernani* is about the only one of the lot that we ever hear now. Then he wrote an opera called *Luisa Miller.* It wasn't much of a success, but it did contain the germ of something new in the way of handling dramatic development through the voice.

The germ developed into a finished product in his next, *Rigoletto.* If you will examine Rigoletto's second-act aria, *Cortigiani, vil razza dannata,* you will find it to be something not quite like anything that Verdi or his contemporaries had ever written before. It is the Verdi dramatic aria. Now, there had been plenty of arias, full of dramatic excitement. Verdi himself had written many of them. But they were conceived on the old *aria da capo* plan, whereby you sang a first theme, then a second, and then sang the first one all over again, coming out, emotionally and dramatically, just where you went in. But *Cortigiani, vil razza dannata* is something different. In it a man starts by cursing a group of courtiers for kidnaping his daughter, then suddenly breaks down and begs them to have mercy and give her back to him. When the aria is over, we have heard not only a vocal solo but a dramatic scene, one that carries the plot along. The music, instead of folding back on itself, goes on to something different when the mood demands it.

Now, this sounds like something very simple to have thought of, but it was a brilliant stroke. For it took away the chief objection to the old-fashioned aria: that it interrupted the action for the sake of giving the singer a chance to show off his voice. In its way, it was as important to opera as the invention of the leitmotiv system, for it enabled the singer, as the former allowed the orchestra, to carry on the action with dramatic and emotional sincerity in terms of formal musical entertainment. Verdi's subsequent operas were more or less a development of his new discovery. In *La Traviata,* in the first act, he even manages to convey the emotional overtones of a scene in terms of the most artificial of all vocal forms, coloratura singing.

The nine years following *Rigoletto* produced seven more operas, four of which, *Il Trovatore, La Traviata, Un Ballo in Maschera,* and *La Forza del Destino,* are still tremendously popular. Then, after five years, *Don Carlo,* and four years later, when Verdi was fifty-eight, the opera that is still one of the most popular in the world, *Aïda.* Then came a long period of silence. Wagner, his exact contemporary, finished his last work, *Parsifal,* at the age of sixty-nine. It was not until five years later, at seventy-four, that Verdi produced *Otello.* One would think that this was an age at which any composer might feel justified in retiring from business. But no. Six years later, at the age of eighty, the incredible old man produced what some musicians consider his masterpiece: *Falstaff*. He died on the 27th of January, 1901, at the age of eighty-eight, having developed a form of operatic writing that many lesser men have since adopted with success. Wagner's music dramas stand alone, waiting for another Wagner to write their successors. In the meantime, let us be grateful to Verdi for having taught us that a man may have less than Wagner's towering genius and still be welcome in the theater.

The Great Romantic

ON SUNDAY, March 28, 1943, almost exactly sixty-two years after Moussorgsky's death, another great Russian died. The passing of Sergei Rachmaninoff cannot be called an untimely end—he went six days before his seventieth birthday—but at any age his death would have been an occasion for mourning.

If you ever heard him in recital, you can have the satisfaction of knowing that you heard one of the great pianists of all time. He was one of the comparatively few who was admired and revered both by the public and by his fellow artists. Any recital of Rachmaninoff's would find in the audience as many of the foremost pianists of this day as could arrange to be there. We shall not soon forget the tall, gaunt figure, as he strode deliberately across the stage and sat down at the piano, looking neither to right nor left. When he had finished playing he would rise, bow stiffly once or twice, with never a change of expression on that wonderful masklike face, then turn and walk back to the wings, as apparently self-absorbed as if there had been no audience at all. There always was an audience, generally overflowing on the stage, and at the end of the program it would bring him out again and again for encores, never letting him go until, with a resigned shrug to the inevitable, he sat down and played the C-sharp minor prelude that the public so loved and that he had so grown to loathe.

He had a reputation for being cold and aloof. He was not. If he seemed aloof, it was because he was an essentially lonely man, saddened by the knowledge that he could never return to his beloved Russia. You would seldom find him at public gatherings, for he was not a ready conversationalist; he had no gift for saying nothing in particular. Besides, he never learned to speak English fluently enough to be comfortable in it. That, added to his natural shyness, made him keep away from strangers. Yet he was one of the kindest and most generous of men, particularly to young composers. He had the essential humility of all great artists who have learned so much that they know how much remains to be learned. When his work the *Symphonic Dances* for piano and orchestra was played in Philadelphia, the audience received it with no great enthusiasm. Vincent Youmans, the popular composer, who was a friend of his, was in the house and, going backstage, told him how much the piece had moved him, what subtle and beautifully wrought music it was, and added a few uncomplimentary remarks regarding the musical perception of the audience. Rachmaninoff said, very simply and sincerely, "Well, at least the orchestra liked it."

The qualities that characterized his playing were just those that characterize his music. Granted the magnificent sweep and power of his playing, the wide range of tone color that he could evoke from the piano, the thing about his playing that fascinated his fellow musicians—and his audiences, too, even if they were not conscious of it—was his monumental grasp of form and structure. He was one of the most articulate players that ever lived. No matter how seemingly complex a given piece might be, he always searched for, and found, the essential line of the music, the succession of themes that gave the music continuity. He didn't neglect the details; they were always there. But he was never lost in them. He was like a great actor, who, no matter how elaborate and varied his performance may be, always keeps before you a clear and consistent picture of the character he is playing.

His music is equally articulate. You may like it or not, but you are never in doubt as to what he is seeking to convey. And you know that he knows. In any strict sense of the term, he is only slightly nationalistic. In form and substance his music is not particularly Russian. Even Tchaikovsky, who was always reproached with being German rather than Russian, went to Russian folk music for much of his melodic material. So far as I know, Rachmaninoff never did. If he is akin to any particular composers, they might be Schumann and Brahms. There is a romantic quality about his music that suggests the former, and a certain all-pervading gravity of utterance that could be called Brahmsian. But he is by no means a German composer.

Let us call him a romantic composer, one who early discovered the thing he could say best and clung to it for the rest of his life. "Romantic" is, of course, more or less a term of mild contempt today. Any music that is consistently melodic and non-astringent is likely to be dismissed as escapist music, and therefore not worthy to be called contemporary.

There is a curious tendency in musical circles today to appraise music in terms of the copyright date, of *when* it was written, as if an artist were a milliner or a dressmaker, unworthy of serious consideration unless he keeps up with the prevailing fashion. I don't think the essential qualities of music change quite so rapidly as that. One of Rachmaninoff's finest works is his third piano concerto. Now, the same critics who characterize it as "a voice from the past, an echo of the romantic eighties," are likely to discuss whether or not a given conductor has done justice to the greatness of Schumann's *Spring* symphony. Sometimes I've had a wicked thought. Suppose the critics could be hypnotized into thinking that

Schumann had written the third piano concerto—and he might have—and that Rachmaninoff had written the *Spring* symphony. I have dared to wonder whether the verdict might not be reversed, whether we wouldn't find them discussing the third concerto as a classic and dismissing the *Spring* symphony as outmoded.

I don't know. I know only that to me his music is not outmoded. And I know, too, that there are millions of others to whom it is not, to whom, as Rachmaninoff himself once said, "Music should bring relief. It should rehabilitate minds and souls." That being so, we can be grateful as we echo the words of George Meredith:

> Full lasting is the song,
> Though he, the singer, passes.

A Writer and a Gentleman

Lawrence Gilman died on the 8th of September, 1939. Six weeks later the New York Philharmonic-Symphony Orchestra, for which he had written the program notes for seventeen years, dedicated its Sunday afternoon concert, an all-Wagner program, to his memory. He would have liked that, for he worshiped Wagner. He left a gap that has not been filled, for he was not only a great critic of music but also one of the finest literary artists of our times.

He was also one of the hardest working. In addition to his work as program annotator, for fifteen years he had been music critic of the New York *Herald Tribune,* writing daily criticisms and Sunday essays that were eagerly read by an army of readers. Also, somehow, he found time to carry on a considerable correspondence with his friends and colleagues. In his thirty-eight years as a critic I doubt if he ever wrote a single paragraph that was not carefully planned, and polished to as near perfection as he could make it. As a newspaper critic he was almost *too* conscientious—so he seemed, at least, to us others, whom he put to shame by his industry. I have a letter from him replying to one I had written in the spring of 1931, suggesting that we lunch together to talk over some things. He writes: "I should like to have lunch with you very much, but I'm faced with the old difficulty about which I've complained to you before: what with score reading, annotating, proofreading, and trying to reconcile the errors in the latest edition of one dictionary with the errors in the latest edition of another, and keeping errors in my own stuff down to a decent minimum (which I don't succeed in doing), I find that lunching and dining are unattainable luxuries. My great meal of the day is early breakfast (after I have read my stuff in two editions of the *Herald Tribune*), about 3:30 A.M. Are you ever up then?" I'm afraid that if I were up at three-thirty in the morning, it would not be because I had sat up reading proof in a newspaper office. In that respect I am not a good type. But Gilman was. No pains were too great for him to take with his own work.

He was one of the gentlest men I ever knew, and characteristically he was at his best when he was writing favorable criticism. It really hurt him to have to condemn anything, although he was too conscientious a critic to shirk doing so when he felt it necessary. He was happiest and wrote his best when he was discussing music that he knew and loved. The one thing that never satisfied him was his own writing. I have never known a man so humble about his own gifts. He simply couldn't get it through his head that he was one of the finest stylists in the English language. After the Metropolitan's production of Debussy's *Pelléas et Mélisande,* in the spring of 1925, he wrote a piece about it that was so beautiful that I had to sit down and write to tell him so. In reply I got this:

"Dear Deems: Your letter reached me just after I'd recklessly read over (a thing I usually have sense enough not to do) that *Pelléas* piece as I was pasting it in my scrapbook, and while I was suffering from the usual hideous reaction. The things I could have improved had jumped out at me in almost every paragraph, and I'd about resigned myself to the sickening conclusion that I never would learn to write decent prose if I kept on until I was eighty. Then your letter came and set me on top of the wave, there to stay until I shall read over some of my stuff again."

In another letter he writes, with characteristic humility:

"I have no pride of opinion as a commentator on music. Nothing is easier than for me to believe that I have failed to put my finger on the strong or weak points of a score, and I believe that if a critic is worth a hoot, he never stops learning that he is in need of learning. I think that a critic can usually learn more from a composer than the composer can learn from the critic. All this, of course, is a violation of the rules of the guild, which insists, as you know, upon infallibility. But then we all know that that is nonsense."

I knew that he had composed and published several songs in his youthful days, but I was surprised—as I think everyone who knew him would be—to receive this piece of information, embedded in a letter written in 1927. He says: "I have in storage a perfectly good four-act Wagnerian music drama, somewhat more impressive than *Götterdämmerung,* written by myself at the age of twenty-two, text and all. It is scored for an orchestra of one hundred and thirty-two, including an octet of tubas, sixteen harps, and the rest in proportion. Through most of the love scene, the strings are divided into twenty-four real parts. Don't you think the Metropolitan would just love to mount it?"

Wagner, as I said, was his god, the one composer who could do no wrong. Several years ago I wrote, because I knew it would interest him, pointing out a harmonic identity between the Klingsor theme in *Parsifal* and the Tarnhelm theme in the *Ring*. To which he replied:

"Thank you for your letter about the Klingsor-Tarnhelm relationship. I had never noticed it. But I'm becoming accustomed to the realization that although I've been studying Wagner's scores, man and boy, for something like thirty-eight years (I used to take the orchestral score of *Tristan* to bed with me when I was sixteen) I still don't know much about them. . . . What a marvelous organizing mind it was!

After hearing yesterday's *Parsifal,* I think I'm convinced that that third act is the most searching thing in all music. Even the *Crucifixus* in the B Minor Mass falls below it, I think, in intensity of expression."

Here is another note, in reply to a suggestion of mine that he make a book out of his newspaper articles on Wagner.

"I have already had a request from four publishers to let them do a book made up of my Wagner stuff. . . . They ought to know as well as I do that there is not enough substance or novelty in any of the stuff I have written about Wagner to justify their republication in book form. I honestly feel this. I have written and am writing those Wagner articles chiefly because I would rather write about Wagner than almost any other subject that I could think of, and partly (and this will strike you as amusing) because I don't feel that he has ever had a square deal. Academic critics and musicians have never yet been willing to admit that his music is the greatest we have; and you know how the modernists sneer at him. The average musician always says that he was 'the greatest dramatic composer.' For heaven's sake, why drag in the drama?"

That was in 1926. Eleven years later he finally did complete and publish that book, a volume entitled simply *Wagner's Operas*. Let me quote, as his testament, what he wrote concerning his favorite among all of the Wagnerian music dramas:

There is nothing that can be set beside it, nothing that yields to the imagination so moving and eventful a retrospect as the close of *Götterdämmerung,* that soaring peak whence we look backward over the long way we came, and see again in memory those unforgettable happenings that were to follow Wotan's primal sin. Only Wagner could have built from the dark, unplumbable depths of Alberich's cupidity and hate, upward across the gulfs and hills and worlds and heavens of the *Ring's* ungirdled universe, into the light of Brünnehilde's selfless and heroic and sacrificial love, where we are "lifted into the great mood and touched with the undying"; so that we are left, at the end, with our inveterate wonder at this boundless imagination which could hold all nature and all humanity in the secret depths of its creative will.

The Little First Viola

YOU CAN count on the fingers of one hand the men who did as much for the cause of music in America as did Frederick Stock, and you might have a finger or two left over. He was born in 1872 in Jülich, Germany, and had his musical education at Cologne University. He had vague thoughts of a career as a concert violinist, and to get some practical experience in playing in public joined the orchestra of an opera house. I think he told me it was in Stuttgart, though I'm not absolutely positive. He was talking one day about the special training and experience that an orchestra musician has to have. "When I joined that orchestra," he said, "I was prepared to play the Mendelssohn concerto at the drop of a hat, but I couldn't play a second-violin part from *Siegfried,* with one eye on the notes and the other on the conductor." He seems to have cleared that hurdle, however, for Theodore Thomas, during a scouting trip abroad, ran across young Stock, liked his playing, and offered him a job. "You'll have to play viola, though," he added. "I've got enough violins."

Stock agreed, and in 1895, at the age of twenty-three, he came to America and took his place at the second desk of the viola section of the Thomas Orchestra—now the Chicago Symphony. For nearly ten years nothing much happened. Not that he wasn't a fine viola player. He was—one of the best in Thomas's orchestra. But it seemed that if rising in the world depended on his own efforts, a fine viola player was all that he was destined to be.

As a matter of fact, to me one of the best evidences of Stock's real greatness, both as a man and a musician, is that he arrived at the position of distinction and authority that he undeniably held almost literally in spite of himself. He was one of the most incompetent salesmen—of himself—that I have ever known. He was a simple man. I think that in his heart he held a naïve belief that if you do your job well, you won't have time left in which to figure how to get ahead. He may have been right. Certainly he never climbed the ladder of success. Climbing was not in his nature. If he got to the top, it's because he was pushed and dragged there by people who believed in him.

Theodore Thomas was the first of them. In 1904 he announced the appointment of Frederick Stock as assistant conductor of the orchestra, much to the disapproval of musical Chicago—first of all, because he had never needed an assistant before; second, because if he must appoint one, why choose an unknown and inexperienced viola player? Thomas's only comment was to the effect that he had been in the orchestra business long enough to know what he was doing. Stock himself rather shared the apprehensions of his critics. He had had practically no experience in conducting, and confessed to his friends that he didn't know whether or not he was going to be able to hold his new position. He and Chicago were soon to find out.

In December of that same year, 1904, Thomas collapsed at a rehearsal. He grew steadily worse, and the young assistant conductor took his place at the two closing concerts of the year. On January 4, 1905, Thomas died. Now, in the early nineteen-hundreds, guest conductors weren't to be had by picking up a telephone, and the problem of filling the orchestra's schedule of concerts was a serious one. The directors finally decided to take a chance on the new assistant and let him finish the season. Meanwhile, they would look around for a conductor worthy to succeed Theodore Thomas. In one sense they never found that mythical conductor, for by the end of the season of 1904–5, they had discovered that they already had him. Frederick Stock was given a contract as permanent conductor of the Chicago Orchestra, a contract that was canceled only by his death, on October 20, 1942.

Any head of an orchestra who can keep his audiences interested and enthusiastic for thirty-seven years, playing an entire season every year with only an occasional guest conductor by way of relief, must have extraordinary qualities. And Fred Stock had. For one thing, he was a wonderful drill-master. Thomas left Chicago an excellent orchestra; Stock left it a great one, one of the greatest in the world, an orchestra famous for its precision, intonation, tone quality, and all-round virtuosity. He was one of the first to break the old tradition of hiring first-desk men from Europe. Whenever he found an American-trained musician who was good enough, he hired him, by preference. And he found some good ones.

Another quality of his was that he was a great conductor. He certainly got credit for that from musicians. I'm not so sure about his audiences. They loved him and they loved the music, but unless they could realize for themselves why it sounded as it did, they got no help from him. As I said, he had no self-salesmanship. He never put on a show in his conducting. He was not particularly graceful, or, to an audience, particularly eloquent. You would know, after watching him for a while, that he must have played in an orchestra himself, for he knew that what orchestra players want first of all on the conductor's platform is somebody to beat time.

So he beat time. Watch his stick, and you would see all the proper movements—down, left, right, up—just as they're set down in Berlioz's treatise on conducting. It wasn't beautiful, but it told the men what they wanted to know. His other gestures were very few. In fact, you might be fooled into thinking that his conducting was perfunctory, it was so easy and effortless. But it wasn't perfunctory. He simply didn't bother to dramatize his own personality, to interpret the music for the eye of the audience. He left that to the ear, and to the orchestra. His hard work had been done at rehearsals.

He was extraordinarily hospitable to new music, working on the theory that since all the old music was once new, there must always be somebody to give new music a hearing. He would give a polished performance of any music that he considered honestly and skillfully written, regardless of whether it happened to appeal to his personal taste. He considered his personal likes and dislikes to be unimportant. As a result, the Chicago Orchestra has a record of "first time" performances during the past three decades that few orchestras in this country can equal. New York, for instance, heard Stravinsky's *The Rite of Spring* for the first time when Serge Koussevitzky brought the Boston Symphony Orchestra to New York to play it in 1924. Chicago had heard it, conducted by Stock, just ten years before. Pieces that are put forward in New York as terrific novelties—such as Gliere's *Ilya Murometz*—have been appearing on the Chicago programs for years. Particularly was he hospitable to American composers, long before many other conductors thought they were worth bothering about, either conducting their works himself or inviting the composers to appear as guest conductors of their own music.

In this connection he never played a rather dirty trick that other conductors have been known to play. You see, once in a while a conductor finds himself under pressure to put a certain new American work on one of his programs. If he likes the piece, all well and good. If he doesn't, he may invite the composer to conduct it himself. That sounds like an honor, and sometimes it is. On the other hand, the important thing about conducting a piece of music is not whether you can keep the orchestra together (any competent musician can do that) but whether you can rehearse it, whether you can get out of the orchestra the kind of performance the piece needs. Now, that's a job for a professional conductor, and, very few composers being professional conductors, the unfortunate guest is likely to give a pretty ungrateful and slovenly performance of his new music. If he were conducting the Beethoven Fifth, the audience would spot the bad performance in a minute and blame him as conductor. But this is music they haven't heard before, and anything they don't like about it is going to be blamed not on the man who is conducting it but on the man who wrote it. So they turn thumbs down on the work, and the regular conductor escapes the blame for having put it on.

Stock never did that. In common with many other Americans, I've been invited by Stock to conduct things of mine with the Chicago Orchestra; and when I arrived, terrified, to take over the final rehearsal, I would find that Stock had already rehearsed the piece thoroughly, that the players were prepared to give such a brilliant performance that the rehearsal was for me, not for them. My only job was to wave the stick and keep out from under their feet.

His rehearsals, by the way, were fascinating to watch. He and the orchestra knew each other so well that everything went with a minimum amount of stoppage and confusion. If something went wrong, he never lost his temper. What was the use? They were good and he knew it. He was good and *they* knew it. His one idea was to fix the mistake, not to fix the blame.

To look at him, you never would have thought he was a great conductor. He was about medium height, perhaps a little under, with a nondescript mustache, rather bulging blue eyes, and a florid complexion that testified to his Teutonic ancestry. His walk was undistinguished, and he was inclined to be stoop-shouldered. He never quite lost a faint German accent. If you had seen him sitting in a corner at some musical gathering, you might easily have assumed that he was one of the orchestra men—say, somebody from the second desk of the viola section. You wouldn't have been far wrong. In his complete simplicity, shyness, and self-effacement he remained, all his life, the little viola player.

I said before that only death terminated his contract. That isn't quite accurate. When we entered the war, in 1917, certain super-patriots in Chicago discovered that he had never got around to being naturalized, that he was, technically, an enemy alien. With no further argument, Stock handed in his resignation, which—and I have friends in Chicago who are a little ashamed of it—was accepted. Needless to say, he was back on the stand as soon as the war was over. The moral of that incident has always seemed to me to be that naturalization papers are not the only things that make an American. If ever there was a great American, at any time during his life in this country, it was Frederick Stock. In the words of one of my correspondents, "Let us not again let men like this go without telling them that we love them. They would appreciate our love. We use many words on the creatures we hate, but never the least word to men who have made us better human beings, who have given us a bulwark against cruelty, bigotry, and stupidity. We have all, all good and bewildered people, died a little with him."

9

Stepchildren

I'D LIKE to venture a guess that at least five out of ten readers of this book have never heard of John Knowles Paine, and would be rather surprised to learn that he wrote some pretty fine music. That's because Paine belonged to what you could almost call the lost generation of American composers. Lost, because its members were born too soon; born, most of them, in the late fifties and early sixties; now dead, most of them, for anything from ten to forty years. If they had been born twenty years later—or even ten—their names would still be familiar and we would know their music, for they were men of talent. But America was not ready for them.

Paine was the oldest, born in Portland, Maine, in 1839. He was the first American to try any of the larger forms of music with any success. His first symphony, written in 1876, was the first of its kind; his oratorio, *St. Peter,* dating from '73, was another pioneer work. So was his grand opera, *Azara,* which resembled so many of its successors in that it has never been performed. His best known music is the incidental music to Sophocles' tragedy *Oedipus Tyrannus.*

His nearest contemporary was Arthur Foote, born in '53 and a pupil of Paine's in the Harvard University music school. In fact, Foote was about the only serious composer of his generation to receive all his musical education in America. If you have ever heard his suite for string orchestra, you'll know why I think that his music is neglected.

A year younger than Foote was George Whitfield Chadwick, who is remembered by many people as the director of the New England Conservatory of Music from 1897 until his death in 1931, but who should also be remembered as a composer. His *Melpomene* and *Tam O'Shanter* overtures and his symphonic sketches ought to be played much oftener than they are.

To say that all of that generation have been neglected isn't completely accurate. Two members of it are very much alive in our consciousness today, and a third is still widely played. The two are Ethelbert Nevin and John Philip Sousa, the one born in 1862, the other in 1856. Curiously enough, both wrote music that made no pretense to classic dimensions. Nevin survives through the sentimental appeal of his piano pieces and songs, Sousa through his magnificent marches. The other composer, Edward MacDowell, born in 1861, is an exception. If he is not played as frequently as a European composer of equal stature would be in his native land, at least he hasn't been as studiously neglectd as most of his contemporaries.

Edgar Stillman-Kelley, for example, was born four years before MacDowell. Two works of his that I'd like to hear—and never have—are his symphony based on *Gulliver's Travels* and his *Aladdin* suite for orchestra, both of which mark him as the first American composer to experiment with fantasy in orchestral music. Horatio Parker, the youngest of the group, was born in '63 and died in 1919. Comparatively speaking, he's forgotten, and yet much of his music, including his superb oratorio, *Hora Novissima,* could be heard today with pleasure.

Now, why were these men pushed aside? Why didn't they get the exploitation that a dozen American composers are getting today? For part of the answer, suppose we turn to a book by Rupert Hughes entitled *Contemporary American Composers,* published in 1901. In the introduction to the book, Mr. Hughes writes, concerning the American composer: "The first and most vital flaw of which his work will be accused is the lack of nationalism." Well, that accusation has a very familiar sound. It's still brought against the American composer, and will continue to be, simply because no two Americans can agree as to what constitutes "Americanism" in music. Hughes goes on to point out that the public at large is inert and indifferent, that it has no interest in listening to music by its fellow countrymen. That, God knows, is also still true. He says that singers generally stick to the lieder that they learned from their voice teachers, without bothering to look for American songs. That, I think, is *not* true today. He says also that the orchestra conductors present almost a solid front against playing American works. That front, at least, is beginning to crack. The conductors are becoming increasingly hospitable.

I think that the real answer is contained in a single five-word sentence from a review of a performance of Paine's *Oedipus* prelude written some years ago by the late H. T. Parker, of the Boston *Transcript*. "The composer was no genius." Remember that sentence. In that brief remark is implied an attitude that still persists on the part of our critics and audiences, an attitude of condescending dismissal that still hamstrings the American composer at every turn of the road.

What *is* a "genius"? Beethoven? Bach? Mozart? Wagner? Haydn? Schubert? Debussy? If any or all of those men are geniuses, then there are a thousand composers who are not. Of course Paine and Chadwick and Foote weren't geniuses, nor did any one of them ever claim to be. But the implication of that sentence of Parker's is that if they weren't, it was hardly worth while to bother with them. And that's our selfsame attitude today—but only, let me remark, toward American composers. I don't think there are many people who would apply the term "genius" to composers like Raff, Max Reger, Borodin, Miaskovsky, Kalinnikoff, Chabrier, Gliere, Lalo, Kodaly, Wolf-Ferrari, and dozens of others in their same rank. Yet their music is played and we listen to it with pleasure, and never question its right to a place on our programs. But let an American venture to write a symphony and succeed, by a small miracle, in getting it played, we don't compare it with Raff's *Leonore* symphony or with Beethoven's first. No. We compare it with Beethoven's *third*. And if it doesn't measure up to the *Eroica,* into the ashcan it goes.

You may have heard of a play that ran for seven years in New York, called *Life with Father*. Now if, at any time during that run, a dramatic critic had come forward to remark that *Life with Father* wasn't as good as *Oedipus Tyrannus* we'd think he ought to have his head examined. We take it for what it is—a play of no cosmic importance, beautifully written and enormously entertaining—and let it go at that. But the minute we hear a new piece of American music, we solemnly start appraising it in terms of immortality. Not that we consciously do so, necessarily, but in the back of our heads—Well, we don't say, "John Doe's symphony in E major is the best symphony written this year." We say, "Will it live?"

Never mind about that. Give John Doe a break. When you hear that symphony of his, ask yourself just one question: "Did I get any pleasure out of hearing it?" If you honestly didn't, perhaps that ends it. If you did, see if you can't manage to hear it again. Listen to some other things of his. Do what you can to give him the thing that any artist must have to go on: the feeling that he's wanted, that he's some use in the world. Give him a chance to learn, in the only way a composer *can* learn: by hearing his stuff played. Perhaps his next symphony will be the best one written in *two* years, or ten, or a lifetime—who knows? You don't. So don't worry about it. Never mind wondering whether it's going to go down through the ages. Concentrate on here and now, and let the ages take care of themselves.

The Underprivileged

MARK TWAIN once remarked that everybody talks about the weather and nobody does anything about it. His remark would have been equally apropos if instead of saying "weather" he had substituted "American opera." I hear a great many people lamenting the fact that we have no such repertoire of native opera as is possessed by, say, France, Germany, and Italy. Few American composers even attempt to write operas, and of the few that are written, only a handful are ever produced. Of those few, a handful, a very small handful, have achieved even a moderate success. As to why this state of affairs exists, the consensus of opinion seems to be that Americans just don't have any talent for opera, that it isn't in our musical temperament.

I believe this is nonsense. I believe that the country that can turn out the world's best musical comedies could, given the right conditions, turn out a respectable quota of viable "grand" operas. I believe that our failure to produce native opera is due to two highly unfortunate conditions which have a common basis.

First of all, the average American opera fails because its composer doesn't know his trade. Oh, he knows music, right enough. He can compose themes and develop them and score them for orchestra. But he knows nothing of the theater. He has never had a chance to know anything about it, and, ten to one, thinks that theatrical effectiveness is a cheap device unworthy of the attention of any serious composer. He is wrong.

You may think that you enjoy *Die Meistersinger* and *Rigoletto* and *La Bohème* for the music alone. You don't. One reason why you enjoy them so much is that Wagner and Verdi and Puccini were superb showmen who were men of the theater to their fingertips.

And not one of them wrote a really successful first opera. Wagner's very first, *Die Feen,* never had a production until his sixty-seventh year, when he was world famous, and was produced then only as a curiosity. His second, *Das Liebesverbot,* ended in a fist fight in the middle of its first (and only) performance. Verdi's *Oberto* and Puccini's *Le Villi* had a moderate reception, but I have yet to see a performance of any one of the three. If three first operas by American composers had been as coolly received, you would never again have heard of either the operas or their composers.

Why should this be so? Because European opera composers are allowed to make mistakes. If their first operas fail, they are not damned forever. If they don't make the big time at once, they have smaller provincial opera houses to fall back upon, theaters whose production costs are low enough to enable them to afford a flop now and then. The American has no such privilege, because he has no small companies to which to turn. He works in a vacuum, theatrically speaking. If he ever does get a production, it must compete with Wagner and Verdi and Puccini in order to survive at all. I don't have to tell you how small his chances are.

Let me be personal for a moment. I have had two operas produced at the Metropolitan, and both were, comparatively speaking, successes. One ran for three seasons and one for four —much longer than any other American works. Why? Were they any better, musically speaking, than a half dozen other operas by Americans? Certainly not. They succeeded because I had had the tremendous—and I think unique— luck to have written incidental music for nine plays before I ever thought of writing an opera. In other words, I had had a chance to watch not the stage but the audience, to learn that the music, however magnificent (as all of mine was, naturally) must always be subordinate to the situation, that the audience is a jury from whose verdict there is no appeal, that in a given situation a single flute can be more effective than Sousa's band, that a scene that is three minutes too long is an hour too long. I had a chance to learn, in short, that the would-be composer of opera must think much more like a stage director than like a composer—a chance for which I shall always be humbly grateful. If other Americans could have that same chance, whether in the spoken theater or in small opera companies, we would have many more stageworthy operas.

Now for the second bad condition. Again I must be personal. I have written three operas. All three were produced. I doubt whether I shall ever write another. I have talked to other composers who also have had operas produced. They feel as I do. We have given up any hope of writing other operas because we can't afford to write them. Not "afford" in terms of money. We never expected to make money out of opera. But we cannot afford not to have our music heard. Say we do get a production. The work runs one, two, or three seasons, and is then shelved for good—a solid one or two years' work relegated to oblivion. We are human. We like to be played. The same amount of time spent on music for the concert hall would—granted the quality of the work—assure us performances for years to come. Wagner could write for the future. We, in case it has escaped your attention, are not Wagner.

The root of this situation lies in the fact that if the Met doesn't produce it, it isn't produced. Heaven knows this is no reflection on the Met. The Metropolitan Opera Association is obligated to produce a large number of operas each season that are a part of the permanent repertoire. Its running expenses are enormous. Financial conditions being what they are, any new production that it makes must have a more than fair chance of being a successful one. Even if the organization could afford to experiment, it would be faced with the physical impossibility of producing more than one or two new operas a season.

Nevertheless, the hard fact remains that the Metropolitan is the only opera company in this country at present that produces any new works at all. It is a very poor theatrical season in New York that does not see upward of a hundred plays, presented by approximately twenty-five different producers. If one can't use your play, you have twenty-four others to whom to submit it. But if it's an opera you have written—if the Met doesn't produce it, it isn't produced. We have one great producing opera company. I wish we had twenty-four little ones as well.

PART FOUR

Development Section

I

Getting a Laugh

SOMEONE asked me the other day what constitutes humor in music. As a matter of fact, there are about six ways of getting a laugh with music. The most primitive is through shock—a sudden and unexpected loud noise in the middle of a quiet passage. The example you all know is the sudden *sforzando* chord in Haydn's *Surprise* symphony. Then there's another kind of shock that comes from a sudden extremely discordant sequence in an otherwise smoothly harmonized passage. There's a very good example of that in Gian-Carlo Menotti's opera *Amelia Goes to the Ball,* where one character makes some invidious remarks about modern music, and the orchestra goes slightly insane for about eight bars. Another way, which comes under the head of slapstick humor but is very effective, is to extract funny noises from the instruments. The famous drunken bassoon player in Beethoven's *Pastoral* symphony is one instance. The clarinet glissando that opens Gershwin's *Rhapsody in Blue* is another. Then there are imitations. The most famous example of those is the section of Strauss's *Don Quixote* where the knight rides through a flock of sheep.

One rather literary method is that of exaggeration, writing music that is all out of proportion to the episode it's supposed to represent. The breakfast scene, with father, mother, and the baby, in Strauss's *Domestic* symphony is a perfect example; that is, it's perfect if Strauss really meant it to be funny in quite that way. I've always wondered about that. Then the last method, which is purely literary, is that of suddenly introducing a quotation. You'll find one in Charpentier's *Louise*, when one of a group of bohemians remarks that an artist's ambition is to be a god—and the orchestra obligingly quotes a passage from the Valhalla music in *Das Rheingold*.

At the same time, I'm not sure that it's possible to be very humorous in terms of pure music. We're told that the shock chord in the *Surprise* symphony is meant to be funny, and so we laugh. But there's an equally heavy shock chord in the first movement of Tchaikovsky's sixth symphony, at which we don't laugh—probably because it's called the *Pathetic* symphony. The animal imitations are funny *if* you know beforehand that they're supposed to be animals. If you didn't, you might be more puzzled than amused. The quotations, of course, don't mean a thing unless you recognize them. Exaggeration, as I said before, is only funny if the composer is conscious of it. As for the funny noises on the instruments and the wildly dissonant passages, with modern music what it is, you simply *must* know beforehand that they are supposed to be funny. Otherwise, you're likely to get into trouble, at an ultra-modern concert, by bursting into ill-timed guffaws at some passage that was meant by the composer to express the suppressed yearnings of man in the machine age.

Music purely by itself, with no literary or pictorial clues to help the listener, can be lively and it can be gay. But I doubt if it can ever be genuinely funny, except by association with some funny sight or natural sound—just as, on the other hand, it can be menacing but never really wicked. It is the child of the arts: cheerful and tearful; too innocent to be evil and too naïve to be witty.

Art Under Pressure

It's curious how ideas get into the air. In the course of a single month I had letters from two correspondents who lived a couple of thousand miles apart, both of whom discussed aspects of the same rather unusual question. The first came from British Columbia, where my correspondent, a clergyman, wrote in part as follows:

"I have a theory that musical expression reaches a high development in a country that is unhappy in its government. Why, I don't know. Perhaps a release. The empire of the Tsars has given us a great number of good composers; so did old Austria-Hungary, and so did Germany and Italy before they became totalitarian. Since then there has been a falling off in the quality of their music. If this theory is correct it is easy to see why the United States and Canada cannot produce good music to any great extent."

The other letter came from Lexington, Virginia. Its writer said: "There is a lot of talk about the stagnation of art in totalitarian countries. Again and again it is asserted that the artist cannot freely create under a despotic government. Aside from the fact that this was not true in the past (if it were, art would just be starting out), it still seems to be utterly untrue so far as music is concerned. Because, how else could you explain the leading roles that Russian composers play in the musical life of our times? Certainly there are refugees like Stravinsky and Rachmaninoff, but of these two the latter, at least, created under a Tsarist regime that was no more liberal than the present one. But there are at the same time artists like Shostakovich, Prokofieff, and Khatchaturian, who add their bit, so that among modern works performed, the Russians are definitely ahead of other nations. Ideologically, I have no sympathy with totalitarianism—I am a refugee myself—but I think it is a serious mistake to judge the artistic standards of a country by its government."

Now, there you have two facets of a very old and many-sided question, which is: Why do certain countries produce great schools of music while others do not? An English composer and musicologist, the late Cecil Forsyth, had an interesting theory about that, which he advanced in his book *Music and Nationalism.* He pointed out, first, that the composer differs from other artists in that outside impressions, while they may affect him emotionally, nevertheless do not form the physical basis of his work. The painter and the sculptor express themselves as artists through more or less literal reproductions of things that they have seen. The poet and the novelist report and comment upon things heard and seen. In Forsyth's words, "They pass these sense-impressions through their minds, and bring forth a 'version' of them colored and modified by their own personalities. The musician, wholly self-centered, passes through the same process, but the creative act begins in a quite different manner in that he looks for his stimulus to nothing outside his own personality." In other words, unless he descends to writing mere imitations of natural sounds, he cannot be objective; he cannot and does not reproduce any phase of the outside world in his music. All that he can express are the emotional reactions to his contact with the world.

It follows, then, that the composer is essentially an introvert, that he looks within himself for the music that he sets down. His role, in world events, is that of contemplation, not of participation. Forsyth then develops the theory that the pursuit and attainment of world power, while it stimulates the creation of the other arts, tends to stifle the development of any musical creative energy in a country. In countries that are expanding, whose people are restless and ambitious, countries engaged in extensive colonial development, you will find, he says, that musical activity is at a low ebb. He cites England as an example, which, for centuries has been pushing out to new frontiers, whose eyes have been turned outward, since Elizabeth's time, to strange things, strange places, and strange faces. This constant reminder of new sights and sounds and ideas has been a great stimulus to her literary artists; she has produced a great race of poets and playwrights and novelists; she has even produced her quota of great painters and sculptors. She has not produced a great line of composers. On the other side he cites nineteenth-century Germany and Austria, "sitting," he writes, "within their own borders, their backs, as it were, turned to their frontiers and their eyes turned inward. In such a nation there is no national projection of energy outward, but there is an intense and cherishing spirit of national pride inward." This, he thinks, makes for the subjective turn of mind that produces great music. As a matter of fact, it is true that as Germany changed from a passive to an aggressive nation, and began to think in terms of territorial expansion, her output of music, whether by coincidence or otherwise, began to decline. Since 1870 her only first-rank composer has been Richard Strauss.* America, too, busy pushing on to new frontiers within our own continent, busy with industrial expansion, has hardly been in a state of mind that is favorable for the development of a school of great music. Now that we have stopped growing, in a geographical sense, we may be starting to grow artistically.

That is one theory. There is also the one held by my first

*I know, I know: what about Bruckner and Mahler? Well, *what* about them?

correspondent, that countries that are unhappy in their governments tend to create music. There's something in that, too. A despotic government, by curtailing its people's freedom of speech and movement, does tend to drive men in upon themselves, and to express themselves in ways that can evade the police and the censors. And among the non-controversial means of self-expression, music is easily the first. My second correspondent rather agrees. He argues simply that the form of a nation's government has no effect one way or the other upon the creative arts. I would hardly go that far. I find it hard—or did—to believe that a painter or a dramatist or a poet living in a modern totalitarian state could paint or write absolutely as he pleased. The musician, however, could very well do so, provided he stuck to pure music, and didn't associate it with subversive titles or poems.

This correspondent cites Tsarist Russia as being just as totalitarian as it is under the Soviet regime. Yes and no. If he means politically, he is right. But Tsarist Russia was only a *political* despotism. Composers such as Tchaikovsky and Rimsky-Korsakoff had no voice in political matters, and were likely to get into trouble only if they engaged in political activities or expressed subversive political opinions. Otherwise, they were free to think and work as they pleased. No government official would dream of telling them what kind of music to write. True, Rimsky's *Golden Cockerel* was banned for a time by the censor, but the objection was to the libretto, not the music. As artists, these composers were free, and fundamentally that was the freedom that mattered supremely to them.

But the modern totalitarian state goes much further than the old-fashioned despots. They told a man what they might or might not say. This despot undertakes to tell him what he may or may not think. It is the medieval church in another incarnation, policing all brands of thought, but infinitely more efficient than its avatar in discovering and punishing heretics. On February 11, 1948, the Central Committee of the Communist party denounced Russia's three leading composers, Dmitri Shostakovich, Aram Khatchaturian, and Serge Prokofieff, and the Soviet music world in general, for creating and encouraging "anti-democratic music." The idiocy of such an indictment is matched only by the abjectness with which the luckless three admitted their guilt.

Shostakovich, Khatchaturian, and Prokofieff have written works that have enjoyed worldwide popularity. But what sort of music are they likely to turn out with their creative gifts in a strait jacket? A composer who is confronted with the fact that even the workings of his imagination may get him into trouble is not likely to let that imagination range very far. It is not even a question of being, as my correspondent puts it, "unhappy in his government." In fact, the more enthusiastic he is about the totalitarian state, the more fervently he believes in complete intellectual and aesthetic regimentation, the more likely he is to practice his art not for its own sake but as the instrument of a political doctrine. Cervantes wrote *Don Quixote* in jail; Michelangelo was virtually a prisoner in the Vatican when he painted the ceiling of the Sistine Chapel; Wagner was a political exile, with a price on his head, when he wrote *Tristan and Isolde*. Physical freedom is not all-important to an artist. You can imprison him, banish him, gag him, starve him; he remains an artist so long as his mind is free. But imprison his mind and you have left only a propagandist.

3

The Grave Robbers

IN A former book* I discussed briefly the sinful practice, among band leaders and their arrangers, of making dance tunes and pop songs out of themes pilfered from the classics. The consensus of opinion (mine) was that we need not take them seriously because they don't survive long—and besides, we can always turn off the radio when they start. That should have abolished them, but it didn't. The swung classics still persist, and so many correspondents have written passionately about them that I venture a few added comments.

One feature of these "special arrangements" of the classics that I find particularly irritating is the cheery impudence with which the arrangers tack their own musical ideas to the originals. A radio orchestra or a night-club band strikes up something familiar, and you say to yourself, "Hm, that isn't too bad—the second theme of the Tchaikovsky *Pathétique*. Tchaikovsky didn't conceive the theme in *quite* that rhythm, but it might be worse." So it goes along for about sixteen bars, when suddenly it arrives at the point where Tchaikovsky began to develop the theme a bit. That doesn't make good dance rhythm, so the arranger is left to his own devices to finish the thing. And his own devices—to put it mildly—are not very good. In fact, it is precisely those little added touches, the closing cadences and interludes that Brahms and Tchaikovsky or Ravel weren't bright enough to think of, that make these swing arrangements so hard to endure. Those, and that ever-

* *The Well-Tempered Listener.*

lasting wire brush on the drums, symbolic, I suppose, of dusting off the classics.

Another thing that I can't get over is the fact that these band leaders and arrangers actually link their own names with those of the composers. Pick up a printed copy of one of these things, and you will read: "*You in My Arms and Murder in My Heart,* music by Wally Pilfer, based on a theme suggested by Beethoven." When you play it, it turns out to be the chorale from the Ninth symphony in fox-trot time, with eight added measures that would have sent Beethoven to a madhouse.

I sometimes wonder if the distortions aren't the result of a subconscious yearning on the part of these ghouls to improve what you might call their musical social standing. Some of them are pretty good musicians, and they must be secretly a little ashamed of some of the bilge that they arrange and conduct. Perhaps this murdering of serious musical themes helps to restore a little of their self-respect, gives them a sense of importance, a feeling that they are playing music that, however mutilated, was originally good music. The fact that the result of their labors is very similar to that of drawing a mustache on the Mona Lisa seems to escape them.

However, these classic themes that are being used for dance music have one characteristic in common. They are all in the public domain—that is, the copyrights on them have expired. So the bandleaders and arrangers can lift them with impunity. I might add, parenthetically, that one arranger was a bit careless about the copyright status of a certain piece that he stole. When it was published as a fox trot, he made the unpleasant discovery that the piece was still copyrighted, with the result, I am delighted to announce, that he not only paid heavy damages for infringement but has had to turn all his royalties over to the estate of the real composer.

But to get back to the non-copyright music. In this country, the copyright on a book or a piece of music (Russian music excepted) runs for twenty-eight years. It can then be renewed for an additional twenty-eight, making a total of fifty-six years during which the composition is protected against piracy. That means that most of these classic themes that are now being played in swing form are at least fifty-six years old. Now, if a theme is so good, has such vitality, that it can remain in public favor for more than half a century, the chances are that it will survive even such mauling as it is getting now.

Moreover, these dance arrangements don't last long. The overplaying to which all popular music is subjected in these days of the radio is so excessive that only one out of a hundred popular pieces lives longer than two or three months. The audience that likes these dance arrangements is a very naïve one musically; it isn't capable of sustained attention to anything, and the one thing that it asks of any piece of music is that it be a novelty. Even though the themes themselves may have lasting qualities, the arrangements have not. They flourish for a while, and then disappear. Already the earlier ones are fading out of the picture. Nowadays you seldom hear *The Lamp Is Low,* for instance, that started out in life as Ravel's *Pavane pour une infante défunte.*

The great English critic, Ernest Newman, once remarked that "Any music worth playing at all is worth playing badly." I think that remark is probably true of these dance arrangements of the classics. Granted that these great themes are mutilated, wrenched out of their context, appallingly orchestrated, and set to words that make one's flesh creep, nevertheless they are still great themes, and I have faith in them. There must be hundreds of thousands of jitterbugs who would run screaming at the idea of sitting through a symphony concert, but who, nevertheless, know the horn solo in the Tchaikovsky Fifth, and the *Pavane* of Ravel, and Rimsky-Korsakoff's *Hymn to the Sun.* They don't know these themes under their own names; but they have them under their skins. And maybe there they will remain, long after the swing perversions have disappeared. Cannibals have to eat a few missionaries before they are sure that missionaries agree with them, and perhaps these partners in the murder of Tchaikovsky will one day realize that he, too, is good for them.

"Mr. Blank Means to Say . . ."

As a matter of fact, there are three kinds of special arrangements: arrangements down, arrangements up, and what you might call arrangements across. The first kind we discussed in the previous chapter. The second is the kind in which a composer takes a theme of humble birth, a dance tune or the like, and improves its social standing by using it as the basis of a work to be taken seriously. Vaughan Williams' arrangements of English folksongs and Brahms' *Hungarian Dances* are good examples, and I have never heard anyone object to them.

The arrangements across are usually referred to more respectfully as transcriptions. In these, a composer rearranges an instrumental work by another composer for another instrument or another combination of instruments. Oddly enough, the critics of this type of arrangement are as acrimonious as those who object to the dance arrangements. Here, for instance, is what one correspondent has to say about what he calls the transcription mania. "It is a mania," he writes, "only insofar as it is a proof of the transcriber's own creative incapacity. For example, a transcription of a Beethoven quartet for orchestra, or a similar transcription of a Chopin piano piece—shall I call them a crime, or merely the top of tastelessness?"

Another correspondent writes to say: "In listening to the musical offerings of the radio, I find that what interests me is the question of historical faithfulness in music. Quite often I find myself being fed a modern orchestral arrangement of a classical piano sonata. Now, it seems to me that if Mozart, for instance, decided to put certain musical ideas into the form of a sonata, and not a concerto or symphony, he knew very well what he was doing and why he did it, and it would seem to be nobody's business to try to doctor up a master's work. Nor, to my mind, can there be much valid reason for orchestrating other compositions for one, two, three, or four instruments, even if these are not written by a classical master. Nine or ten years ago one conductor offered the subscribers of the New York Philharmonic-Symphony Orchestra a lot of modern orchestrations of sixteenth-century Italian mandolin and guitar pieces.

"Another historical aspect of music," he continues, "in which I usually find myself in emphatic disagreement with modern practice concerns the use of the harpsichord. Here, of course, faithfulness to the composer would seem to demand faithfulness to the instrument for which he wrote. Yet I am convinced that if Bach, Handel, and Mozart could be brought back to life and asked to make their choice between a first-rate harpsichord or clavichord of their own time and just an average piano of today, they would unanimously vote to donate the ancient instrument to the junkman."

You'll notice that my second correspondent goes in on one side of the controversy and comes out on the other—which is probably a clue to the answer to the whole question.

I think that much of the music we hear is more tampered with than we realize. Many people who violently resent the slightest alteration in any composer's score would be amazed, I imagine, to know how often they listen to performances that are, technically at least, a gross violation of the composer's explicit directions. For one very common example, several famous conductors, when they program a Beethoven or Mozart symphony, use double the number of wood-wind players that are called for in the score. By doing this, they get the richness and sonority of the large string section of the modern orchestra, and at the same time preserve the balance in tonal volume between the strings and the comparatively weak wood wind. I once heard Walter Damrosch conduct a performance of Beethoven's Ninth in which, in the vocal quartet of the last movement, he used four singers on each part. It may or may not have been historically justifiable, but I must say that the florid counterpoint of that passage emerged with more clarity and distinctness than I've ever heard before or since. When Arturo Toscanini on one occasion conducted the entire string section of the NBC Orchestra (the basses silent, of course) in two movements of Beethoven's F major quartet (Opus 135), he was violating the *letter* of Beethoven. He was also presenting a performance of that music that I have always remembered—and I mean pleasantly!

It seems to me that you can't lay down any hard and fast rule as to the propriety of any transcription. Every one has to be considered on its own merits, more or less. You can say that music written for a solo instrument should never be arranged for the orchestra—and then you're confronted with Moussorgsky's *Pictures at an Exhibition,* which most people accept as an orchestral work, but which has been transcribed for the orchestra by both Maurice Ravel and Leopold Stokowski from Moussorgsky's original piano score. Then there are Stokowski's transcriptions of Bach's "Sarabande" from an *English* suite, the adagio from the organ *Toccata* in C minor, and the *Passacaglia* in C minor. These are magnificent orchestral works, that give symphony audiences all over the world a chance to hear certain Bach masterpieces that would otherwise survive only in an occasional organ recital. On the other hand, I once heard three Bach chorales, orchestrated by a famous modern composer, that were so extravagantly colorful that they produced the impression of somebody with a box of water colors touching up a Rembrandt etching. Of course, in the case of the organ, it must be remembered that that particular instrument is the closest of all to the orchestra. Fundamentally, it's a collection of wind instruments, played by means of a keyboard, so it's the easiest of all to transcribe for orchestra without hurting the quality of the music.

A musical composition is not a painting. It is much more like a play, in that it requires performers to give it substance. And if you can compare the themes of a work to the plot and dialogue of a play, you can, if nobody's looking, compare its instrumental dress to the scenery and costumes. And just as you can give a Shakespearean production in modern clothes, you can, within reason, produce a piece of classic music in terms of the modern orchestra. There is, I think, just one question we should ask concerning any transcription: Does it convey the music as the composer intended? Does it make the particular impression that he wanted it to make?

Now that question, answered honestly, will admit a great many orchestral transcriptions and rule out a great many others. I agree with my correspondents in their dislike of orchestrations of piano music in general. If Ravel's transcription of Moussorgsky is faithful to the spirit of the original, as in my opinion it is, that's probably because Moussorgsky wasn't a very good pianist, and therefore didn't write music that was particularly pianistic. Chopin, for example, is another story. His music is so utterly designed to exploit the particular virtues of the piano, is so completely piano music, that any attempt to translate him into terms of the orchestra generally ends up by sounding like an orchestration of a piano piece; at best, it sounds like somebody else's rhapsody for orchestra, based on themes by Chopin. So Chopin's a good man to leave in peace.

Now, leaving aside the aesthetic merits of the case, and considering only the principle of the thing, the question as to whether a transcription is ever justifiable, you might be surprised to know that at least two great composers, Bach and Beethoven, if their own practice means anything, would vote yes. Bach, for instance, arranged sixteen of Vivaldi's violin concertos for the piano, and then went back and arranged three of them for the organ as well. He took a Vivaldi concerto for four violins and arranged it for four harpsichords, changing rhythms and melodies when he felt like it, and even adding extra parts. He arranged several of his own violin concertos for the piano. Beethoven never hesitated to make piano arrangements of his own works, if he thought they would sell better, going so far as to arrange his second symphony as a trio for piano, violin, and cello.

Hamilton Harty's orchestral transcription of three Handel dances is a good example of what a sympathetic transcriber can do for a classic composer. The orchestra of Handel's day was a pretty thin and haphazard affair. In the string section, the cello was invariably treated as a sort of junior double bass, playing the double-bass part an octave higher. The wind section comprised pairs of flutes, oboes, and bassoons—no clarinets—a couple of trumpets, and a pair of hunting horns. The harpsichord played a very important role, with the conductor —who was generally the composer—filling in the harmonies from a single-line figured-bass part. Handel himself wasn't a particularly interesting orchestrator. Even when he took pains with his orchestration—and that wasn't very often—his instrumentation lacked variety and contrast to our ears. Consequently, when a skilled musician, and an admirer of Handel's, like Sir Hamilton Harty transcribes his music for a modern orchestra, in a conscientious effort to make that music sound the way Handel would have *liked* to have it sound, he is doing the composer a great service.

To me, the convincing argument in favor of certain transcriptions—granted, of course, that they are made by honest craftsmen who understand the composer they're transcribing—is that they make accessible to us a vast store of good music that otherwise we would hardly ever hear. If Bach transcribed Vivaldi violin pieces for the piano and the organ, it was because he was living in an age when good violinists were rare and pianists and organists were comparatively plentiful. Similarly, if we hear orchestral transcriptions of Bach, we are hearing music that, as I said before, we probably would seldom hear. Incidentally, don't forget that the technique of the performance has to be considered, too. The number of organists who can play Bach really well is not overwhelmingly large; and I'd rather hear an orchestral transcription of Bach, played superbly by a first-rank symphony orchestra, than the original organ version played devoutly and badly.

Then, too, I think we're justified in guessing as to what one of the classic composers would have done if he had had at his command the performing resources that we have. If Bach had lived in a country that possessed nearly three hundred orchestras, as we do, would he have confined some of his preludes and fugues and toccatas and chorales to the organ? I think not. To me, certain orchestral transcriptions of Bach's music sound more expressive of the vastness and eloquence of Bach's musical thought than his original versions.

And there I leave it. If a transcription sounds like someone's attempt to improve upon the original, to be a medium for satisfying the transcriber's vanity, don't bother to listen to it again. But if it sounds like a sincere attempt, first, to make the music more generally accessible, and second, to preserve the substance and the spirit of the original, you may safely listen to it with no outrage either to your own taste or to the memory of the composer.

5

The Illiterate Art

OF A Saturday night, on the air, I heard a number of Chinese classical songs, including two folksongs that are five hundred years old. The next afternoon, seeing that a favorite of mine, Stravinsky's *Firebird* suite, was likewise on the air, I got out the printed score and followed it while the orchestra played. The score comprises seventy-seven pages, approximately twelve by fourteen inches in size, averaging from twenty to thirty separate instrumental parts to the page.

?

Oh, nothing much. I was just wondering.

The *Firebird* suite is pretty generally considered as being typical first-rate music of our time. The folksongs, simple, square-toed, a bit monotonous, were probably about as good as any music of *their* time, not only in China but anywhere in Europe or Asia. Between their primitive simplicity and the gorgeous color and thematic variety of the Stravinsky work yawns an abyss. Now, that seems very strange. The period of those songs is the early middle fourteen-hundreds, say the Hung-hsi era of the Ming dynasty. Now, the Ming dynasty has given us masterpieces in the plastic, graphic, and literary arts that still hold their own with the best that we have. Ming porcelains, for instance, still bring fantastic prices, because they still rank among the finest that the world has produced. But where is the Ming music? Where are the musical masterpieces that we would have the right to expect from a period that was so fruitful in the other fields of art?

Suppose we go back still further, to Greece in the age of Pericles, two thousand four hundred years ago, and consider the state of the arts there and then. Once more we are in the midst of masterworks. Aeschylus, Sophocles, Aristophanes, and Euripides were writing poetic dramas that are still being played, twenty-four centuries later. Socrates was formulating a philosophy that is still vital. The *Iliad* was already a classic; Sappho had been dead nearly two hundred years. Herodotus was showing the way to future generations of historians. Phidias was creating sculpture that has not been surpassed. Architects were designing structures of such perfection of design that the Doric, Ionic, and Corinthian orders are still the foundation of any architectural student's education.

And what of Greek music? What of the great symphonies, oratorios, music dramas that we would expect, as a matter of course, to have been the fruits of that golden age?

All that we know of Greek music is that they did have some kind, because we know that the choruses of the Greek dramas were sung, or at least intoned, and that poets were also supposed to be singers. We know, too, that the Greeks had flutes, pan pipes, and several varieties of harps. Of actual Greek music of that period, all that we possess are a handful of fragments that have been translated as primitive and more or less formless tunes. Music in Greece, in the year 450 B.C., was still in its infancy, and remained in practically the same state of arrested development for upward of sixteen hundred years.

Why? Briefly, I think it was because, outside the songs of the common people, music, so-called serious music, was in the hands of mathematicians and theologians for thousands of years. It was they, rather than the musicians, who took charge of the art and evolved ponderous philosophical and ethical theories about it—and never advanced it an inch. They spent —and here was the stumbling block—hundreds and thousands of years laboring under the delusion that since poetry and music were so closely allied, both were branches of the same art, and could be treated exactly alike; and, so thinking, they wasted countless centuries trying to *write* music just as they would write poetry. And of course, they failed, for a simple reason.

In a written line of poetry or prose, the letters that form a word stand, fundamentally, for just one thing: a thought. So long as the letters are in such order that they spell out intelligible words, the thought can always be grasped. You may slant the lines of the poem or the play or story up or down; you may write them upside down; you may write them backward; you may make the lines wavy, if you please; you may write them small or large. No matter. Reading them, you can always grasp the author's ideas. Furthermore, even if you don't know the *sound* of the language, you can still grasp the sense of the author's message. The fact that scholars today are still fighting over the proper pronunciation of Latin doesn't prevent their being able to *read* Latin fluently, even though their pronunciation might send an ancient Roman into gales of laughter.

Now, if you happen to be familiar with the language in which a line of words is written, it can also stand for sounds —in other words, for the language as it is spoken. Give an actor a script of a play to read. He can sit down and read it, in silence, to himself. Or, using the same script, he can read you the play aloud. But even in that case, the *thought* comes first. If the words don't make sense as written, your reading them aloud won't make them mean a bit more.

But consider music. A line of written or printed music, as we know it today, has no thought in it at all, in the literary sense. Even if you are an expert sight reader, and can read a line of printed music as easily as you can read a line of printed English, the musical symbols make no sense at all until you have mentally converted them into sounds. That line of music isn't a line of writing at all. It's a diagram, a blueprint, a set of directions. What it conveys to your brain is merely a silent order to utter a sound with your voice, press down a key of a piano, push down a valve in a trumpet and blow, stop a string and draw a bow across it. When you have performed that—not intellectual but *mechanical*—operation, the sound comes forth.

One other difference between words and music. You may read aloud your line of poetry fast or slowly; you may space the words widely or run them together; you may raise your voice or lower it. The result may not be uniformly pleasant, but the *sense* of the words remains unimpaired and unchanged. If you do those same things in playing or singing music, you produce a different kind of music with every operation. Music exists in space and time simultaneously. Not only the pitch but the duration of the notes as well is vitally important. Our musical ancestors never grasped these inherent differences between music and words. There was one secret that they never solved, a secret so childishly simple that it seems incredible that they could have *avoided* solving it. But avoid it they did. And the secret is this. In order to preserve a musical composition, in order to transmit it, undistorted, from one person to another, you don't *write* music; you *draw* music. You must evolve a set of two-dimensional characters that indicate not only pitch but duration.

That is what the ancient Greeks, and their musical descendants for sixteen centuries, never succeeded in doing. The Greeks did evolve a set of modes, which were something like our modern scales, and they did use the letters of the Greek alphabet to represent the pitch of the various notes. But they had no way of showing how long the notes were to be held. That is why music, in Greece and in other ancient civilizations, was the servant of poetry. It couldn't exist without poetry, because the quantities and accents of the words were the only clue to the rhythm of the notes. As an inevitable result, music, for thousands of years, was vocal music. What instrumental music there was existed purely as an accompaniment to singers. Anything remotely approaching an orchestra, in our sense of the word, was unthinkable, as there existed no such things as orchestra parts. Whatever the instrumentalists played, they had to play by ear. In other words, there was no way of preserving or transmitting music except by memory. The music that singers sang existed only in their recollection of what some previous singer had sung. Imagine the state of the drama at the time of Shakespeare if, up to his day, there had been no way of preserving a play except by word of mouth, and you will realize why music remained a monophonous infant while its sister arts were reaching full maturity.

The first attempt to improve on the Greek notation was made in the Christian church some time around the third or fourth century, A.D. The monks, noticing that the Greeks indicated a rising inflection of the voice in poetry by an upward stroke and a falling one by a downward stroke, hit on the idea of applying these marks to the music of their chants. Eventually they evolved the neumes, a sort of musical shorthand, a series of squiggles and pothooks and dots which, when placed over the words of passage, formed a rough graph that served to remind the singer of the tune he was to sing. They worked pretty well, except for two fatal drawbacks. They weren't any use to the singer unless the tune was one that he already knew, and, being so very vague, made anything like formal part-singing out of the question. Then along about the tenth century some unknown genius had an inspiration. He drew a red line over the text, called it the F line, and drew a letter F at its left end. That line survives today as the fourth line of our bass clef, and the bass-clef sign, which looks like a left-handed C with two dots on its back, is a distorted form of a Gothic F.

About a century later, a great man came up over the musical horizon. He was a Benedictine monk named Guido d'Arezzo.

The inscription under his portrait in the church at Arezzo, "*Beatus Guido, Inventor Musicae*"—"Blessed Guido, Inventor of Music"—is hardly an exaggeration, for he was the man who made real harmony and counterpoint possible—in other words, was the founder of music today.

Guido's aim was to devise some means of writing down music that would enable someone to sing it who had *not* heard the tune before. The first thing to be done, he realized, was to invent some way of indicating the pitch of a note more accurately than the neumes were capable of doing. So, keeping the existing F line, he added a line some distance above it which he called the C line (this is our modern middle C). Then he drew two black lines, one under the F, and the other between the F and the C. Now, by putting dots on the lines and in the spaces, he had a system whereby he could indicate a complete scale; in other words, he had invented the musical staff that we use today. You'll notice that his staff has middle C at the top and then goes down into the bass clef. That's because all church singing was done by male voices. Sopranos and altos didn't become fashionable until later.

Now, while Guido still used the neumes, he changed them considerably, leaving out some of them and thickening others so that their ends bore an approximate resemblance to our modern notes. A singer reading his notation couldn't read a line of music *without words* at sight, because he had no means of knowing what the rhythm was. But given the words, he could sing the exact notes, so far as pitch was concerned. The words then gave the rhythm.

This was about the year 1000. Within a hundred and fifty years the neumes had turned into notes. These notes differed from ours, in that they were square or lozenge-shaped instead of round. But their shapes and sizes, and the presence or absence of their tails did give exact directions as to the duration of the notes. At last music was freed of its slavery to the voice, and could be preserved and transmitted from one generation to another without having its existence dependent upon someone's recollection of it. Instrumental music, however, was still in the future. The earliest attempts at writing harmony and counterpoint in this newfangled method of notation were all made in the field of vocal music. Moreover, for some time, musicians didn't quite dare to be composers on their own hook. Up to the thirteenth century, almost all so-called "composition" consisted in making up counter melodies over a bass that was some traditional church tune.

But real composers were on the way. The first—if not in fact, certainly in survival—was John of Fornsete, an English monk in the abbey of Reading, in Berkshire. About the year 1240 he composed a round for four voices that is still sung, the famous *Sumer Is Icumen In*. Between his death and the birth of Johann Sebastian Bach lie only four hundred years. The marvel of the art of music is that it developed from a collection of simple hymn tunes to the *Ring* trilogy in less than nine centuries. And what delayed that development so long? A silly little problem in the mechanics of notation.

6

Wasted

What would be the state of music today, I wonder, if that problem of notation had been solved in Pericles' time? There were geniuses in the other arts in those days. Who is to say that about the middle of the fifth century, B.C., there were not musical geniuses as well, potential great composers whose gifts went to waste because they had no way of getting their musical ideas written down, and so were never able to develop or communicate them?

Suppose we imagine, for example, Mozart in a previous incarnation, born, with all his genius, in Athens of about the year 465 B.C. What was the possible story of his life?

As a child he gave evidence of possessing an extraordinary musical ear, and soon knew by heart all the old folksongs that his mother sang him. By the time he was seven he could play the chelys, or seven-stringed harp, better than most grownups. His father even bought him a kithara, or phorminx, a larger harp of eighteen strings, supposed to be played only by professionals. He taught himself to play the aulos, which was a sort of cross between a flute and an oboe. By the time he was twelve, everybody was predicting that he would become a great poet. They thought thus because, to a Greek, music and poetry were virtually one and the same thing. They did not conceive of music without poetry. Accordingly, he was sent to study musical theory with the best philosophers of the day; for music, as everyone knew, was a branch of philosophy as well as of poetry.

Guided by his tutors, he learned the seven modes and how to improvise in them, and was also taught the ethical concepts of every mode. I must explain about those modes. Today we have three scales, the major, the minor, and the chromatic; and these are the basis of all our melodies. The Greeks had seven, which were the basis of all their melodies. If you want to know what they sounded like, play (or ask someone to play) a scale of C major on the piano. Now, that is, approximately, the Lydian mode. Now, using only the white notes, play a scale beginning on the D above middle C. That's the Phrygian mode. I won't bore you with any more names, but if you play the white-note scales beginning, successively, on E, F, G, A, and B, you will have played the rest of the Greek modes.

Now, each mode was given its own—not emotional but *moral*—quality. Emotion wasn't associated with music. Today we talk of "bad" music, meaning that, structurally, or perhaps emotionally, it is weak and banal. But when a Greek spoke of "bad" music, he meant just that. The southern Greeks despised the Lydian mode, because they considered it weak and effeminate. The northerners, on the other hand, frowned upon the Phrygian mode because it typified loose morals to them, and considered the Lydian mode very chaste and austere. It was as if we should say to a composer, "You mustn't write that hymn in the key of D minor. That's an immoral key. Put it in C major, where it belongs."

This may all sound to you a little bewildering, but our young Greek Mozart accepted it as a matter of course. He also learned the Greek letters that were written down as symbols of the various notes. We use letters for the names of the notes, too. Thus, C, D, and E are the names of three consecutive notes of the scale. The Greeks used letters in a manner that might puzzle us. Consecutive letters, to them, meant octaves. Thus Delta Epsilon, that is, D-E, meant our middle C and the octave above it; M-N meant our F and its octave.

His musical education completed, our young genius embarked on what gave promise of being a highly successful career as a professional musician—that is, as a singer of poetry—using airs that he had learned by rote and accompanying himself with plucked notes on the kithara. But he ran into trouble very soon. He developed an abnormal fondness for the Lydian and Hypodorian modes, and was frequently caught using them for poems to which they were inappropriate. In other words, he was drawn to our two scales of C major and A minor. He created a great scandal by singing a poem about Achilles in the Dorian mode, which was reserved for love poems, instead of the Hypodorian, which represented military valor. Moreover, he horrified the musical scholars by insisting that the pitch at which a song was sung had nothing to do with its moral effect. Before long he began to be looked upon, in the best musical circles, as a young man who had begun well, but was degenerating into a musical anarchist. As one of the doctors wrote: "I flatter myself that I am just as tolerant of modern music as anyone, but when musicians deliberately descend to sheer noise and ugliness, it is, in my humble opinion, time to call a halt."

Not that he was universally unpopular. Many of the common people liked his singing and his unorthodox methods, especially when he even dared to make up music that no one had heard before to go with the poems. They said it was pleasant to hear, and that was enough for them. Let the philosophers worry about the moral values. What they wanted was a good tune. However, such people were peasants, and ignorant, and their opinions on music were of no importance whatsoever.

But soon his struggles began, struggles in his own mind. One day, idly strumming his harp, he plucked three of the strings at once. The result was a beautiful sound, quite different from the sound of any one note. Startled, he tried another combination of strings. Again, another new sound. Wildly excited by this time, he spent hours trying out fresh combinations of sound, sometimes two, sometimes three, even four notes at once. Some of the most beautiful he noted down, putting the letters one on top of the other.

The next day he played them to a sympathetic friend, who was delighted. He also played him a new air that he had made up for the aulos, an air that had no words to go with it, whose rhythm was not like that of any poem. "Why not put the two together?" the friend suggested. "Why not accompany the new air with some of those new harp sounds?" He seized on the idea at once. He taught the air to his friend, who was also a skilled aulos player, and together they practiced until they had evolved—though they didn't know it—the first instrumental solo with a harmonized accompaniment that the world had ever heard. Laboriously he wrote down the Greek letters that represented all the notes of the new composition. The next day, when they tried again to play it, the friend had forgotten the air and could not read it from the letters. They showed him what notes to play, he explained, but gave him no clue as to how long to *hold* the notes or when to stop playing and wait for the harp.

No matter. That day they worked out a new air and a new harp accompaniment. A week later, when they tried to play the first one, neither could remember it exactly, and the letters of the alphabet gave them only a vague clue as to how it went. To make matters worse, it was as if a gate had been opened in his brain. Day and night, his mind seethed with ideas for new airs and chants, wonderful melodies that came so fast that he couldn't possibly write all of them down in his crude alphabet notation. Even when he had managed to write some of them, a flood of new melodies would occur to him, and when he tried to go back to the earlier ones, he had forgotten them, and what record he had managed to make of them was too inexact to be of much use.

Sometimes he would go to the theater and, seeing *Medea* or *Agamemnon* or *The Trojan Women* and hearing the actors intone their lines and the chorus wailing between scenes, he would suddenly hear, in his own mind, another kind of speech for the actors, something nobler, freer, more varied in rhythm than the monotonous march of the hexameters. He could hear an imagined chorus singing not one melody but three or four at the same time, the combined voices forming those wonderful new sound combinations that he had picked out on the harp. He would hurry home and try to set them down, but the marks that he made could be read only by himself. He could hear, too, other airs that were not for voices or harps or flutes, airs that could not be sung, that refused to go with the rhythm of poetry, that went too high and too low for human voices, that could be played only on instruments whose sound he could dimly imagine, but which he had never heard—and never would hear.

He tried to teach other singers to make this combined music, tried to teach other harp and flute players to read the instrumental airs that he had written down in letters; but his efforts only bewildered them. As time went on, his efforts grew more and more persistent, more and more agonized. But he never succeeded in writing down his music in such a way that anyone else could even guess what it sounded like. His friend the aulos player finally grew bored with his insistence, and began to avoid him. Even his family grew weary of the incessant wailing of his aulos, the everlasting twang-twang of his kithara, the frantic scratching of his reed pen. His father forbade him to make those outlandish sounds in the house. So he took to wandering about in the streets, playing his kithara for any passers-by whom he could induce to listen.

He had abandoned any hope of setting down the airs that he made up, but he always had plenty of new ones. Some of those who heard him play would smile indulgently and tap their foreheads. Others would declare that there was something arresting in the queer stuff the little mad poet played, and would take him to an inn and buy him wine.

His body was found one morning at the foot of the north wall of the Acropolis. Whether he fell or jumped will never be known.

The Dislike Is Mutual

WHEN Hugo Wolf was writing music criticism for a Viennese weekly he had this to say about the music of Johannes Brahms. "Brahms' symphonies," he wrote, "are disgustingly stale and prosy, and fundamentally false and perverse. A single stroke of the cymbal in a work by Liszt expresses more intellect and emotion than all of Brahms' symphonies and his serenades put together." Now, Wolf was no fool about music. He stands, at least in my opinion, on a level with Schubert, Schumann, and Brahms, as one of the four great composers of German lieder. The only way to explain his complete Brahms-blindness is to fall back on the reflection that composers are regrettably erratic in their likes and dislikes of the work of other composers. What the critics have said about them are nosegays compared with what they sometimes say about each other.

One of the most critical and caustic commentators on other men's music was Debussy. We have access to his opinions because he printed them in the years when he was writing articles for *Gil Blas, La Revue Blanche, Figaro,* and other French papers and periodicals. He, by the way, didn't care for Brahms, either. All he could think of to say about Brahms' violin concerto was that it was "very tiresome." He observed that Frederick Delius, the English composer, "wrote some very sweet and innocent songs, music with which to rock to sleep the convalescents of rich neighborhoods," and that a song of Grieg's was like "a pink bonbon filled with snow."

Delius, by the way, is the only composer on record, so far as I know, who had absolutely no use for anybody's music except his own. Eric Fenby, who acted as his musical amanuensis during the years when Delius was blind and paralyzed, used to sneak off in the night and play phonograph records of other men's music, just to relieve his nerves; and Delius would invariably catch him at it and stop him.

But to get back to Debussy. He didn't like Schumann, and he didn't like Schubert. He said that Schubert's songs were "like dried flowers," and that "the trouble with the *Unfinished* symphony was that it couldn't make up its mind to be unfinished." Mendelssohn he called "a facile and elegant notary," and remarked of Beethoven's famous song *Adelaide,* "I think the old master must have forgotten to burn this one." He had his likes, though. Chopin was one. Bach, whom he called "a benevolent God, to whom musicians should offer a prayer before starting to work," was another. Curiously enough, he was very fond of Liszt. He said of him, "His fire and abandon tend to compensate for his faults. I prefer these qualities to kid-gloved perfection, even though Liszt, in his worship of the Muse, sometimes does address her with unseemly familiarity and unceremoniously take her on his knee."

Moussorgsky and Rimsky-Korsakoff were particular favorites of Debussy's, and so was the younger Richard Strauss, whom he called "one of the dominant geniuses of our time." He had a quaint, sneaking fondness for Massenet, for whom he was always apologizing. He once wrote of him that "Massenet's brethren could not readily forgive his power of pleasing. . . . It must be admitted that this gift is not indispensable, particularly in art. To take but one example, Bach never 'pleased,' in the sense of the word as applied to Massenet. Has one ever heard young milliners humming the *St. Matthew Passion?* I think not. But everyone knows that they wake up in the morning and sing *Manon* and *Werther*. Make no mistake. This is a delightful sort of fame, the secret envy of many of the great purists who can only warm their hands at the somewhat pallid flame of the approbation of the elect."

Incidentally, despite that rude remark about *Adelaide*, Debussy was a tremendous admirer of Beethoven, particularly of the Ninth symphony, which he called "the most triumphant example of the molding of an idea to the preconceived form." His abhorrence of Wagner, of course, is historic. Wagner obsessed him; he could never stop writing and talking about him. But I think his disapproval has been misunderstood. His quarrel with Wagner was much more as a writer for the theater and as a bad influence on French art than as a composer pure and simple. He was a fanatic Wagner-lover as a young man, and only grew away from him as his own theories of opera matured. He once described Wagner's use of the leitmotiv system in his music dramas as "a play in which every character presents his visiting card every time he enters the room." At the same time he could, and did write, "In *Parsifal*, the final effort of a genius which compels our homage, Wagner tried to drive his music on a looser rein and let it breathe more freely. . . . Nowhere in Wagner's music is more serene beauty attached than in the prelude to the third act of *Parsifal*, and in the entire "Good Friday" episode. . . . The musical beauty of the opera is supreme. It is incomparable and bewildering, splendid and strong. *Parsifal* is one of the loveliest monuments of sound ever raised to the serene glory of music."

Edvard Grieg, whom Debussy described as looking from the front like a genial photographer and from the rear like a sunflower, was infinitely generous in his estimates of his fellow composers. The list of his favorites ranges from Mozart, Sinding, and Schumann to Tchaikovsky, Chopin, and Arthur

Sullivan. He gave the American Edward MacDowell valuable encouragement and help; he was so excited when he first heard Strauss's *Death and Transfiguration* that he sent the composer a telegram of congratulation; and he was a tremendous admirer of Verdi, whom he called "the last of the great ones. I would go so far," he once wrote, "as to say that side by side with Wagner he was, on the whole, the greatest dramatist of the century."

He was an ardent admirer of Brahms' music, and he and Brahms were great friends. Brahms liked his music, too, which was unusual. Brahms' likes and dislikes were highly unconventional, and he had very little use for the music of most of his contemporaries. Bizet, however, was one of his enthusiasms. An Anglo-French journalist named André Ternant quoted Debussy as saying that he had met Brahms in Paris in 1887, and that they had gone to the opera together to see *Carmen,* which, Brahms told him, he had already seen twenty times. He added that if Bizet were still alive he would go to the ends of the earth to embrace him. In view of Hugo Wolf's remark about the Brahms symphonies, you won't be thunderstruck to learn that Brahms didn't care for Wolf's songs. However, I don't think his opinion was colored by personal considerations. In Brahms' lieder the voice is supreme, the accompaniment being always subordinated to it. So that naturally he wouldn't like Wolf's songs, in which the piano part is fully as important as the voice—sometimes even more so.

Brahms' so-called feud with Wagner was less a personal matter than a breach forced upon both composers by their overzealous admirers. To the Brahmsians, Wagner was everything that was formless and deliberately extravagant in music, whereas the Wagnerites held Brahms up as a horrible example of pure mathematics and no feeling. With each man being used as a club with which to beat the other, they could hardly be expected to be on very close terms. Brahms, being a strict classicist, disapproved utterly of Wagner's habit of developing his themes in accordance with the stage action rather than in terms of pure music. But as a talent he admired him tremendously.

He first met Wagner in 1864, when they spent an evening together and Brahms played his variations on a theme by Handel—which, by the way, Wagner admired and praised. That's more or less of a record, for Wagner, as a rule, was too much preoccupied with his own music to pay much attention to that of the composers around him. Brahms always followed Wagner's career with interest, and made a special journey to Munich in 1870 to hear the first performances of *Das Rheingold* and *Die Walküre*. He was a great collector of autographs and manuscripts, by the way, and one of his particular treasures was the manuscript score of *Tannhäuser,* which the pianist Karl Taussig had given him. Apropos of that, a few years ago another collector of manuscripts, the late Richard Aldrich, the famous music critic of the New York *Times,* showed me a letter in his collection that Wagner had written to Brahms in 1875, asking if he might please have the score back. Brahms reluctantly returned it, but I don't think that the episode particularly endeared Wagner to him.

In his own way, Brahms could be as biting as Debussy. One of his biographers tells of his listening to a fairly dull work by a friend of his and at the end turning to the unfortunate composer and saying, "Tell me, dear friend, does composing actually amuse you?" Another story is that he was listening to a performance of a setting of Schiller's *Das Lied von der Glocke,* composed by Bernard Scholz. Every once in a while he would nod his head approvingly, to the great delight of the composer, who was watching him. When it was over, he shook hands cordially with Scholz, and exclaimed, "I tell you that *Lied von der Glocke* is really an indestructible poem!"

Still, composers can be generous as well as critical. Let me quote something that one composer once had to say about another: "Years have gone by since I raised my voice in a territory so rich in old remembrances. Many new and significant talents have appeared, and music has seemed to show signs of acquiring new strength. . . . It seemed to me, who followed the progress of these chosen ones . . . that in these circumstances a musician would inevitably appear to whom it would be granted to give the highest and most ideal expression to the tendencies of the time. . . . And he has come, a young man over whose cradle Graces and Heroes stood watch. . . . He has shown us by every sign, even outwardly, that he is one of the elect. . . . His fellow musicians hail him on his first progress through the world, where griefs may perhaps await him but laurels and palms also. We welcome him as a strong defender."

That is an extract from an article published in the *Neue Zeitschrift für Musik* on October 28, 1853, written by Robert Schumann, concerning a twenty-year-old composer named Johannes Brahms.

The Mongrel Prima Donna

THE saxophone is, next to the violin, probably the most widely heard and widely played instrument in this country. At the same time it is an instrument that is almost never heard at a symphony concert, or any other gathering devoted to the playing of serious music. The saxophone, in the minds of most of us, is incorrigibly associated with jazz and dance music. On the occasions when we do hear it in the hands of an artist, playing such music as Debussy and Ibert have written for it, our attitude is likely to be a combination of amused admiration and patronage, much as if a slum child should suddenly begin to recite Greek poetry.

It's curious that this should be so, for the ancestry of the saxophone is utterly respectable, and the instrument is a comparative latecomer into jazz music. It was invented by the great Belgian instrument maker Adolphe Sax, who seems to have had no idea of the amount of trouble he was laying up for future generations. The actual invention was almost an accident. Sax had been experimenting with some improvements in the ophicleide. That is a brass bass instrument, the ancestor of the bass tuba, differing from its descendant in that instead of producing its various notes by means of valves, it employed holes and flaps in its sides. It suddenly occurred to Monsieur Sax to see what sort of tone he would produce on the ophicleide if instead of using a cup mouthpiece, he used a clarinet reed. So he tried it. And the result—you know the result.

One of the first to write for the instrument was the opera composer Meyerbeer, who was always on the lookout for new orchestral effects. It found its most cordial reception, however, among composers of band music. Only a few years after its invention, no French or Belgian military band was complete without its choir of saxophones.

In this country it was virtually unknown until the eighties, when a great saxophone virtuoso named Lefèbre came over to tour with Patrick Gilmore's band, and brought the instrument to public attention. Shortly after, Sousa added saxophones to his band, and the instrument was launched.

The man who probably had more to do with really selling the saxophone to America was a vaudeville performer named Tom Brown. How many of you, I wonder, remember the Six Brown Brothers? Whether they were really brothers or not I don't know, but I do know that under Tom Brown's leadership they toured the vaudeville circuits from 1911 to 1926, playing a sextet of saxophones that enchanted their audiences. People began to buy saxophones and practice them and organize saxophone clubs long before the sax was a recognized instrument in the standard dance band. H. W. Schwartz, in his book *The Story of Musical Instruments,* estimates that between 1919 and 1925, more than five hundred thousand saxophones were sold in the United States—an average of over eighty thousand a year.

You see, people discovered that the saxophone is as easy to learn to play as the cornet, without rendering the beginner as socially undesirable as the latter instrument. It "speaks" easily—that is, it's easy to produce a tone on it. Its fingering, though much like that of the clarinet, is also much simpler; it doesn't require the breath control of the oboe, nor the manual dexterity of the flute and the bassoon. Besides, the standard B-flat soprano saxophone is pitched in a register that is very effective for solo work. Incidentally, the saxophone is as difficult to play well as it is easy to play badly, but that doesn't bother the average amateur.

The saxophone, contrary to the usual assumption, came into the dance bands only within recent years. The legend is that it made its first appearance in Joe Kaiser's Novelty Orchestra in New York in 1921. It soon spread to all the other bands, for economic reasons. The band leaders discovered that its curious, half-human tone quality made it an ideal solo instrument for putting over popular songs in dance arrangements; and as it is a much more powerful instrument, in its middle register, than either the clarinet or the violin, three saxophones could easily do the work of two clarinets, a bassoon, and half a dozen violins. Today, a trio of saxophones is an indispensable ingredient in any popular band or orchestra.

In the symphony orchestra, however, it hasn't done so well. Several of the French composers, notably Massenet, Berlioz, Saint-Saëns, Meyerbeer, and Ibert, have written for it. Bizet uses it in his *L'Arlésienne* suite; Ravel uses it in his orchestration of Moussorgsky's *Pictures at an Exhibition;* and Strauss employs a quartet of saxophones in his *Domestic* symphony. But when you've named these, you've named practically all of the existing serious literature for the instrument.

There is a very good reason for this apparent neglect. In the theater and motion pictures there is a variety of actor who is known to his fellow workers as a "scene stealer." He's a type of performer who, even when he has nothing to do, manages to attract attention to himself and distract the attention of the audience from the other actors by killing their performances—by wiggling his hands, making faces, moving about during other people's important speeches, and so forth. He is not loved by the profession.

Now, the trouble with the saxophone is that it is the scene stealer of the orchestra. Every orchestral instrument has to perform two functions. It must, on occasion, be prepared to execute solo passages; at other times it must be able to drop out of sight, as it were, to become a background for the solo passages of other instruments or groups. The other wind instruments can perform this double function to perfection. If you will listen to the cello passage—the so-called "glance" theme—near the beginning of the prelude to Wagner's *Tristan and Isolde,* you will notice that it is accomplished by soft plucked chords on the violas and double basses. What you will *not* notice, unless your ears are very keen, is that the stringed instruments are backed up by three bassoons and a bass clarinet, playing so softly that you are not conscious of their support. This is one of dozens of examples that I might cite where wind instruments provide a harmonic background that is felt rather than heard. But the saxophone can't do this. Its tone color is so pronounced that when the rest of the orchestra is playing very softly, it is always audible. On the other hand, when the orchestra is playing mezzoforte or louder, the saxophones which ordinarily play in approximately the same register as the French horns haven't anything like their power. In other words, the saxophone isn't soft enough or loud enough to be completely useful in a symphony orchestra. The same is true of the piano, which is a valuable solo instrument because it insists on standing out from the rest of the orchestra, but by the same token can never be useful as a rank and file orchestral instrument. Another instrument that has dropped out is the flageolet. This is a sort of cousin of the flute, and sounds like a flute. But whereas the flute is played by blowing across a hole near the top of the instrument, the flageolet has—or had—a whistle mouthpiece. This means that the flute player can play his higher notes by increasing the tension of his lips, while the flageolet player can only play them by blowing twice as hard. In other untechnical words, the flageolet simply could not play softly the moment it got above its lowest octave. So out went the flageolet. The fate of all these instruments is an illustration of a grim truth: that if you insist upon being a prima donna, you'll never get a job in the chorus.

9

Dream of the Long-Lost Strad

Most of the Strad letters arrive during April and May—a phenomenon not unconnected, I fancy, with spring housecleaning. What is a Strad letter? Here is a typical one:

Dear Sir: Some time ago a young friend of mine told me that she had an old violin. It was believed to have been a Stradivarius. The friend sent me a copy of the inscription in the instrument, which is as follows:

Antonius Stradivarius Cremonensis, Faciebat Anno 1714.

Two concentric circles appear at the end of the inscription, with "A.S.," topped by a cross. My wife attempted to locate some source that would tell us how we could determine whether the violin was genuine or some replica of an original. The only information we could get was something on the life of Stradivarius in the public library here in Louisville. I would appreciate it very much if you could advise me how to determine the value of the instrument, or refer me to someone who could and would honestly appraise it for us. The violin is located in North Carolina and is in the possession of a country family. I understand that it has been handed down for at least three generations.

There are three great names in the history of violin-making, belonging to three violin-makers, all of whom lived and worked in Cremona, Italy, during the seventeenth and eighteenth centuries. They were Nicolo Amati, Giuseppe Guarnieri, and Antonio Stradivari. As a matter of fact, there were two famous Amatis. The first of them, Andrea Amati, was one of the earliest, if not *the* earliest, of all the violin-makers. Certainly he was one of the first to evolve the square-shouldered violin from the round-shouldered viol that was its immediate ancestor. His two sons, Antonio and Girolamo, were also violin-makers; but they were all overshadowed by the great Nicolo Amati, his grandson, whose instruments are still treasured by violinists who are lucky enough to own them. He died in 1684.

The second of the great ones was Giuseppe Guarnieri, or, as he signed his violins, Guarnierius. He was a third-generation member of a family whose founder, Andrea Guarnieri, had been a pupil of Amati.

But the greatest of the three, probably, and certainly the most famous outside musical circles, was Antonio Stradivari. He was born about 1644—no one knows just where—was a pupil of Amati, and spent his entire professional career in Cremona, where he died at the age of 93, making violins up to the day of his death. He also found time to marry twice and have eleven children. He worked hard and saved his money, and toward the end of his career was so prosperous that he even got into a simile that was popular in Cremona: *"ricco come Stradivari"*—"as rich as Stradivari." His violins became so famous that many of the best ones have names—the "Viotti," "La Pucelle," the "Boissier," the "Dauphin," the "Messiah." He made violas and cellos as well as violins; his cellos, in fact, are the most valuable of all. Paganini had one of his violas, and virtually every famous violinist, from Sarasate on, has had at least one of his violins.

They are the most expensive violins in the world. You can pick up a fairly good one for fifteen thousand dollars. That won't be a first-rate specimen, of course. For a really fine one you will have to pay twenty-five or forty thousand; while one of the really great ones will cost you about fifty-five thousand dollars.

There has been a great deal of argument as to what makes his violins so perfect. One legend, that was long popular, had it that their wonderful tone was due to a secret varnish, of which only he had the formula, that was based on the rosin from a tree that grew only in Northern Italy, and is now extinct. However, it has been pretty well established that all the violin-makers of Cremona of that period used more or less the same varnish. Besides, while a fine varnish helps to preserve the wood of a violin, nobody has yet proved that it has anything to do with its tone. The truth is, probably, that the perfection of his instruments is due to a very simple cause: the tremendous labor and skill that he put into the making of them. He worked for Amati, as an apprentice, for about eight years before he ventured to put out a violin under his own label.

But to return to the people who hope they own genuine Strads—let's look at the probabilities. In the course of his professional career, from 1666 to 1737, Antonio Stradivari is estimated to have made 1,116 instruments. Of these, 540 violins are known—that is, we know where they are, and who owns them. We also know of 12 violas and 50 cellos. There are about a hundred additional, whose existence is fairly definitely established. That's a total of 702 instruments out of 1,116, leaving 414 unaccounted for. Now consider, for a moment, that the violin is one of the most perishable of all musical instruments. You can break it across your knee; you have only to drop it on the floor to ruin it; you have only to sit on it to destroy it—to say nothing of the fact that it's as inflammable as tinder. Considering that, it would seem that the chances of many of those 414 missing Strads having survived for two hundred years are pretty remote; and the chances of anyone's running across a Strad that hasn't been identified in two centuries are about one in a million.

Now, the label that my correspondent describes is absolutely correct. Stradivari always signed his violins—in Latin —"Antonio Stradivari, of Cremona, made it in the year so and so." But considering the comparative abundance of paper and ink, a Stradivari label is too easy to copy to mean anything by itself. In fact, a label that one of my correspondents describes reads: *Antonius Stradivarius Cremonensis Faciebat Anno Millessimo - septingentesimo - septuagesimo.* And then, in the left-hand corner: *Made in Germany.*

It is definitely not the label that makes a violin valuable. Workmanship counts, of course; but even that isn't of primary importance. What makes a Stradivari violin worth its fantastic price is, of course, its wonderful tone. Even a genuine Strad, if it hasn't a good tone, isn't very valuable except as a museum piece.

On the other hand, tone is something that it doesn't take a violin-maker to discover. If you or one of your friends have an old violin with a Stradivari label in it, don't spend time and money, and hope, to get it into the hands of an expert. At least, don't start off that way. The first thing to do is to find out who is the best violin teacher in your town, take your violin to him, and ask him to play on it and tell you whether or not it has a good tone. Don't ask him to tell you if it's genuine. He probably couldn't tell you, in the first place. In the second place—and I can't emphasize this too strongly—a violin is *not* like a signed Rembrandt, or a Cape of Good Hope stamp, or an 1804 dollar. Its age and authenticity and scarcity have very little to do with its value. It is *a musical instrument,* and it's worth a lot of money only if it's a superlatively good one.

Now, it won't take that violin teacher ten minutes to tell whether your old violin has a good tone or not. If he says it's worthless—well, you don't have to accept his verdict as conclusive. But if two or three violinists tell you that it's worthless, then you'd better forget it. But suppose the teacher says that it *is* a good instrument, and has a fine tone. He'll undoubtedly be sufficiently interested to get it into the hands of some dealer not too far from where you live. If the dealer offers you twenty dollars for it, that probably means that he thinks it's worth about forty. So take the twenty. But if he offers you two hundred—well, then you may begin to get excited. For that means that you have an offer of enough to pay the expense of a special trip to San Francisco or Chicago or New York or Philadelphia to put it into the hands of one of the expert appraisers.

But don't bother those experts, don't make that trip, unless you've been offered enough to pay for it. Otherwise, you are probably in for a disappointment. Even under the most encouraging conditions, the chance of your finding yourself the owner of a genuine Stradivari is an extremely slim one. The expert will examine it, front and back, tap it, draw the bow across the strings, shake it, hold it up to the light—and all the other mysterious things that experts do. Then the probabilities are that he'll nod his head approvingly and say, "M-hm. Nice tone, pretty good specimen. Made in Mittenwald, Bavaria, about 1890."

Assembly-Line Music

I'VE had a suggestion made to me. It comes from a correspondent who has a new plan for writing opera, which, I imagine, he would also apply to the writing of a symphony or some other orchestral work. Here is what he has to say:

"After looking at the orchestral scores of some of Wagner's operas, almost anyone will agree that the writing of such music is an almost superhuman task, or, at least, a job for two or three men. Now, suppose that a man with musical ability would gather around him a group of composers—let us say five. These five, after the leader had set before them the libretto of the opera, and maybe an opening theme or some idea he wishes to incorporate in the opening measures, will retire to adjoining rooms where each will be able to jot down his musical inventions and developments of the opening measures, with a piano or any other musical instrument to aid him.

"At a given time," my correspondent writes, "these five will meet the leader, and each will give his rendition of what he has so far composed. These renditions will be written down on a blackboard, and the leader will choose the measures he likes best. With the measures that are chosen, another group of five arrangers will harmonize and orchestrate them, and then submit them to the leader for his final decision as to the best arrangement. He continues to take the best tunes, leading motifs, and the like, and the best harmonizations and arrangements, and keeps sending the groups back to work on new ones until the opera is completed. Now, of course, someone would have to finance such a project, or else a group of friends would have to join together to work on it. In any case, if such a plan were worked to perfection, it seems to me that music could be produced in a comparatively short time, or even in mass production."

Now, on first reading that letter I took it for granted that its writer was jesting. Then I read it over again, and decided that he was in earnest. Even so, it was so obvious that the scheme was absurd that I wasn't going to waste time thinking about it. Then I did, and the more I thought about it, the more fully I realized that just laughing at it wasn't enough; that the proposer of the plan could show that while it had never been tried in the field of opera and symphonic works, there are fields in which it is in operation—and successful operation—at this very moment.

He could point out, for instance, that that is precisely the way in which the script of many a successful motion picture is written. The next time you go to the movies, take a good look at the screen credits for the feature picture. The authors' credits are just as likely as not to read: "Screen play by John Doe, George Spelvin, and Michael Whoozis, from an original story by James Frammis and Joseph Doakes, based on an idea by Milton Portisan, inspired by certain incidents in the life of Ghengis Khan." I remember hearing a worried Hollywood producer say, "You know, I'm at my wits' end over this picture. I've had fourteen writers on the script, and it isn't right yet!" That was an extreme case, but it's by no means unusual for a studio to put five writers on a single script.

He could point out that the musical score of a picture is sometimes the product of the labors of two, or even three, composers—to say nothing of the passages that are borrowed from Brahms and Grieg and Rimsky-Korsakoff.

He could point out that the profession of play doctor is a

respected one in theatrical circles, a play doctor being an expert who comes in while a play is being tried out and rewrites the original author's script. If that revision isn't successful, the producer may call in still another play doctor to rewrite the efforts of the first two.

He could point out that César Cui, Borodin, Moussorgsky, and Rimsky-Korsakoff once agreed to work together on a single opera, *Mlada;* Cui to write the first act, Borodin the fourth, with Rimsky and Moussorgsky splitting parts of the second and third acts between them.

He could also point out that it was not unusual for the Italian old masters to entrust portions of one of their paintings to apprentices.

So what's wrong with my correspondent's idea? If it works for motion pictures and plays and paintings, why shouldn't a successful opera or symphony be turned out by a committee of composers?

First of all, let me call your attention to certain significant facts. The average motion picture exists solely for the purpose of entertainment. The motion-picture industry rightly calls itself an industry. It is interested primarily in making profits, and not in producing works of art. That's an honest attitude, and a perfectly legitimate one. However, once in a while you do run across a picture that is not only entertainment but worthy to be called a work of art, and what do you find? That nine times out of ten, it is the work of one man—one man, who wrote, directed, and produced it. If you write a play, and if your name happens to be Anderson or Sherwood or O'Neill or Odets or Wilder, you don't call in a play doctor. The most significant feature of that collaborative Russian opera that I mentioned is the fact that it was never produced; and if collectors are absolutely sure that a given painting attributed to an Italian old master is the work of his apprentices, they don't want it.

There is a great difference between entertainment and art. True enough, any work of art must possess entertainment value, in that it must hold your attention and make you glad you heard or saw it. But there's something beyond. You might compare entertainment value to flavor in food. Roast beef tastes good; so does a chocolate éclair. But there they part company. You can live on roast beef, but you won't last long on an exclusive diet of chocolate éclairs. Now, a real work of art is something more than entertaining. It almost literally nourishes you. Now that nourishment is the stimulus, the release, the inner satisfaction that you get from your contact with the mind and spirit of the artist. If you like one picture by a certain painter, you'll probably like his other pictures, because, however they may differ in subject matter, they are all the expression of his particular artistic point of view, a point of view to which something in you responds. If you like Beethoven's *Eroica* symphony, you like it not just because it's a symphony but because it is a Beethoven symphony. That particular composer says something, musically, that has meaning for you. If he and a few friends should collaborate on a symphony, the result of their labors would be not more meaning but no meaning at all. Some of Europe's great cathedrals were the work of many architects, because it took centuries to build them. Otherwise, I think you'll find that the work of art that endures is a one-man job. What makes it worthy of your attention is not its form or its subject, or even its materials, but the fact that it is the expression of a personality with which you are sympathetic. It's pretty safe to say that the symphonies that mean something to us will continue to be those turned out by such as Beethoven and Tchaikovsky and Brahms, rather than the product of the Little Giant Symphony Associates, Inc.

Of Thee They Sing

LATE in the winter of 1941 I was suddenly swamped by the arrival of a flood of poems, sheet music, and manuscript music, generally accompanied by a letter that read, approximately, "I understand that you are looking for a new national anthem, and enclose herewith one that I have written. Will you please have it sung in the near future?" This was all rather bewildering, inasmuch as I really didn't know that I *was* looking for a national anthem. The mystery was finally cleared up by the arrival of a newspaper clipping, headed, "Taylor Asks a Singable Anthem," and going on to say that I believed that the war would produce an American national anthem that was possibly more singable than *The Star-Spangled Banner.* Then I remembered that a short time before, when I had been in Boston, I had talked to a couple of newspapermen, one of whom asked casually if I thought we needed a new national anthem. And I said, *as* casually, that the one we have is rather difficult to sing, and has words that aren't particularly appropriate, and that it was barely possible that this war might produce one. Meanwhile, I said, the *Battle Hymn of the Republic* might be a good one. One of the interviewers turned out to be a Virginian, so that was the end of *that* suggestion. Then Lowell Thomas quoted the interview on his news broadcast, and finally, the United Press picked up the item.

The whole trouble was that the end of that interview never got into circulation. I'd like to repeat now what I said then: That when you've said that the words of a national anthem aren't of universal appropriateness, and that the music isn't particularly singable, you haven't said a thing. An anthem like *The Star-Spangled Banner* doesn't appeal to your critical sense. It appeals to a set of emotions and memories and loyalties that have absolutely nothing to do with the intrinsic merit of either the words or the music. You can write a song with better words and better music, but that fact isn't going to make it a national anthem. No one knows and no one can predict what gives a certain song a nationwide appeal; and no one can stimulate or manufacture that appeal. Why, out of all the popular songs of the time, did the British army in World War I elect to go to the front singing *It's a Long Way to Tipperary?* Why did the French soldiers march into the trenches singing not *La Marseillaise* but the slightly improper *Auprès de ma Blonde?* And why, in World War II, did the favorite song of the British and American armies turn out to be—of all things—the German-born *Lili Marlene?*

Take the case of *La Marseillaise* itself. Claude Joseph Rouget de Lisle was a captain of engineers, quartered in Strasbourg. One night he happened to hear the mayor of the city say that it was a pity the young soldiers had no patriotic song to march by. That same night, the night of April 24, 1792, he wrote the words and picked out the music on his violin of something that he called *War Song for the Army of the Rhine.* It was sung at the mayor's house the next day, arranged for a military band the day after, and played at a review of the National Guard on the 29th. Nearly two months later a baritone named Mireur sang it at a banquet at Marseilles. It caused such a sensation that it was immediately printed and distributed to the volunteers who were starting for Paris. It was that song that they sang as they marched to the attack on the Tuileries Palace on the 10th of August, 1792. The people picked it up and sang it in the streets. They called it first *La*

Chanson des Marseillais—The Song of the Men of Marseilles —and finally just *La Marseillaise.*

That was the birth of one national anthem. How another will be born nobody can say. There is only one way to find out. If you think you have written one, have it sung in public—anywhere, by anyone, except me. If it is really what you hope it is, within a month it will have swept the country.

The Foot in the Door

I AM NINETEEN years old. When I was young, I was given piano lessons, which I detested with the healthy hatred of most children. But ever since I was twelve or so, I have gone off on my own hook. I started being able to read music, even if I couldn't keep time, and for some years drove the family mad with one finger. However, this One soon blossomed into Two, Three, Four, and Five; and finally I even learned how to use the pedal, in a fuzzy sort of way. I started off and spent three months memorizing the first movement of the *Moonlight* sonata. There I rested on my laurels for some time until the family gave me the music for the second movement. To show that I was steadily improving, let me point out that it took me only a month and a half to learn to play that. About a year ago I was seized of a sudden burst of energy and learned, all in a short space of time, Chopin's prelude in C minor, and *The Little Shepherd* and *The Golliwog's Cakewalk* of Debussy.

Not being content with these accomplishments—and now we approach the crux of the matter—I began to compose at an early age, and if you think that *Yankee Doodle* or the *Largo,* à la One Finger, drove the family mad, you should have heard me rap out my own harmonies and rhythms. Of course I have gone far, since then, with composition. Two or three years ago I composed a small suite for piano, and had the sarabande from the suite played at a student program in high school. I have jotted down a good many things since then—some organized, some merely bits of melody or odd harmonies that I ran across in my keyboard doodling. I took a half-year course in elementary harmony at high school, but lost interest in its dull conformity. I have read, rather carefully, Forsyth's book on orchestration, and have studied musical scores—orchestral and instrumental—with an eye to analyzing their form and construction.

And that is the full extent of my musical education. My compositions, most of them, I dare not write down, since I am unable to play them without great difficulty. I talked to a famous composer and teacher last semester, and he advised me not to study music at all—simply because a composer has such a rough time of it. Only one in a thousand ever gets anywhere, he told me, and that one mainly by good fortune. I am rather at the crossroads now. In my sophomore year, I feel that it is time for me to begin to decide definitely what vocation I intend to follow. I am extremely interested in composition, have developed some skill at the piano through long practice, have a more or less sketchy notion of the technique of composition, and know what pleases my own ear. What shall I do?

There are, I should say, three ingredients that go to make up a composer, or any other artist: talent, urge, and technique. It's obvious, simply from reading his letter, that my correspondent has at least one of them. Anyone who has taught himself to play the piano, who reads books on orchestration and studies scores simply because he wants to, and whose greatest pleasure is to make up his own music certainly has the urge to be a composer. And that urge, that drive, is very important. In fact, I have an idea that the difference between a professional and a dilettante, is not, primarily, one of talent but of impulse. The dilettante loves to compose music—when he doesn't happen to have anything more important to do. The professional may hate the drudgery of composing—and there's a great deal of drudgery about it—but he feels so guilty, when he's *not* composing, that just for his own peace of conscience he sticks to it.

But the urge isn't everything. The mountains of dull books, bad paintings, indifferent poetry, and tedious music with which the world is filled is proof of that. You can't be a successful artist without talent. On the other hand, there's not much point in any artist's worrying about his talent. He can't manufacture any more than he has, and whether he has any or not is a matter that the public, present and future, is going to decide, anyhow. But technique is a different matter. Any artist who is content to be a sloppy workman is betraying himself and his art. I have no particular reverence for formal technical education. I believe that any gifted artist can teach himself technique. On the other hand, he may spend years wasting valuable time in making mistakes and painfully correcting them, when he might have avoided them by a few weeks or months of strict technical training.

And so I would say to my correspondent: whether or not you take up music as a career, learn your trade. It won't take long. If you have worked out things for yourself as far as you have, you'll probably find that most of the rules of musical technique are merely a confirmation of your own suspicions. And even if you turn to something else, as your major career, you're better off being a skilled dilettante than a bungling one.

As to the possibility of making a career of composing, that depends upon what you mean by "career." Ordinarily, the word is applied to the profession out of which one makes a living. If you insist upon that definition, don't be a composer. Offhand, I can recall very few composers of symphonic music who ever made a living out of it. A composer of opera and ballet can, with luck, live on his fees, but not a composer of absolute music. Beethoven came fairly close, but even he had patrons, and was, besides, a piano virtuoso. The lifetime earnings of the man who today is buried beside him, Franz Schubert, amounted to precisely $2,875.

The composer of serious music must either be subsidized or subsidize himself. In other words, he must face the necessity of making his living not out of his compositions but out of some activity that doesn't involve composition, whether it is teaching, lecturing, playing, conducting, or writing. He must be prepared to follow two parallel careers. If he has the courage to do this, he has at least one compensation. He can practice his art with the knowledge that his motives are pure. He need never ask himself, "Am I doing this for the money there is in it?"—for the simple reason that, comparatively speaking, there is *no* money in it. His problem is a simple one. It is not "How much can I get out of my art?" but "How much can I give to it?"

These remarks, needless to say, do not apply in the field of popular music and musical comedy. That field is so special and complicated that I couldn't discuss its problems with any authority. I was in it briefly many years ago, but while I had the firm intention of becoming a second Victor Herbert, nobody was interested. So I shall leave any discussion of that branch of music to Rodgers and Hammerstein.

Assuming, then, that my correspondent has resigned himself to pursuing a career as a composer of serious music, ignoring any vulgar monetary consideration, what does he do next? Here, first of all, is what he does *not* do. It is a letter written to a friend of mine who is head of the music department of an important radio network:

Dear Mr. Blank: About two weeks ago I wrote you and stated that I had a manuscript to submit for your approval for your program. I am still awaiting your reply. Fortunately I do not depend upon music for a livelihood, but I am only one of hundreds of American composers who give up in despair, because such persons as you, and Soandso and Soandso, refuse even to acknowledge receipt of a letter. Or you might say that they only recognize a composer who has won recognition by being handed a prearranged prize in some unsuspected fixed competition. In plain English, it is the old story of who you know, and not what you know. My experience in trying to get a number played in the popular-music field has also been enlightening. One must pay, and pay dearly, unless you have a close friend or relative who happens to be an orchestra leader.

And so on. Of course, that letter is rather an extreme example. The average struggling composer, I imagine, after having written to a frantically busy program director, waits longer than thirteen days for an answer before deciding that he is being ignored. But the point of view and the attitude that it reveals are far from unique. I know, and I meet, a good many beginning composers, and I hear from dozens more than I meet. And a serious proportion of them are convinced that the world of music is one gigantic conspiracy to keep them in obscurity and their music unplayed. They tell me, as they will tell you, that conductors never look at scores by unknown composers, that singers and instrumentalists don't want new music, and that the only hope for an unknown who wants his music performed is either bribery or influence, or both.

Now, there is just enough evidence in support of that attitude to make it understandable. It is perfectly true that a new score by Igor Stravinsky or a new song by Irving Berlin gets more attention from conductors and band leaders than a manuscript by George Spelvin or Joseph Doakes. Concert artists do favor music by well-known composers over music by unknowns. And I'm willing to believe that there have been occasions when music was played not because it was good but because somebody paid to have it performed or knew somebody's uncle or brother-in-law.

In other words, a beginning composer has something of a struggle to get started. He always has had, and always will have. So have, and will have, beginning lawyers, doctors, poets, painters, actors, playwrights, and elevator operators. There are several reasons why, and none of them is the result of a criminal conspiracy.

The first reason—and one that too many novices overlook—is that the beginner's work may not be so good as he thinks it is. I can remember a time when, looking at my own pile of rejected manuscripts, I said to myself, "All right. Just wait till I get somewhere—if I do. I'll show you publishers up. I'll have every one of these things published, and print the names of the people who turned them down." Twenty years later I remembered that vow, dug out those early manuscripts, and tried them over. And I breathed a little prayer of thanksgiving that they were still manuscripts.

Another reason is that in order to get a start in any profession, it is not enough to be merely as good as the worst members of that profession. I've often had a young composer hand me a fairly bad piece of music by a fairly successful composer and say, with a snort, "Look at that stuff. You tell me my music isn't as good as *that?*" Well, if it isn't *better* than that, why should the publisher or the performer make a change? Names do count, do influence people, in music as in anything else. If people prefer publishing and performing a piece of new music by a known composer to that of an unknown composer, it's for two very simple reasons. One is that the composer's reputation brings a certain number of customers into the concert hall or the music store. The other is that the composer's reputation is more or less of a guarantee that the music will not fall below a certain level of merit. Even if the conductor or performer isn't overenthusiastic about it, or doesn't completely understand it, he has faith enough in the composer to give the music a chance. Furthermore, if the music doesn't turn out well at performance, he knows that the listeners will criticize the composer and not the interpreter's taste.

What, then, *is* the beginner to do, in order to get a hearing? What would I do if I were a young composer with a symphony that I wanted played? I think I would begin at the beginning. I would not take it to the office of a major symphony orchestra, or address it vaguely to the music department of NBC, CBS, ABC, or Mutual. I would submit it to one of the "B" orchestras, those with an annual budget of less than a hundred thousand dollars. There are over two hundred of them in the United States, and, having less money and prestige at stake, they can afford to experiment and risk making occasional mistakes. If there were no minor orchestras near me, or if they all turned me down, I would take thought. I would say to myself, "They may be right, and they may be wrong. In any case, my music is down on paper and won't evaporate. So I can afford to put it in storage for a little while." Then I would sit down and turn out something that didn't demand quite such an elaborate apparatus to perform, say, something for a small orchestra or a string quartet. I would go through the same procedure with that. Meanwhile, I would subscribe to a music magazine and keep my eyes open for possible prize contests. Despite the opinions of the author of the letter that I quoted, no prize contest that I ever knew anything about was ever, as he puts it, "fixed." I can assure him, as a veteran judge at such affairs, that nothing warms the jury's hearts so much as to find a flash of talent among the tons of spoiled music paper through which they have to plow. Prize contests are bores to the judges, and they seldom unveil any unsuspected geniuses, but the fact remains that they are a reasonably effective means of attracting attention to a young or little-known composer; and they are at least one field of music where prestige and reputation count for nothing at all.

If I couldn't get a performance for my string quartet, I would take still more thought. I would write a song or a short instrumental piece. I would *not* try to get it published, just then. A piece of music is not a book. Fundamentally, its survival depends not on publication but on performance. So after a performance I would go. I would try all the small radio stations—the smaller the better, because, as I've said, the little ones can take a chance. Failing them, I would go after local singers and instrumentalists. I wouldn't mail it to Heifetz or Rubinstein or Melchior. I would try Mr. Brown, who sings in the First Congregational choir, or Miss Smith, who gives recitals and teaches piano on the side. I wouldn't consider these people unworthy of my attention. I would remember that one of the world's early masterpieces, Purcell's *Dido and Aeneas,* was written for performance by a girls' boarding school in London.

If Miss Smith and Mr. Brown failed me, I would begin *really* at the beginning. I would get myself invited to parties, and would bring my music with me and find an excuse to play it, or get one of the guests to hum it over with me. I might not be invited to the same house more than once, but I would persist. And then, *maybe,* some evening one of the guests would say, "Let *me* try that on the piano," or "Let *me* sing that song." And then I would know that I was on my way, with nothing to stop me but the limitations of my own talent. I would say to myself, "I have heard my music performed by someone else. Someone besides myself has liked it. I am a composer."

13

The Door Opens

Now that our beginner has established, in his own mind at least, the fact that he actually *is* a composer, that he can write music that arouses somebody else's interest, what next? Where does he go from there?

Well, he should capitalize on that interest by making it as easy as possible for people to play or sing his music. If somebody who really plays or sings well likes something of his, he should see that that person gets a copy of it—whether that person is a professional or an amateur. Apropos of that, the wife of one novice composer writes to me: "You mentioned letting others play compositions. Friends have asked for copies of my husband's two best compositions for piano—one a waltz, the other a ballade. After he had spent two evenings laboriously copying the waltz, I objected. If they are good enough to be played they are good enough to be stolen. And neither is copyrighted."

I think she was foolish and a little unkind. Why, for instance, did she let poor Caspar Milquetoast waste two evenings of hard work if she wasn't going to let him make some use of his copy? Aside from that, she reflects an attitude that is very common among amateur composers, the assumption that their musical ideas are necessarily so unusual and invaluable that the world around them is full of musical burglars who are just waiting for a chance to steal them. In the first place, my spies report that there is a copyright bureau in Washington where music, even if it is in manuscript, can be registered, and so protected. In the second place, if a composer is so unfortunate as to have one of his compositions pirated (and that happens far less frequently than you think), while he will naturally feel resentful over having had his property stolen, he can take comfort in the fact that—to reverse my correspondent's statement—"any music good enough to be stolen is good enough to be played." If his music is *that* good, it won't be long before he finds performers and publishers. I find that as a rule the composer who is just starting his career tends to have delusions of grandeur regarding the uniqueness of his musical ideas. Look over the notebooks of any mature composer, and you're likely to find that the sketches for the music that he rejected outnumber those that he used by about five to one. Yet the beginner tends to assume that because a given composition took him a lot of time and hard work to write, it must therefore have some merit. Unfortunately the world is not interested in how hard you work. It is interested only in how good the results of that work are. If a composer, having tried all possible avenues of approach, continues to find no welcome for his music, he can fairly assume that there may be something wrong with the music. If they don't want your song or your symphony, don't waste time beating your breast. Write another.

Another thing that the young composer ought to do is ask himself, "Do I honestly have to write music?" I know that sounds like superfluous and rather absurd advice, but it isn't. Remember the story of the elder J. P. Morgan's banking partner, who said, "Mr. Morgan, do you think I can afford to keep a yacht?" To which Mr. Morgan answered, "If you can ask me that question, you can't." Not long ago someone sent me a sheet of music paper covered with sketches for musical themes, with a note saying, "Please look these over and tell me whether you think I ought to keep on writing music." The question is not ought I to write music? but can I *help* writing music? So many of the would-be composers who write to me show by what they say that their basic motive for composing music is not a pure one. They want to make a lot of money; they want to be talked about and admired; they want to see their names on printed music, and on programs. Well, all these things are highly pleasurable, and desirable, and a person would be more —or less—than human if he didn't want them. But they don't come first. People write to me threatening to stop composing unless they get their music played and published. If they can stop, if lack of recognition and applause and financial return can make them cease to compose, then they never were composers. Fundamentally no artist of real talent practices his art for money or fame or even because he gets pleasure out of it. He does it because he must, because he feels less uncomfortable when he's painting or writing or composing than when he isn't. Wagner wrote a trilogy of music dramas in the full knowledge that no opera house in existence was equipped to perform them. Bach had plenty of performances, but if he had waited to find a publisher for the bulk of his music, he would have had to wait until eighty years after his death.

Granted that the young composer we're discussing has a real, individual talent, will he ever get a satisfactory hearing? Will his talent ever be recognized? The answer to both those questions is, I think, an unqualified yes. Where that hearing and recognition will come from, and when, is another question. No one can answer that. But while he is still in the struggling stage of his career, still looking for help, I could suggest that he try not to make it difficult for people to help him. If a famous singer or instrumentalist gives a concert in his home town, I would say to him, "Don't pester the artist while he's trying to get a little rest before the concert, or while he's hurrying to catch the train after the concert. Find out from his manager when he's likely to have leisure time, and get permission to mail your song or sonata. Don't ship the score of your symphony, uninvited, to an orchestral conductor in the middle of the concert season. Find out what time of the year he makes up his programs, and *ask* if you may send it then. There's a legend that publishers never look at music by unknown composers. They do; but being human, they are likely to be prejudiced against manuscripts that come without return postage, or are accompanied by long letters explaining how good the music is, or are written in pencil or in a hand that no one can read."

Nobody who has not seen it at first hand has any conception of the mass of worthless music that descends upon the desks of editors, publishers, conductors, performers, and radio directors. They are to be forgiven if their recognition of genuine merit is sometimes less than instantaneous. Sooner or later they do recognize it and reward it. If all of the world's unrecognized great composers, living and dead, could by some miracle be gathered together in one room, I have an idea that the room would not have to be a large one. The mute, inglorious Milton upon whom Thomas Grey lavished such poetic commiseration must be a very lonely man, for there are not many of him.

Let us take specific instances. Suppose we glance briefly over the careers of two great composers, Richard Wagner and Franz Schubert. How and when did they get their start?

Take Wagner first. He began composing when he was a student in Leipzig. Outside of school time he had taken a few lessons in harmony from a violinist named Müller, and with this meager equipment he set up shop as a composer. Beginning in the summer of 1829, when he was sixteen, he composed a piano sonata, an aria for soprano, some incidental music to a pastoral play that he wrote himself, and a string quartet. Nothing happened, and none of these works has survived. He had a friend named Dorn, eleven years his senior, who was director at the Leipzig Theater, and in 1830 he managed to persuade

Dorn to give a hearing to an overture in B flat that he had written. It was put on the program of a benefit concert on Christmas Day, and was simply announced as a "New Overture." No composer's name was given—which, in a way, was lucky; the new work not only failed to impress the audience, but amused them.

Nothing daunted, he went back to work. In 1831, when he was eighteen, he wrote three more overtures, with no success, as well as a piano sonata in B flat, and a cycle of instrumental and vocal pieces based on Goethe's *Faust*. About this time he began serious study of musical theory with Theodore Weinlig, who was cantor of St. Thomas's Church, the one at which the great Bach had held the same position. Weinlig was enough impressed with his pupil's talent to go to the publishing firm of Breitkopf and Härtel and recommend that they publish the B-flat piano sonata, which they finally did, in 1832. Thus, at nineteen, Wagner first saw a work of his in print. In the meantime he had written a polonaise for piano, four hands, and another piano sonata, in A major. So far as I know, neither was ever played.

The next work of his to get a performance was an overture in D minor, which he heard played on Christmas day, 1831, at another benefit concert, by the Gewandhaus Orchestra. In April of '32 a semiprofessional organization known as the Euterpe Society tried out an overture of his in C major. Nothing more was heard of it. His sister Rosalie was an actress in the Leipzig Theater company, and thanks to her intercession he was allowed to compose an overture and some incidental music to a play called *King Enzio,* which had several performances. At the opening performance his name was not given, as the management, remembering the fiasco of the B-flat overture, was a little timid about the possible attitude of the public. But the music got over pretty well, and at the second performance, in March, 1832, the nineteen-year-old Richard Wagner had the thrill of seeing his name in print on a program. In April, at a benefit concert (he seems to have run to benefits), he had a performance of a scene and aria for soprano.

In the summer of '32 he visited Vienna. By flattering the head of the conservatory there he managed to get his D minor symphony tried out by the school orchestra. But the youngsters couldn't play it, and finally gave it up. That same summer he was at the home of a Count Pachta, who lived near Prague, and fell violently in love with his younger daughter, Jenny. The young lady was amused by him for a while, but finally, to quote his own words, "proved unworthy of my love." He had already written a song called *Evening Bells* for Jenny, and when she finally turned him down he commemorated that tragedy by writing the first sketches for an opera entitled *The Wedding*. Returning to Leipzig, he finished a symphony in C major. This was first tried out by the faithful Euterpe Society, and later, in January, 1833, received a public performance by the Gewandhaus Orchestra. The audience liked it, and the critics wrote of it with approval. Young Wagner was at last established as a composer worth watching.

Here we leave him, on the eve of his career. He was twenty years old, and had been studying and composing for four years. During that time he had composed twenty works, ranging from incidental music, a song cycle, a string quartet, and various piano pieces, to overtures, a symphony, and sketches for a grand opera. In the four years he had had five performances, one of which was a disaster, and two of his pieces had been published. Most of the rest were never heard again.

Schubert started composing in his twelfth year, shortly after he had entered the Imperial Convict School as a student and choir boy. In addition to his academic studies, he sang, played the violin, and studied musical theory with the Court *Kapellmeister*, Salieri. The first piece of music of his of which we have any record, and which is still in existence, is a twelve-movement fantasia for piano, four hands, written in May, 1810, when he was thirteen years old. Of his life at that time, all we know is that he lived in a state of semi-starvation, and depended for his supply of music paper upon the generosity of an older friend of his, Joseph von Spaun.

From his fourteenth year on, he composed incessantly. In 1812, when he was fifteen, he turned out nine works, including an overture for orchestra, two quartets, and an overture for string quartet. That same year his voice broke, and he had to leave the choir. In the national library in Vienna there still exists a copy of a Mass, on the flyleaf of which is written, "Franz Schubert crowed for the last time, July 26, 1812."

In his sixteenth year he composed twenty-one works, including a cantata in honor of his father's birthday, and his first symphony, which had a tryout by the school orchestra. That same year, 1813, he entered the normal school, and in '14, in order to escape conscription, he got a job as a schoolmaster. He also actually heard something of his performed outside the Convict School. This was his first Mass, in F, which was played and sung in a suburban church. Among other songs that he wrote that year was one of his masterpieces, *Gretchen at the Spinning Wheel.*

In 1815, the eighteen-year-old schoolteacher turned out 189 compositions, of which 146 were songs, including the immortal *Erl King*. The following year he tried to get a position as teacher in the Government Music School, but was turned down in favor of a musician named Franz Sokol. That's all we know about Sokol. What we know about Schubert is that he gave up teaching entirely, went to live in the house of a Professor Watteroth, and wrote 131 compositions. In that year, 1816, he received the first money he ever earned from writing music. He composed a cantata for chorus and orchestra, called

Prometheus, for which he got twenty dollars. It was never published, and we now have no trace of it.

His twentieth year marked a turning point; for it was then that one of his friends introduced him to Johann Michael Vogl, the court baritone. Vogl, who was the Eddy-Thomas-Tibbett of his day, consented to look over some of Schubert's songs. Among them was the *Erl King,* and we must give Vogl the credit for recognizing its greatness at once. He made it part of his repertoire and sang it at private parties all over Vienna. Schubert, meanwhile, was having a comparatively unproductive year, writing only sixty-eight works. Incidentally, how he managed to live nobody knows. He had a room, with Professor Watteroth, but no money. As a rule, unless one of his friends took him to dinner, he had no dinner.

In 1818 he finally got a position as a sort of tutor and private musician to Count Esterhazy, of Vienna and Hungary (this was, of course, not Haydn's patron). He wasn't very happy, and before the year was up came back to Vienna to live with his friend the poet Mayrhofer. The following year he wrote an opera, called *The Twins.* There was considerable applause the opening night, but Schubert refused to take a curtain call. He had no dress clothes. The opera had six performances, and then disappeared. He tried another one, *The Magic Harp.* He was to get a hundred dollars for it, but the management went bankrupt and he got nothing. His first taste of any kind of success came in the year 1821. Remember that he had been composing steadily for eleven years. He had written well over four hundred compositions, just three of which had had public performances, and of which not one had been published. And he was absolutely penniless.

In '21 came a break. Vogl sang the *Erl King* at a public charity concert in the Kärnthnerthor Theater in Vienna. It was enthusiastically encored, and people began to talk about this

Schubert. His friends decided that some of his songs ought to be published. After being turned down by all the publishers they finally published two albums of his songs by private subscription, and sold out both editions. Schubert made sixty-six dollars out of the deal. At last he was started. He paid his debts, and in a moment of financial inspiration sold the plates and all his rights in both collections to the publisher Diabelli for three hundred and fifty dollars. Incidentally, out of one of the songs alone, *The Wanderer,* Diabelli made nearly fifteen thousand in the next few years, and systematically swindled Schubert for the rest of his life. That didn't matter to Schubert. His music was being played, and he was, if only for the moment, out of debt and free to write more music.

He was twenty-four years old. He had seven years left to live. He was very happy.

PART FIVE

Recapitulation

I

The Worried Neophyte

IN ONE respect the young painters and writers seem to me to be better off than the young composers. The young painter is free to paint in almost any style he pleases, from Picasso's latest five-star final period to Grandma Moses. No matter what style he elects, he will find plenty of company. So, too, in the case of the young writer. So long as his work is reasonably intelligible, his critics don't care very much what style he chooses. But the young composer finds himself virtually obligated to take one of two warring sides. On the one side there are the conservatives, and on the other the radicals, with the liberals a negligible and lonely minority. Witness this letter from a New York music student:

> As a student, my main study is the piano, but I feel increasingly drawn to creative work. The trouble is that I have at present bogged down into a sort of Franck-Strauss-MacDowell imitativeness, and am in urgent need of getting my musical individuality clarified, or rather, of being told whether I am on the right track, if there is such a thing. My chief difficulty is that I feel that so long as I continue to write in the idiom most congenial to me, I shall only be repeating what has already been better said; while if I try to write in a more so-called "contemporary" idiom I shall be insincere.

Now, at first blush that sounds like a purely personal and rather technical problem, one to be discussed in private rather than here. But in a sense it's a problem that concerns all of us who listen to music. For we are the public. We are the people for whom music is written, whether the composer thinks so or not, the people who are going to keep a given piece of music alive for generations, or sentence it to a speedy death; who render a verdict from which there is no appeal, regardless of the fact that we're not even conscious of rendering it. So we have a sort of vested interest in the work of any beginning composer and the way in which he goes to work. For we're going to have to listen to it, eventually, and he is going to spend his life trying to please us, through the medium of what he *calls* "self-expression."

I think my correspondent is worrying unnecessarily about what he calls his "Franck-Strauss-MacDowell imitativeness." Any beginner has got to use some pattern, some model, in order to get the hang of how it's done. I know of no first-rank composer who began his career by writing music that was absolutely his own, that sounded like nothing that had ever been written before. Beethoven's first symphony might have been written by Mozart. Wagner's *Rienzi* and much of *The Flying Dutchman,* and even parts of *Tannhäuser*, might have been written by Meyerbeer. The three composers that my correspondent mentions were also imitators in their day. Strauss and Franck were strongly influenced by Wagner at the beginning, while MacDowell's early works made it very easy to guess that he had studied composition with Joachim Raff. I've always been struck by the fact that the art of musical composition is one branch of human activity in which it is considered particularly disgraceful to have legitimate parents. My young friend can rest assured of one thing. That he will pass through two periods in his professional career, and only two. During the first, people will be busy pointing out how strongly his music resembles that of other, older composers. During the second, granted he is successful, people will be busy pointing out how strongly the music of other, younger composers resembles his. At no point in his career will anybody bother to point out how strongly his music resembles itself.

In the second point that he raises—his perplexity as to whether to write in the style that comes natural to him, which he feels is old-fashioned, or in a more up-to-date style, which he feels would be artificial with him—there he furnishes an example of the paradoxical pressure under which contemporary composers have labored during the past fifteen or twenty years. Go back over the careers of composers during the past hundred and fifty years, and you'll find that the hostility that they encountered was exactly the opposite of what they have to contend with today. Mozart, Beethoven, Schumann, Wagner, Brahms, Strauss, Debussy were all criticized, not only by the public but by their fellow composers, for *not* writing in the traditional style. Today, the young composer is under constant pressure not from the reactionaries but from the radicals. If he wants to avoid being jeered at by his contemporaries, he must be a revolutionary whether he feels like being one or not. Hear from another worried correspondent:

I am a composer. My tastes happen to be with Bach, Brahms, Mozart, Handel, and the Russians. The music that I write is in strictly classic form, and can scarcely be called revolutionary. Last spring I heard a lecture by a certain eminent composer and teacher and was so impressed that I arranged for an interview, in the hope of getting a criticism—at fifteen dollars a criticism. So off I trotted with a piano concerto. The eminent one looked it over, said there were only five or six passages in it that couldn't have been written by Scarlatti, and told me that I shouldn't write antique music in modern times.

What I want to know is this: why has any teacher, however eminent, the right to say, "You mustn't write antique music in modern times"? If I were earning—or trying to earn—a living by composing, the answer might be the obvious one that you don't attract much attention unless you write something sufficiently startling to be called "modern." I know all this business about expressing the mood and spirit of the times. But why isn't music good no matter when it was written? I wonder if this is something that is really answerable.

Well, it is, but, as you will find out, dear reader, not in one sentence. Let me begin by saying that the eminent composer, if he meant what he was saying, expressed himself badly. I think what he was driving at was the fact that a composer who writes strictly in the style of the classic masters—or, as he puts it, Scarlatti—runs the risk of saying nothing in his music that they haven't already said better in theirs. Besides, we tend to identify a given means of artistic expression with the greatest men who employed it, until we wind up by assuming that it's their property. There were other Elizabethan dramatists besides Shakespeare, and they, too, wrote blank-verse plays, using the same English that he did and stealing the same plots that he stole. But because he emerged as the greatest poet and playwright of the lot, they all sound, now, like imitations of Shakespeare. There were contemporaries of the classic master composers who wrote music that, in structure and idiom, had much in common with theirs. But we have accepted that kind of music as so completely theirs that we subconsciously resent any contemporary composer's undertaking to express himself in the same terms. And so we don't judge him fairly. As a matter of fact, we're not nearly as critical of the classic composers, most of us, as we are of modern ones. Anybody who writes in the style of, say, Mozart, and thereby challenges comparison with Mozart, has the dice loaded against him.

Before we go on with this discussion it might be a good idea to define our terms. People talk a lot about the classic style and the ultra-modern idiom, but nobody bothers to explain what they are. Just what is the classic style? And how does the modern style differ from it? Suppose we take the first one first. What are the elements that have distinguished good music written, say, from the time of Mozart up to the later works of Brahms or the early works of Richard Strauss? Individually, of course, the classic composers differed among themselves to a great degree. Those differences, in fact, constitute what we call their individualities. Nevertheless their works possess certain fundamental characteristics in common—just as, for instance, all buildings that were erected before the advent of steel construction had certain structural elements in common which they don't necessarily share with the modern steel-framed building.

First of all, so-called classic music in the symphonic style possesses the element of unity. It is consistent within itself, has an unmistakable beginning, middle, and end. This element is particularly evident in the matter of tonality. A classic symphony in C major, while it may digress into several other keys in the course of its development, does begin and end in the key of C major. When it's over you have a pretty definite impression of having heard something in the key of C major.

Closely allied to that element of tonal unity are those of balance and contrast. Music is, of course, not the only field of art in which these two elements are important. Any work of art must have some sort of form—of shape—if it is to produce any coherent impression. In architecture, for instance, that is classic in feeling, you will find that a building is made up of a series of balanced and contrasted elements. If there's a wing at the left, it is likely to be balanced by a wing at the right. If the main body of the building is tall, the wings are likely to be short. In good prose you're likely to find long sentences alternating—that is, contrasting—with short ones. In poetry you'll find one line rhymed—that is, balanced—with another. In music you will find one eight- or sixteen-bar section balanced by another of equal length, a fast movement contrasting with a slow one.

But the matter of form in music goes far beyond that. Music is so vague, so fluid, that it tends to require some sort of rather strict pattern in order to have it make sense at all. Now, there are a number of those patterns to which the classic composers adhere pretty faithfully.

The simplest is the song form, and the most primitive song form is the folksong, which is likely to be built on two or four simple phrases that balance one another. A good example of that is *Comin' Through the Rye,* which consists of four four-bar phrases which are identical in rhythm and slightly different in notes. Another, slightly more complicated example is Schubert's *Who Is Sylvia?*, where the musical setting of the words just repeats itself from stanza to stanza. Then there's the AB song form—in other words, any song that consists of a verse and a chorus. Then there's the ABA form—first strain, second strain, first strain. Some of Schubert's songs are of a kind that the Germans call *durchkomponiert*—literally, "composed through." That is, songs such as his *Der Doppelgänger*, in which he abandons any strict musical balance and just sets the words as they come, relying on the meaning and mood of the poem to give his setting coherence. But that hardly counts, because Schubert was a great genius and often went a hundred years ahead of his time.

The classic symphony is made up of strictly formal elements. Its first movement is written in sonata form, which in turn is in three sections. In the first section, two main themes are introduced, generally contrasting. In the second section they are developed—or, as I've heard that process described, torn to pieces. In the third section they are put together again. The second movement is a slow movement, generally written in that ABA form. The third is a fast movement. That's often written in rondo form, which is ABACAD—that is, a string of beads in which the alternate beads are identical. The last movement can be in almost any of those forms, or perhaps in the form of a theme and variations. A string quartet is like a miniature symphony. The typical violin or piano concerto is like a symphony in form, except that the fast movement and the finale are usually telescoped into a single movement. Now, these forms, as I say, were very strictly observed, their strictness going even so far as to impose certain conventions in orchestration. Beethoven was criticized because he used a bass drum in the finale of the Ninth symphony. Schumann's *Rhenish* symphony was criticized because it has five movements instead of four. As for César Franck's poor old D minor symphony, its first critics denied that it was a symphony at all; first, because it was in three movements, and second, because he used an English horn in the slow movement.

And so, you see, in music in the classic style the composer introduces and arranges his musical thoughts in the framework of a formal, prescribed pattern, just as the classic architect, regardless of the originality of his ideas, sticks to his classic orders—Doric, Ionic, Corinthian, Byzantine, Romanesque, Gothic, Renaissance—what you will. It was music designed to be listened to—and is still listened to by most people—as fundamentally an arrangement of beautiful sounds; and these sounds, no matter what emotions they might in themselves arouse, were arranged within the limitations of a framework that was almost mathematical, that fundamentally had no emotional basis at all.

Another characteristic of music written in the classic style is recognition—or, to put it more bluntly, repetition. The composer is anxious to have you recognize his themes, to grasp them, to retain them in your memory. So he impresses them on your ear by the only means at hand, by playing them over again. He balances one theme with another; then he balances one section with another section by reiterating his themes.

When Beethoven introduces the chorale section of the last movement of his Ninth symphony, he plays the entire tune straight through four times without a break before introducing any subsidiary material. Even when a composer doesn't repeat his material verbatim, he keeps you reminded of it by reintroducing parts of it in recognizable form.

That material is in general characterized by another element, one for which I cannot find a more elegant term than tunefulness. You might, I suppose, call it lyricism, but then you'd be likely to suggest comparisons between lyric and dramatic and be involved in complications. Tunefulness is, I think, the best all-round term for the quality I mean, that of being a definite melody, one that can actually be whistled or sung. Think of the main themes in Mozart's best-known symphonies, most of those in Haydn and Beethoven, the themes of Schumann and Tchaikovsky. A large proportion of them could have been written as songs if their creators had chosen so to treat them. You could put words, God forbid, to the slow movement of the Beethoven *Eroica*. Tchaikovsky has been dubiously honored by having had half a dozen of his best themes stolen by the Broadway song writers. It seems to me that the classic composers were strongly influenced by the early traditions of music, which were predominantly vocal, so that their themes, consciously or not, tend to stay within the confines of the human voice. I say "tend." On occasion they do break away from the vocal tradition. To sing the opening measures of the finale of Mozart's G minor symphony, for instance, one would have to be a coloratura soprano, and a phenomenal one, at that.

Still another element that characterizes classic music is its rhythmic regularity. Not that the rhythm of a given bar or phrase is necessarily rigid; but a classic symphonic movement that starts out in one rhythm is likely to finish in that same rhythm. If the composer does shift, his variation is a comparatively simple one: from three-four to four-four, or from two-four to six-eight. When he makes a change, he keeps up the new rhythm long enough for you to become fully conscious of it. Even Wagner, radical as he was in other ways, is extremely conservative as to rhythm. The King's prayer in *Lohengrin* is in three-four time, but all the rest of the entire opera is in common time. The five-four movement of Tchaikovsky's *Pathétique* symphony was a sensational innovation when it first appeared, but Tchaikovsky, once he had established his exotic rhythm, stuck to it for the entire movement.

Lastly, in the harmonic scheme of the classics you find a strong element of consonance, which is to say that the chords employed in the course of a given piece are generally those that are pleasing to the ear. Of course, the minute you begin to talk about any chord's being "pleasing to the ear," you get into trouble, because tastes in harmony are as various and as divergent as tastes in food. The chord that tastes like ambrosia to you may taste like tripe to me. Let's play a little safe, and put it that the harmonic structure of the classic symphonic works is such as to be pleasing to the ear of the average listener. Discord, dissonance, has of course always been employed by all composers, from Palestrina on up the line. But it is used *as* dissonance, in small quantities, for contrast, as a sort of musical red pepper, to heighten the flavor of the consonant chords.

Such, I think, are the six characteristics that distinguish the music of the classic composers. Notice one thing about the list. All six are elements of design and ornament in classic architecture. First, unity—in other words, symmetry—the quality of being recognizable as a definite design. Next, balance and contrast, elements applicable to any formal pattern, whether architectural or textile. Then repetition, the characteristic of any architectural design. Next, tunefulness. We'll have to translate that one a bit, but isn't it fair to say that the element of a tuneful, vocal theme is a smooth, graceful line? Then, rhythmic regularity, as applicable to a cornice as to a sonata. Last, consonance. Again to translate, a pleasant and harmonious color scheme in a building or a room.

Now, I think that analogy is significant, for it seems to me that what we call the classics in music, particularly the abstract classics—the symphonies and quartets and sonatas—are music conceived in terms of a formal pattern, music whose coherence and emotional power are derived from the arrangement of balanced elements into a symmetrical and harmonious whole. In other words, if von Schelling could call architecture "frozen music," the classic composers could be said to have regarded music as liquid architecture. The modern trend seems, rather, toward music conceived in terms of literature, drama, and painting. But of that, more later.

Heterodoxy

SO MUCH for the distinguishing musical elements of the classical school. How many of these elements do we find in modern music and to what degree, if any, are they modified? Suppose we take the first element, *tonal unity*—that is, sticking to one principal key. Here we find almost a complete breakdown. Even when a modern piece is written in what is, technically, a definite key, its composer doesn't hesitate to modulate into all sorts of keys that haven't the slightest family resemblance to the original. If Haydn wrote a sonata in the key of C, for instance, he might go into the key of F in one section, or into G in another. He might go into A minor, or, if he were very venturesome, into E minor. All those keys have certain notes in common with the basic chords of his original C major. He would hardly venture further. Even in music that was supposed to be intensely dramatic the classic composers were very hesitant about using sudden modulations for dramatic effect. As a friend of mine once remarked about a scene from Gluck's *Orfeo*, "The hero enters in the midst of a terrific tonic and dominant thunderstorm."

It is possible that one reason why they were all so chary of changing from one key to another was that the so-called tempered scale had been in existence for only two or three generations. This is no place in which to go into a discussion of it, except to say that in the tempered scale—that is, the scale to which the modern piano is tuned—sharps and flats are synonymous; D sharp, for instance, is the same *sound* as E flat.

In other words, a composer can switch from a sharp to a flat key without any shock to the ears of his listener. In the old, untempered scale that was used up to Bach's time, the sharps and flats were *not* the same. E flat, for instance, was lower than D sharp. If you shifted from D sharp to E flat, you sounded out of tune. So the conservatism of the classic masters in the matter of shifting from one key to another may have been partly the result of an ancestral remembrance of the horrors of the untempered scale.

Nowadays, of course, that limitation has disappeared entirely. Take such a work, for example, as Debussy's *The Afternoon of a Faun,* which is by now such a classic that even the most obstinate conservative can listen to it without a shudder. Yet the *Afternoon of a Faun* is written in the following key signatures: E major, C major, A flat, D flat, E major, C major, E major. Now, Haydn might have managed that shift from E major to C major, but he would have hesitated a long time before going from D-*flat* major to E major. Besides, the idea of making seven drastic changes of key in a piece that is only a hundred and ten measures in length would have seemed fantastic to him. Even our popular music displays a tonal daring that would have been beyond the average symphonic composer of the classic period. Take Jerome Kern's popular classic *Smoke Gets in Your Eyes*. Any one of us can sing it, and yet in its middle section there is a sudden modulation from E-flat major into B major—three flats into five sharps—that would have made Haydn's jaw drop.

The man who struck the first really serious blow at the old conception of unvarying tonality was Wagner. If you want to see why his *Tristan and Isolde* was bewildering to many of his contemporary hearers, just look at the opening measures of the prelude—or listen to them, rather—and remember that they were first heard by people to whom music composed in a definite key, and employing the chords common to that key, was obviously the only kind of music that *could* be written. I remember once reading a harmonic analysis of the *Tristan* prelude written by an earnest German musicologist of the late nineteenth century, in which he endeavored to trace the various keys into which the music modulated. That poor man's struggles reminded me of nothing so much as a chameleon going to pieces on a Persian rug. Most of the prelude to *Tristan* is written in no definite key at all, and the fact that its harmonic progressions sound perfectly logical and inevitable doesn't alter the fact of its essential defiance of definite tonality.

I think that independence of tonality has advanced the art of music greatly. It has tended to make music more colorful and more expressive. Now, some of you may object that Mozart, after his fashion, is just as colorful and expressive as Wagner is after his fashion. Let me put it in another way. Naturally, what a composer manages to express in his music is, in the last analysis, up to him as an individual creative talent. At the same time, this new harmonic freedom has enriched at least the raw materials of music. I once heard a high-school English teacher remark casually, "Of course any of my fourth-year students write better prose than Milton did." And when I looked properly incredulous, he explained that the contemporary English language is infinitely richer and more subtle and expressive than the language that Milton had at his command. And that's what these moderns (and in this respect I call Wagner a modern) did for the language of music. One of the most effective devices in music, for instance, is a sudden and unexpected modulation from one key into another that has nothing in common with its predecessor. And when it's skillfully done, it produces a definite emotional effect upon the hearer. One of the best and simplest examples of this is the so-called "Fate" motive from Wagner's *Ring* cycle. Now, it consists of three notes and two chords. The first is a tonic chord of D minor, which goes to a dominant-seventh chord of F-sharp minor. At least, that's the way a professor of harmony would describe it. As a matter of fact, the *effect* of that modulation has nothing to do with those two keys. You play a chord of D minor on the piano; then stop for a second or two and play a dominant-seventh chord of F-sharp minor. If you don't play the piano, ask someone who does to play those two chords separately. Now, the effect of those two, sounded apart, has nothing in common with the magical effect that Wagner produces by sounding one immediately after the other. Beethoven could have written that particular modulation. I doubt if he ever did, and I doubt if his strong sense of tonality would have allowed him to do so.

The second characteristic of music of the classical period was *formal balance and contrast*. The music of Haydn and Mozart and Handel and Beethoven is held together, so to speak, by being written in accordance with certain rather strict rules as to form, and however eloquent their musical content, the forms themselves were almost mathematical in their rigidity.

And then certain composers, particularly the opera composers, began experimenting with the framework. The earlier operas, up to the middle of the eighteenth century, were merely a series of formal numbers that relied for their appeal upon the same abstract musical qualities as the symphonies possessed. They were merely more or less beautiful tunes, almost devoid of any specific emotional or dramatic pretensions. Then Mozart, notably in *Don Giovanni,* showed that music could be so adapted to a particular scene in a drama as to produce a tremendous and exciting *dramatic* effect, an effect that had very little to do with the classic beauty of symphonic music. Then Gluck went still further, and deliberately went after dramatic appropriateness first and formal balance second. Weber continued his work. Schubert helped. A song like his *Erl King* has a certain quality of emotional intensity that you won't find in any of his symphonies. Then came Berlioz, whose operas were failures, and yet who wrote intensely dramatic music in his *Fantastic* symphony. Then Liszt, taking the cue from Berlioz, developed the symphonic poem, which introduced a narrative element into music. Then Schumann explored the pictorial possibilities of music, putting definite titles to many of his pieces. Then, supremely, came Wagner, who abandoned the symphonic and song elements almost completely, in his music dramas. By the last quarter of the nineteenth century we had a whole library of music by men who traveled far afield from the road taken by the classic symphonists. People talk of the Romantic School. That's too narrow a term. They weren't a school. They didn't all belong to one country, and while they did get ideas from one another's music, they didn't consciously work together. To call them the Romantic Race would be more precise, I think. Some of them wrote orchestral music; some wrote piano music; some wrote operas. But whatever they did, they greatly developed the richness, flexibility, and expressive power of music. And as a natural consequence, they developed new forms, in which they could put this increased expressiveness to use. Opera since Wagner's time no longer takes its form from strict musical forms.

On the contrary, the form of the music is determined by the situations of the libretto and the presumed emotional states of the characters. Even in *Carmen,* and Puccini's operas, which do abound in arias and duets, these set numbers are not put forward as such. They are imbedded in the plot, and serve to carry the plot along. The arias are presented as dramatic monologues or soliloquies, and the duets are dramatic scenes. The symphonic poem and the ballet are far more popular forms among modern composers than the symphony or the concerto. In other words, the composers have tended to get away from the architectural conception of music, and have gone in for music that undertakes to speak in terms of painting, poetry, storytelling, and the drama.

Compare the output of these two races of composers. The reputations of Haydn, Mozart, Beethoven, and Brahms rest largely upon their symphonies, overtures, and chamber-music works, formal pieces whose titles are almost never descriptive, but exist purely for identification. Now look at the work of the moderns. The six compositions upon which Richard Strauss's fame rests are all symphonic poems, every one of which tells a story or paints a picture. The five most popular works of Stravinsky were composed as ballet-pantomimes. Edward Elgar's is a familiar name because of his *Enigma* variations, a series of musical portraits of his friends. Respighi's three Roman poems are musical impressions of architecture—*pictures* of architecture, mind you—landscapes, and Roman history. Sibelius has written symphonies, to be sure, but he has also written the descriptive *Finlandia* and the *Swan of Tuonela*. Ravel is perhaps best known for his ballet-pantomime *Daphnis and Chloë*, and second best for his *Mother Goose* suite of nursery stories. Consider just the titles of Debussy's best-known and most popular works: *The Sea, Clouds, Sirens, The Afternoon of a Faun, Through the Streets and Byways, The Perfumes of the Night, The Morning of a Holiday*. I could go on almost indefinitely with a list of modern works whose main outline and internal structure are determined not by any fixed pattern but by a story or some sort of visual impression.

Here the composer runs a risk, that of sticking so closely and literally to his program that his music becomes meaningless without it. My own experience as a listener is that when I first hear a new piece of program music, I pay close attention to the program, using it as a sort of pair of musical water wings to keep myself afloat. Then, as I become more familiar with the music, I find myself beginning to forget about the program and to hear the music just as music. Roughly, I should say that the difference between program and absolute music is very much the difference between a ballad and a sonnet. I read a ballad for the story, and a sonnet for the poetic ideas. After I'm familiar with the story of the ballad, unless it has poetic qualities as well as narrative ones, I get tired of it. I don't get tired of the sonnet, because I never did read it for the story. And so with the program music. It may sound brilliantly successful when it is first played as a ballet, say, with stage action to give it structure, or as a symphonic poem with an elaborate narrative program note. But fitting his music to a dramatic or pictorial program doesn't in the least relieve the composer of the responsibility of writing music that can stand on its own musical legs. If it doesn't mean anything without the program, sooner or later it doesn't mean anything even *with* a program.

3

Short and Hot

ONE of the simplest devices that the classic composers use in order to give their music clarity and coherence is, as I said before, that of repetition. In any classic symphony or sonata or string quartet you'll find the composer not only putting his main themes through all sorts of transformations—in other words, developing them—but also returning to them in their original form, repeating them note for note. Frequently he'll do this with an entire section. Mozart, for instance, in the first movement of his symphony in D major, puts a so-called double bar line after the 142nd measure—in other words, directs the conductor to play the entire 142 measures over again. Beethoven does this sort of thing. So does Schumann.

Even the most devoted purists among present-day conductors have no hesitation in ignoring directions like that. Unless you have looked at the printed score you're not necessarily aware that they are making cuts in the classic symphonies; but making cuts they are. And they make them because, if they didn't, their audiences would probably grow restless. I've often thought how slow to grasp a given musical passage eighteenth- and early nineteenth-century audiences must have been, compared with the audiences of today. On the average we're much quicker on the uptake, so to speak, than they were, and consequently have much less patience with literal repetition. I know that in my own case, every once in a while, listening to a classic symphony, I find myself thinking, "Yes, I know about that. You said that before. Come on, get on with it.

What happens next?" Or words to that effect. It isn't just a matter of being familiar with the piece. I find the same thing happening with works that are not particularly familiar; and mine is no unique case. I think that the average layman today, no matter how ignorant, musically, he may consider himself to be, is much more receptive of music, much quicker to grasp the composer's message, than the listener of Beethoven's time.

Now, we find this impatience reflected in present-day music —that is, music written within the past fifty years. Whether consciously or unconsciously, the contemporary composer tends to assume that his hearers are going to get the gist of his ideas without much reiteration, and so don't want to be told the same thing twice over in the same way. Take a familiar example that I've cited before: Debussy's *The Afternoon of a Faun*. It opens with a four-bar chromatic passage for the flute. Now, Debussy reintroduces that phrase no less than ten times, yet never once does he merely repeat it verbatim. Sometimes he changes the intervals, sometimes the harmony, sometimes the rhythm; whatever he does, he always manages to give you a fresh slant on that passage. No two versions of it are ever exactly alike. That tendency is widespread throughout modern music. Not only do our composers today avoid literal repetition, but you'll notice that their works tend to become shorter and more compact. They say their say and get it over with. They tend to write sinfonettas and sonatinas instead of symphonies and sonatas. Even when one of them writes a comparatively long work, as Elgar does in his *Enigma* variations, he divides it into a large number of brief sections, instead of a few long ones.

Now, I like that tendency to brevity. In the first place, it forces the audience really to listen to the music. You can't just sit and bathe in a piece of present-day music, paying no particular attention to any given section because you know the merry-go-round will bring it back a little later. If you miss the point of one passage in a modern symphony, you've missed it for good. It may, and probably will, reappear, but it will have changed its costume. So, whether you're conscious of it or not, you tend to listen more attentively, and therefore more intelligently.

Besides, that knowledge that he has an alert but rather impatient audience is a good thing for the composer, because it forces him to be very critical of his material and his handling of it. When he sits down to compose a symphony, he can no longer just knock together a handful of themes and trust to luck to say something significant in the course of fifty minutes. He's got to present themes that really mean something, and say something reasonably important with them inside half an hour, or even less. If he doesn't, his hearers, spiritually at least, will walk out on him. There is much less diffuse and repetitious writing in music today than there was a century ago, even among the masters. In the eighteenth century, most novels were as long as *Anthony Adverse*. Today, a novel as long as that is a phenomenon, just as the Bruckner Eighth, a symphony that lasts an hour and nineteen minutes, is a lonely exception to an almost universal rule.

Of course, this conciseness, like any other good thing, can be carried too far. A good composer today, even though he may not repeat his themes literally, does repeat them. And he must, because repetition in some form or other is still necessary to make music coherent. Dmitri Shostakovich went through a phase in which he avowedly wrote music no two bars of which were alike. That might work in vocal music, where the sense of words lends sense to the musical setting. But he extended it to the field of instrumental music. And the net result was that you heard just a lot of bars of music, with no particular connection between them and no particular beginning or end. Happily for him, and for us, he gave that up before long.

Then, too, it's one thing to avoid saying too much, and another to avoid saying anything at all. When composers start writing compositions that are eight, and twelve, and fourteen measures long, as certain ultra-modernists have done, the net result of their labors is not likely to be impressive. Julius Caesar's "I came, I saw, I conquered" is a model telegram, but it's hardly what you'd call a literary treat. Some of my younger colleagues seem so anxious to avoid repeating something they've already said that they neglect to say it in the first place.

When we come to the element of rhythm, we find modern music differing from the classics in two rather entertainingly antipodal respects. In recent years one school of composers has taken various dance rhythms—tangos, rumbas, boleros, fox trots, Charlestons—and applied their patterns to what is intended to be serious music. In other words, these particular moderns have gone back to the past with such a vengeance that they have skipped over Beethoven, leaped over Mozart, and vaulted over Haydn and Bach straight into the astonished laps of Couperin and Corelli, whose dance suites they proceed to emulate.

To me, these experiments have not been strikingly successful. The few that have succeeded are generally pieces that utilize the archaic dance rhythms of the seventeenth and eighteenth centuries, rhythms so deliberate that one hardly feels them as dances—for example, Ravel's *Pavane for a Dead Princess*. In the faster rhythms the moderns haven't done so well. After all, the very essence of a dance rhythm is its appeal to the feet. And it's a well-known fact that the feet are farthest south from the head and the heart. A symphonic work that says its say in terms of a floor show is going to have a hard time making any very deep emotional appeal. Whatever way you slice it, even a good piece like Ravel's *Bolero* is still a bolero.

On the other hand, another school, scorning anything so regimented as a dance rhythm, demands, and practices, rhythmic freedom to the point of anarchy. Where the classics stick pretty consistently to their two-four, three-four, and four-four time signatures, these moderns have made all sorts of experiments with five-eight, seven-four, nine-four, twelve-sixteenths —practically any sort of time combination you can think of. Nor do they stop at establishing these odd rhythms; they mix them up, so that you will find passages of sixteen or eighteen measures, sometimes whole movements, with no two bars in the same time. I think they have yet to prove that they're on the right track. The rhythm of a piece of music is not only what makes the music come to life, but its alternation of strong and weak beats forms a pattern that enables the listener to grasp the outline of the themes, and follow them in their course. A certain degree of variety in the placing of those beats does give the music an element of surprise, of unexpectedness that is a source of pleasure. But there is a definite limit to the listener's capacity to keep up with those variations. Change the time on him just once too often, and you confuse him. He loses his sense of direction. The beats don't fall in the places he expected. And so the themes begin to elude him, and to lose their outline.

Now, in tennis it's a good idea to drop the ball where your opponent doesn't expect to find it. But music isn't tennis; and if you keep your listener running all over the court, he's likely to get tired and not want to play any more—or, rather, not want *you* to play any more. In some of the scores by some of our young modern composers, those dazzling successions of constantly shifting time signatures look very exciting, and undoubtedly furnish healthful exercise for the conductor and the players at rehearsals, but they don't necessarily work out in performance. I think Stravinsky has led a large number of young composers astray in this respect. There are passages in *The Rite of Spring* in which no two bars are the same in length. But *The Rite of Spring* was written for the stage, for pantomime. His rhythms are visual as well as aural, so that the audience can literally *see* those irregular beats reflected in the movements of the dancers, and can follow the music with its eyes as well as with its ears. But what *looks* logical in the theater may *sound* incoherent on the concert platform. Put too much rhythm, too many kinds of rhythm, into a piece of music, and you're in danger of completing the circle and coming out with no rhythm at all.

I mentioned the fact that music written in dance rhythms isn't likely to have much emotional power. Neither, I think, is music likely to have much emotional impact if it changes rhythm too often. When a regiment crosses a bridge, the soldiers are ordered to break step, because if they didn't the regular vibration might break down the bridge. Similarly, a more or less regular rhythmic beat in music has a profound effect upon the nervous system of the listener, tends to break down his emotional resistance, where music with no regular beat may produce no emotional reaction in him at all. But this, say a certain school of modern composers, is all to the good. They don't *want* their music to have any emotional content. They want it to arouse our interest, to stimulate our minds; but on no account do they want it to be emotional. They don't call it emotional. They call it sentimental. To hear some of them talk, you would think that the slow movement of the Ninth symphony belonged in the same category as *Hearts and Flowers*.

4

The Human Clarinet

THREE chapters ago I commented on the tendency of the classic masters to compose themes that were prevailingly *vocal* in character. When we come to modern music, I think we shall find composers inventing themes much more adapted to instruments than to voices. For one thing, many of their melodies go far beyond the compass of the human voice. (Yes, I know that that has always been true of violin music; but I am discussing themes in general—abstract themes.) Take, for example, the opening theme of Strauss's *Ein Heldenleben.* Any human being, living or dead, who could sing those first eight measures, transposed into no matter what key, would be not a vocalist but a museum piece. Moreover, the last two measures of the phrase illustrate another non-vocal tendency in modern music, in that they contain intervals that are quite foreign to the theoretical key of the melody, and which a singer would have great difficulty in singing in tune. I think it is no coincidence that the field in which ultra-modern music has been least successful is that of writing for the voice. The wide leaps and out-of-key intervals that characterize this music put physical and intellectual burdens upon the soloist that are simply beyond the powers of the average singer.

In the old days it was quite possible for a singer to have a highly successful career in concert or opera and be, musically speaking, illiterate. A tenor could, and can, learn the role of Manrico in Verdi's *Il Trovatore* without being able to read a note of music, simply by having the airs played over and over for him until he had memorized them. If he should get lost in the middle of an aria, he had only to cock an ear to the orchestra, which would either be playing the actual tune, or else would give him the harmonic background that would help him to pick it up again.

Nowadays, when a singer studies a piece of music written in the modernist idiom, he must be an all-round musician. He must be an expert vocalist, in the first place, in order to stand the strain of singing over a range that wouldn't be any too easy for a clarinet to cover. He must, of course, be able to read music perfectly, in order to cope with the intricacies of the rhythms and the intervals. Also, he must have an ear so perfect that he can sing the piece through with no accompaniment at all; for if he misses a few notes, he is sunk with all on board. When he goes to the orchestra for help, he's likely to find it playing in a different key and in a totally different set of rhythms. Since we're on the subject of vocal music, let me point out one phase of it that I discussed in a previous book, and which the modernist composers, in my opinion, have rather overlooked. And that is that the human voice is the one musical instrument whose player must *hear* the note, in his imagination, before he can produce it. You can set a highly complicated passage, bristling with sharps and flats, in front of a trumpeter or an oboe player, and while he may have some difficulty in reading the notes at sight, he can, when he has mastered the fingering, produce them accurately. Hand that same succession of notes to a singer, and he must memorize them with a completeness that is demanded of no instrumentalist. When he goes from one note to another, he must imagine, and almost literally hear, that interval before he can bridge it. If he can't, he can't sing it. Now, that seems almost too obvious to mention, and yet I have mentioned it to composers who had never thought of taking it into consideration. That, I think, is why you hear so few completely successful performances of ultra-modern choral works. There is a definite limit to the average singer's capacity to master exotic note-relationships. Once you pass that limit, once your music is so complicated that he can't hear it in his mind's ear, he either breaks down completely, or, as we have all heard upon occasion, sings out of tune.

5

Comes the Revolution

Now we come to the element in modern music wherein it differs most conspicuously from the music of the past. All the other elements that we've discussed—tonal, melodic, and rhythmic freedom, terseness, unorthodox form—all these may or may not have been noticed by you. In any case, I doubt whether they have impressed you very forcibly either way. But the thing about modern music of which the average listener is most conscious, and about which he feels most violently one way or the other, is its unorthodox harmony, its persistent use of dissonances—intervals that a great many people call discords. Harmony, to the classic composers, meant consonance—literally, "sounding together." In other words, a normal chord of music was made up of notes that combined to produce a pleasant impression on the ear. And two notes, to be consonant, couldn't be less than three steps apart.

For instance, strike the middle white key on the piano—middle C. Now skip one white key and strike the one above that. Now do the same over again. Those three notes, at intervals of a third, are a consonant chord, the common chord of C major. Now, to the classic harmonists, any interval of less than a third was a dissonance—that is, "dis-sounding"; in other words, a combination of notes that was, theoretically at least, *not* pleasing to the ear—or, at any rate, not for very long. Dissonant chords, when they were used at all, were always considered as being sort of halfway steps between two consonant ones. So much for pure theory. Needless to say, all the classic masters, from Bach on, violated this theory incessantly, in actual practice. But the *theory* still held, even to them. Dissonance was always considered to be something away from the normal. Now of course, the minute you begin to talk about what is pleasing to the ear and what isn't, you get into an endless argument that eventually resolves itself into "I like it," or "I don't like it." And the composers, being closer to music, and familiar with it through long handling of it, tend to get used to certain dissonant combinations, and even to enjoy them, before their listeners do. The lay listeners sometimes catch up with the composers within a comparatively short time, because, being technically ignorant, they feel free to like what they do like as soon as they get to like it—if you follow me.

But the critics, being more or less familiar with the rules of the game, are so conscious of what rules the composer is breaking that even after they get used to his dissonances, they are still outraged by his lawlessness. Frequently, during the nineteenth and early twentieth centuries, the progress of music has been a procession, headed by the composer, with his lay audience somewhat in the rear, and the critics a bad third, wringing their hands.

Whence came this instinctive reaction to so-called "consonant" chords? Let me seem to digress a bit. Go to the piano. If you haven't one, borrow one. And be sure it's in tune. Now find the lowest C. On the standard piano keyboard it is the third white key from the bottom. Having located that, find the eighth white key above it, counting the lowest as number one. Now find the eighth white key above that. Hold that one down, without letting it sound, and strike the lower C sharply with your left hand. On a well-tuned piano, the second C will hum its proper note as you strike the lower one. Now find the eighth white key above the second C. Hold it down, strike the lowest C again, and once more you'll hear the proper note sung by the upper string. Now find the second white key above the upper C. Repeat the holding and striking process. Do the same with the second white key above that. Every time you struck the lowest C, the key you happened to be holding down sang its proper note in sympathy.

What's the point? Simply this. Those sympathetic vibrations that you heard were the so-called natural harmonics, or overtones, of that low C. Sound, of course, is vibration, and every vibrating medium that produces a note gives off a series of—well, you might call them junior vibrations, whether it's a vibrating string, as on a piano or violin, a vibrating membrane, as in a kettledrum, or a vibrating column of air, as in a trumpet or a flute or a clarinet. On a violin or a harp, these overtones are produced by touching the string lightly at certain so-called nodal points, so that its vibrating length is shortened, and the sounds produced are, consequently, higher. On a wood-wind instrument the overtones are produced by boring holes in the tube of the instrument. On a brass instrument, like a trumpet, they are produced by variations in the opening of the player's lips and the tension of his lips.

I have a theory as to the origin of harmony that the world, as yet, doesn't share. In fact, I made it up only yesterday morning, and am consequently very fond of it. In the earliest music there were no stringed instruments outside of harps and lyres. Except for accompanying singers and poets, they weren't particularly useful because their sound was comparatively weak—particularly their overtones, which were the weakest of all. In the case of the wood-wind instruments, such as flutes and pipes and primitive oboes, the overtones didn't figure much in the player's consciousness, because by boring a number of holes in his instrument he could produce several different sets of overtones. In other words, he could play tunes. But the primitive brass instruments, the buccinas and early trumpets—in fact, all brass instruments before the invention of valves—could play nothing *but* those harmonics or overtones. Since there were gaps between the playable notes, the only tunes they could play were what we would call bugle calls, which are all based on the natural harmonics. Now, if you'll strike again that series of keys, you will notice that it contains the notes C, E, and G—in other words the so-called common triad of C major.

Now, here's where my theory comes in. When primitive men began to play together, in the prehistoric equivalent of an orchestra—and I see no reason to assume that such gatherings never took place—the flutes and reed pipes played the tunes. (Incidentally, I believe that they had tunes to play. I think the art of inventing melodies is a good deal older than we think.) As I say, the wood winds played the tunes. The harps and lyres twanged away, I suppose, in a sort of running tinkle that didn't make much difference one way or the other. Now, the brass, besides being able to play nothing but their harmonics, were the loudest of all the instruments. Since they couldn't skip about like the wood winds, they probably filled in with whatever notes they had in common with the wood winds. So that the ears of man, for hundreds of generations, were filled with the sound of those fundamental harmonics. Not only that, but it's impossible not to believe that on occasion the brass players sounded several of those harmonics at once, whether accidentally or not; so that they produced octaves, fifths, thirds, and perhaps even complete triad chords. And then, finding that these combinations of several simultaneous notes were rather pleasant, they probably began to play them deliberately.

Consequently, when men began to evolve harmony as a conscious branch of the art of music, they undoubtedly built on an ancestral inheritance of response to these natural tonic and dominant chords. In addition, since we are products of Nature and tend to obey the laws of Nature, it was almost inevitable that we should tend to vibrate in sympathy with the laws of acoustics. In other words, when you attempt to evolve a system of harmony that is *not* based on these natural harmonics, you are, literally, going against Nature. Not that that's necessarily a sin. If it were, the airplane and its inventors would be excommunicated.

But does such a system actually go against Nature? One school says that it very definitely does not, the school that expounds the theory of the twelve-tone system, music without a tonic, music that is not based on the chords of any definite key. Now, this is a subject which a large number of people have no hesitation in discussing very fluently, without going to the trouble of determining what it's all about. Just what *is* twelve-tone music? The easy thing is to say, "Oh, it's a theory of music based on ugliness and discord"—and let it go at that. But that isn't a very clear answer. If you ask me to describe anchovy paste, and I say, "Well, it tastes nasty," you have a right to complain that I haven't given you a very accurate description of anchovy paste. So putting aside the question of how it sounds, for the moment, let's find out what these twelve-tone composers are after.

Luckily I can give you a completely authoritative analysis of what they're after. At the time I was discussing this subject on the air, I received a letter from Arnold Schönberg, the inventor of "twelve-tone composition," enclosing a copy of a lecture that he delivered at the University of California. In it he expounds his theories in detail. I am taking the liberty of paraphrasing his remarks; for inasmuch as his subject is a pretty complicated one, his language at times becomes so technical that it might be difficult for the lay reader to follow him. I shall try to simplify it as much as possible without doing violence to the author's intentions.

Dr. Schönberg begins by pointing out that in the last hundred years our conception of harmony has changed a great deal, through the development of chromatic harmony—that is, chords that don't necessarily belong to the basic key in which the music is written; and that, as a consequence, modern music wanders about from one key to another with the utmost freedom. Gradually, through this chromatic development of harmony, our ears have grown to tolerate, and even take pleasure, in dissonant intervals that would have been very disagreeable to our ancestors. There are harmonies in a work like Strauss's *Till Eulenspiegel* or Debussy's *La Mer,* in parts of Wagner, that would have been unbearably ugly to a musician of the eighteenth century.

But according to Dr. Schönberg, what distinguishes dissonance (or discord) from consonance is not a greater or lesser degree of beauty, but a greater or lesser degree of *comprehensibility*. Now, that's a very important point, and I'd like to repeat it in other language. What the Doctor is saying is, in short, that when you hear a series of chords that are strongly dissonant, whether or not they sound beautiful to you depends on whether or not they make sense to you. If your ear finds a certain degree of musical logic in that progression of chords, you like it. If not, you don't.

I wrote just now of our common chords being based on natural harmonics. Well, Dr. Schönberg points out that as we leave the lower harmonics of any instrument, and go into the more remote—that is, higher—ones, we find notes that are utterly foreign to the simple, basic chords. In other words, if you're going to talk about "natural" harmonics, these dissonant ones are just as natural as any others, acoustically speaking; and if we find them strange, it's because they are less familiar. Accordingly, he decided that, logically, there are no such things as dissonances—that no notes are foreign to any given chord; and he evolved a school of composition that treats dissonance and consonance as one and the same thing.

"Whether one calls oneself conservative or revolutionary," he writes, "whether one tries only to imitate old styles or is destined to express new ideas, whether one is a good composer or not, one must be convinced of the infallibility of one's fantasy, and one must believe in one's inspiration. Nevertheless, the desire for a conscious control of the new means and forms will arise in every artist's mind, and he will wish to know *consciously* the laws and rules that govern the forms that he has conceived as in a dream. . . . The conviction that these new sounds obey the laws of nature and of our manner of thinking, that order, logic, comprehensibility, and form cannot be present without obedience to such laws—this conviction forced the composer [he is referring to himself] on the road of exploration. He had to find, if not laws and rules, at least systems, or advice [I think he means opinions] to justify the dissonant character of his harmony, and reason for the succession of such chords. After many roundabout ways, which demanded approximately twelve years, I laid the foundations of a new procedure in musical construction which seemed fitted to replace the losses of formal differentiation granted by the former harmonies."

That last sentence is pretty tough, isn't it? Dr. Schönberg previously pointed out that sticking to a key, or a regular progression of chords, gave a piece of music coherence. Abolish chord progressions, and you destroy that coherence. Hence his search for a system that would still leave the listener with some feeling of form and balanced structure. This new system he calls "A Method of Composing with Twelve Tones Which Are Related Only with One Another." In other words, a system of composing by which you take the twelve notes of the chromatic scale and use any two or three or four of them in combination, regardless of whether they bear any relation to any chord—in the old-fashioned sense of the word.

Now, his procedure in composing is, in its essentials, as follows: He takes the twelve notes of the chromatic scale and arranges them in any order he chooses. The resulting group he calls a "set" of twelve tones. In old-fashioned terms, it would be called a phrase. As I said, he decides the order in which they are to occur, taking care, however, to use all twelve and not to repeat one of them, even in the octave, until all twelve have been used. Now, this "set" is the theme of his composition, and he creates the entire work by the incessant repetition of the notes in the order in which they originally occurred. He may, of course, cause them to be played higher or lower, and is at liberty—in fact, is obligated—to introduce variations, to alter their rhythmic relation to one another, in as many ways as he can. In order further to avoid monotony, he employs the devices of florid counterpoint: inversion, retrogression, and retrograde inversion. In English, that means that he can first play the theme "straight," so to speak. Then he can invert it—that is, cause the notes to go down where they went up, originally, or up where they went down; or he can play the theme backward; or he can play it upside down *and* backward.

He explains his prohibition of octaves or repeated notes by saying that "To double is to emphasize, and an emphasized tone could be interpreted as a root or even as a tonic, whose consequences must be avoided." Even a slight reminiscence of former—that is, conventional—harmony is prohibitive, because, as he says, "False expectations of consequences and continuations would provoke disappointment." In other words, if you get the idea of consonance in your ear, you'll become conscious of dissonance—which this theory denies. He also insists on the incessant use of just one arrangement of the twelve notes because introducing another arrangement might result in repeating one or more notes too soon. His accompaniment is likewise based on "chords," or, rather, note combinations that, again, are various phases of the original group of twelve notes. In writing for orchestra he may use six, eight, ten, or a dozen independent parts, since his system forbids any doubling of notes in octaves.

In conclusion, Dr. Schönberg points out that his invention of repeated sets of twelve notes is closely allied to Wagner's invention of the system of leading motives. In both cases the idea is to convey a sense of unity and balance in a composition that otherwise doesn't necessarily possess any definite form. Whether or not the hearer is conscious of where that sense of unity comes from is not important.

The Defense Rests

It was just about at this point, when these chapters were being delivered as broadcast talks, that the letters began to arrive, all of the same general nature, all intended to be anything but complimentary, and all of which I found flattering. The writers accused me of swallowing ultra-modern music whole, and of trying to sell the radio public a lot of stuff that I ought to know better than to praise. I found them flattering because I had been trying to state the case for modern music as fairly as was humanly possible, and apparently I succeeded. For I don't mind confessing that I find about ninety per cent of modern music unbearably dull and dishearteningly sterile. And so, warning you to accept that only as one man's opinion, let me give you some of my reasons for that opinion.

Suppose we start with the most conspicuous characteristic of such present-day music, its extremely dissonant character. A whole school of composers, whether or not they accept the entire Schönberg twelve-tone theory, deny that there is any such thing as dissonance. Any one combination of notes, they say, is just as harmonious as any other. If one happens to sound ugly to us, it's only because our ears aren't accustomed to it. Well, that's an argument. Logically, the history of music bears them out. But right there, I think, they make a mistaken assumption that has affected many artists: the assumption that art is susceptible to the same kind of logic that governs science. It isn't. There are, for instance, such things as good taste and bad taste in art. There are not in science. You can reason your way to a scientific discovery; you can't to an artistic discovery. Take this question of dissonance, for instance. Next time you're in a night club or at a symphony concert, listen to the bass drum, and try to determine what note it is playing. You'll find that it isn't playing any one discoverable note. It's making a definite sound; it's making a noise. And since it isn't playing any one note, it doesn't clash with any of the notes that the rest of the orchestra may be playing. As a matter of scientific fact, that bass drum *is* playing notes. All of its overtones are sounding at once, and there are so many of them that no one of them is distinguishable. If you go to the piano and strike a chord of A flat with your left hand and a chord of A natural with your right, the result will probably sound discordant to you. But if you lay a stick of wood on the black keys, and another on the white keys, and push both down so as to strike all the keys at once, the result will probably *not* sound discordant. It will just be a noise. In other words, if you keep adding discordant notes to a chord indefinitely, you eventually reach a point where your ear no longer hears that combination of notes as a chord. The notes melt and run together, so to speak, to form a single sound that is neither consonant nor dissonant. In other words, a simple noise. Just where that point it, just how many different notes a chord can contain and still *be* a chord, nobody can prove by any logical process. All I know is that while there's no theoretical limit to the amount of dissonance to which the ear can grow accustomed, sooner or later the ear revolts, and refuses to hear any dissonance at all.

Moreover, I'm not at all sure that I want to get *too* used to dissonant harmonies. I think there's a vital need, in all art, for ugliness—ugliness that is avowedly ugly, without claiming to be the same as prettiness, so as to supply an element of variety and contrast. Suppose there should arise a school of cooks that decided that "bitter" and "sweet" were mere words, that the difference between them was purely imaginary. And suppose they should flavor their cakes and stews and puddings with anything they chose to pick out of the kitchen cabinet. And suppose, after conscientiously sampling their fare, our palates finally attained a degree of toleration that enabled us to eat anchovy ice cream and roast turkey with hot chocolate sauce and mustard pie with equal relish, to be indifferent as to whether we used sugar or curry powder or red pepper in our coffee. It might be done, but think of the fun we would miss as our food began—and it inevitably would begin—to taste all alike.

To change the metaphor, it seems to me that many modern composers are producing the same effect as would a school of painters who should suddenly elect to abandon the violet end of the spectrum, and the middle, and to use nothing but various shades of red in their pictures. Think of what they'd be giving up, to gain what? A picture painted entirely in red has no more real color values in it than a picture painted in black and white, and many of the excessively dissonant works of some ultra-modern composers have no more real harmonic contrast than the excessively consonant music of the thirteenth century. When I say that I'm afraid I'll never get used to certain present-day works, I'm wrong. What I'm really afraid of is that I *shall* get used to it. I want to hear music in which dissonance is conceived *as* dissonance, in which it is set against consonance so as to furnish contrast. To me the net effect of a good deal of modern music is one of monotony, lack of expressive power, and the chief cause of that is the rather Pollyannish insistence of its composers that there is no such thing as ugly music. Suppose you're writing a tone poem in which two lovers are supposed to be sitting by the sea in the moonlight. Then the woman makes a confession that drives the man mad with jealousy, and he strangles her.

Well, if your love scene has been conceived in terms of the most acrid kind of dissonant harmony, what have you left for your murder? What's the fun in strangling the girl to the same kind of music that accompanied holding her hand?

Now, when I say that I find the thematic material of much ultra-modern music as essentially dry as its harmonic scheme, I am expressing a purely personal opinion, one that I can't possibly prove. Time alone will show whether I'm right or wrong—for after all, a piece of music lives or dies not by the way it is harmonized but by the vitality of its themes. There is one comment that I could make, to back up my opinion, and that is that unless I have completely misunderstood Dr. Schönberg, the twelve-tone system of composition requires the composer to build every one of his themes out of all twelve notes of the chromatic scale, without repeating any of them. If this is so, then the composer is virtually forbidden to have a spontaneous inspiration for a theme. If he should happen to hear, in his imagination, a theme that contained only two notes, with one of them repeated three times—like the opening of the Beethoven Fifth—he would have to reject it. Two-note themes aren't allowed.

In fact, the essential weakness of much ultra-modern music, to me, is its purely negative character. It sounds not so much like a discovery of something new as a running away from something old—a flight from the obvious. Its composers seem to be driven by a fear of saying something that has already been said. I think a great deal of the blame for this state of mind lies on the shoulders of the music critics. Read a typical review of the first performance of a new work by a younger composer. No matter where the performance took place or who the critic is, he will write substantially as follows:

"Mr. Blank's new symphony, though it contains some

promising material, is conventional in form, and pays copious tribute to the influence of Brahms, Puccini, Ravel, and Strauss." And so on. If one of his melodies goes up a sixth and then comes down two half steps, it's stolen from Wagner. If he uses a couple of whole-tone chords, they're stolen from Debussy. If his main theme is solid and diatonic, it's cribbed from Brahms. If the piece contains half a dozen dissonant chords, they're cribbed from Schönberg. I'm not exaggerating—much. This sort of tune-detective obsession is common to music critics all over the world today. Their attention seems always directed not upon what the composer has to say that is his own but upon what he owes to his musical ancestry. If Brahms had written his first symphony last week, it wouldn't have a chance. Every critic would point out that the second theme of his last movement was stolen from the Ninth symphony—and that would be that.

Now, the present-day young composer, exposed to this sort of cross-examination with every work he produces, almost inevitably has it borne in upon him that the supreme crime in music is to write even a phrase that is suggestive of some other music. And it is small wonder, therefore, that he embraces a theory and practice of composition that at least give him the assurance that his music will sound like nothing ever written before.

I can't find any other period in the history of music in which the theory and practice of the art was in an equal state of confusion. There is being written, at the present time, music that Beethoven would not have found incomprehensible—the music of Sibelius, for example. And it exists side by side with music that Richard Strauss must find utterly beyond him—Arnold Schönberg's *Pierrot Lunaire,* for instance. We have three distinct modern schools of composition, all of them differing violently among themselves. Hundreds of composers today are groping their way along a road so misted in uncertainty that they have little or no notion of what their destination may turn out to be.

That remark of mine at the beginning of this chapter, to the effect that I found ninety per cent of ultra-modern music dull and sterile, was one that I ventured to make over the air. I made it deliberately, in the hope of stirring up a little reaction. I got it, to the tune of several hundred letters and postcards—a heavy mail for a symphony broadcast. I was dumfounded at the unanimity of the writers' opinion. Out of the lot, there were just four who sharply disagreed with me. The rest said that they hated most ultra-modern music, and were glad to find somebody who agreed with them.

Now, that is a curious and rather disturbing state of affairs. It is customary for the defenders of any contemporary composer to point out that Mozart, Beethoven, Wagner, and Brahms all had to endure a tremendous amount of unpopularity and misunderstanding before their music finally triumphed. But that is only a half truth. The abuse and misunderstanding that fell to their lot came, most of it, from the music critics and other composers. During the major portion of their careers all four of those composers were, literally, *popular* composers. Whenever the general public got a chance to hear their works, it liked them. But today the situation seems to be reversed. Many of the ultra-modern composers are ardently praised by their confreres and the more advanced music critics—and are *not* liked by the public.

Granted that to desire to be popular is an unworthy ambition, granted that the public doesn't know as much as the critics, granted even that it is stupid and trivial in its tastes, the fact remains that it invariably responds to real greatness. The public isn't always very bright in the field of politics, because politics requires clear mass-thinking. But in the field of art, which requires only emotional and spiritual response, the verdict of the public is almost invariably just, because mass-*feeling* is generally sound. When we agree that Wagner's critics were wrong, we are only saying that the public was right. When the critics don't like a composer, he has the right to claim that he's ahead of them. When the public persists in not liking him, he has cause to worry.

Today we are all worried, both the composers and the public. The former don't seem very certain as to what they're composing, and the latter certainly has no very clear idea as to what it is hearing. I believe that the only thing that any of us can do, as listeners to this new music, is to take absolutely nothing for granted. If a new piece is written in this strange and dissonant idiom, don't refuse to hear it for that reason. And don't swallow it whole, for that same reason. Never mind who the composer is or what its title is. Put it on its own. See whether you can find signs of life in it. If you can, put it aside for future reference. If you can't, forget it.

What are those signs of life? I have no formula, but I have a clue. There is a quality that, I think, distinguishes all great music, the quality of discovery. It's a hard thing to define, but it's unmistakable when it exists. Not long ago, over the air, I heard two choruses by Guillaume Dufay, a Flemish composer who died in 1474. Hearing that music, simple and naïve as it may sound superficially, I suddenly realized that to Dufay it had been a new and wonderful thing, something that had come to him out of the void, mysterious and beautiful. And so it was still that to me, four and a half centuries later. I find that same quality, that quality of transmitting something that is new to the composer, and therefore new to me, in the music of Mozart and Beethoven and all the other greats. Mozart's chord progressions are commonplaces to any music student today. But they weren't commonplaces to him. They were discoveries; and they still are. What is there about the main themes of Wagner's *Ring* that makes them so unforgettable? They're nothing but a lot of bugle calls.

How did he manage to make of them something that we had never heard before? I don't know. All I know is that they are no longer bugle calls. They are Wagner. I find that same quality in Stravinsky's *The Rite of Spring*. It's brutal stuff. But Stravinsky didn't invent it; he heard it. I find that quality in Debussy's *Afternoon of a Faun*. The opening phrase is only six notes of a chromatic scale, but hear those six notes once and you will not forget them. I find that quality in Alban Berg's *Wozzeck,* written on the twelve-note system that has aroused such controversy. It's bitter music and often repellent music, but hearing it, you know that Berg didn't cook it up. He thought, musically, in those terms. He wrote it that way because he had to write it that way. And you agree that he had to write it. What matters, fundamentally, is not whether a piece of music is ancient or modern, sweet or bitter, but whether it gives you a sense of the miracle of creation, whereby a composer suddenly discovers a way of saying something that has never been said in quite that way before, and manages to convey to you the mystery and wonder of that discovery.

PART SIX

Coda

I

Barbarian America

THEY tell a story concerning the late Calvin Coolidge, to the effect that when he returned from church one Sunday, Mrs. Coolidge asked him what the minister's text had been. To which, with his characteristic conciseness, Mr. Coolidge replied, "Sin."

"And what did he say about it?" asked Mrs. Coolidge.

Said Mr. Coolidge: "He's against it."

I was reminded of that story when I read the letter from which I'm about to quote. It runs as follows:

"I much appreciate your efforts for music in this country, but you engage in a Sisyphean task. There are a few really musical spirits in America, but *few*. The majority of Anglo-Saxons simply cannot bear the higher altitudes of Western music, and the foreign elements born here immediately become of like quality. The very imported musicians are corrupted promptly, and cease producing the 'inner sacredness' of great music. Instead, they pander to the demand for showmanship for the barbarian ears of the Americans. I no longer go to concerts here, preferring to listen to music by radio, and of that, preferably recorded.

"And who," he continues, "may I be? An American who went abroad when young, with as thick a shell of American as ever was; who learned, step by step, incident by incident, shock by shock, how utterly provincial and barbarian his country is in all the really 'top drawer' things of Western civilization. Nor am I against the American as such.

[Thanks, pal.] I enjoyed the Americans who in Paris opera and orchestras were laboring at their art, without reaching for easy money, but I have seen no conductors there called American.

"I doubt whether we shall have more of Western music in the grand style. Bach, Beethoven, Mozart, Wagner, Liszt, Meyerbeer—that *galère* have passed, with none like them. Smaller men, imitators, panderers to 'money' demands, to the tunes of the mob—yes. The barbarians close in; the 'people's' music is never great music. Fewer and fewer can hear. The emperors and the courts and the courtiers have passed. For whom should great music be written? Just a few days ago I was writing to a friend, and I said, 'The Anglo-Saxons have never produced more than a third-rate musician, no artist worth the mention after his day.' And I stand upon it. Yet to listen to this people, you would think us the Athens of modern culture, the depository of all Western achievements, the Messiah of future humanity. We can tell ourselves, over the radio principally, and in the Sunday supplements, that we are wonderful, but that doesn't make it so; never."

I should like to comment upon the last part of that letter first—the part about us Anglo-Saxons. I suspect my correspondent of using that term much as the Germans used "Aryan"; I doubt if there's a pure-blooded Anglo-Saxon in the world. He probably means the Americans of British descent—meaning Norman, Welsh, Scotch, Scotch-Irish, and Manx. Also, I'm a little baffled by his announcement that he shuns concerts in favor of the radio and records. If our orchestral concerts are the barbarian orgies that he implies them to be, whence comes the civilizing influence of the radio that conveys their horrid goings on to his ears? And, considering that the conductors and orchestras that make the recordings are the same that play the concerts, why are the records so much better at producing the inner sacredness of great music? However, let us get on to more important matters.

When my correspondent speaks so wistfully of the courts and the courtiers, and so disrespectfully of what he calls the "people's" music, I think he hasn't read his musical history thoroughly enough, or hasn't thought about it thoroughly enough. If you want to catch a glimpse of the musical taste of the courts, of their real degree of sensitivity to music, read Mozart's letter to his father, written from Paris when he was twenty-two, describing how he played at the invitation of the Duchesse de Bourbon, in a room so cold that his fingers were numb, on a piano that wasn't even in tune, while the Duchess and her boy friends sat around and had a drawing lesson, completely ignoring him. I think my unknown friend is confusing the people who supported the composers with the people who supported their music. The Duchess may have paid Mozart—as a matter of strict fact, she didn't; the honor of playing for her was supposed to be enough—but it wasn't her presence that made Mozart's *Paris* symphony a success. The audience that heard Beethoven's Ninth symphony and pronounced it great wasn't composed exclusively of kings and counts and electors and dukes. It was composed of people very much like you and me. As a matter of fact, there was rather a scandal at that first performance, because the public gave Beethoven more rounds of applause than they gave the king. It is never the patrons or the critics that make a piece of music live from one generation to another; it is the barbarian public. If Beethoven still lives, he does so partly because the crew of a merchantman still likes to hear his Fifth symphony played from phonograph records, because a man driving to a factory or an office likes to tune his car radio to a morning symphony program. Don't forget that. Lincoln's remarks about fooling the people hold good just as much in the field of music as in the field of politics.

Furthermore, I think my correspondent forgets how little time we've had. Read LeGrand Cannon's novel, *Look to the Mountain.* It is the story of two young people who set up housekeeping in New Hampshire in the seventeen-seventies. They needed a new house, so the boy cut down trees, shaped the logs, and built it with his own hands. That was the only way to get a house. They needed land on which to grow things, so he cut down more trees and pulled the stumps. That was the only way to get a field. Most of the Indians were gone, but they were still a threat. The two told the time of day by looking at the sun. They kept track of time by cutting notches in a log. If they forgot to cut the notches, they lost count. It might be Sunday or Wednesday. When they needed meat, the boy went out and shot it.

Yet the year they moved into their log cabin, Bach had been long dead. Haydn had yet to write *The Seasons,* and Mozart's opera *La Finta Giardiniera* had just been produced in Munich. What did they know of Haydn or Mozart? They had barely heard of Boston!

Then consider the fact that up to the middle of the nineteenth century there were thousands—hundreds of thousands—of Americans, living under those same conditions. To parallel that stage of national culture in Europe, you'd have to go back nearly a thousand years. I think we have done not so badly.

Not that I would wish to abolish my pessimistic correspondent. On the contrary, I think that he and those who think as he does perform a highly salutary service. So long as a certain umber of persons are vociferously dissatisfied with their country's progress in the arts, that country is likely to progress. Once a nation is content to rest on its laurels, you may be pretty sure that the laurels are going to fade. Consider what happened to Germany during the past half century or so. Of course, her gradual decline in musical importance is partly explained by the fact that after 1870 she became so increasingly preoccupied with military prowess that her people had less and less time for the arts. But I think there is another reason. For so many years the world had agreed that Germany was the supreme music-loving and music-producing nation that she finally agreed that that was so. If a German composed it, and a German orchestra or opera house performed it, it was, *ipso facto,* good. With what result? Nothing written since 1914 by Germany's last great composer, Richard Strauss, has had the breath of life in it. Such composers of any importance as she has produced within the past two decades, men such as Kurt Weill, Jaromir Weinberger, Paul Hindemith, Arnold Schönberg, are refugees here.

But even before the war, in the early thirties, Germany—and Austria, too—were showing signs of complacency. I have heard some of the music festivals in Munich and Salzburg, and they were first-rate. The Vienna Orchestra was a good one, one of which no large American city would be ashamed. But *only* that. It wasn't a bit better than any major American orchestra. The performances of opera were excellent, just as good as some that the Metropolitan puts on in New York. But no better. For years our best performances of music have been fully equal to those of Germany; and I'm not sure that our average hasn't been better. But, with that curious inferiority complex that has so long haunted us in the arts, we've gone along assuming that of course we couldn't possibly measure up to the standards of Germany and the rest of Europe.

And what of the audience? Too many people will point out that we hear more jazz over the radio than any other kind of music; that the night clubs play nothing but jazz, jazz, jazz. And what do you think is the staple musical fare on the European radio? What do you think the night clubs in

London and Paris and Rome play—Brahms' *German Requiem?* If we hear a lot of jazz here, it's for the same reason that they hear a lot of jazz there, the reason being that the audience for the lightest kind of music is, and always has been, infinitely larger than the audience for the best, in this or any other country. We tend much too much to assume, as my correspondent does, that artistically speaking, we are all barbarians, and that every other country is a nation of art lovers.

To refer to another branch of art for a minute, we hear much of the brave days of Good Queen Bess, when all London flocked to the Globe Theater to see Shakespeare's plays. What we *don't* hear so much about is that a couple of blocks beyond the Globe Theater there was another structure, exactly like it in design and seating capacity, called the Bear Garden, to which those Londoners who didn't care for Shakespeare could go and watch a fight to the finish between a bear and a pack of hunting dogs.

There have always been bear gardens, and perhaps there always will be. But we don't have to assume that they are *all* that we possess. I think it's about time that instead of moaning about our lack of musical taste, we take a little time to look around us and try to realize how astonishingly our musical taste has grown during the past quarter of a century. Two things have contributed to that growth, the automobile and the radio. Symphonic music has traditionally been a strictly urban affair. A symphony orchestra is composed of people who must live near one another, so that they can meet to rehearse as well as to perform. And audiences have generally been composed largely of city dwellers, because, as a group, they were the only people who could conveniently attend the concerts. The automobile has developed an immensely larger audience by making it possible for people to travel twenty, thirty, or even forty miles to hear a concert.

Then radio came, and increased the audience still further, because it did away with the necessity for actual physical presence at a concert. That meant that people living far in the country could hear a symphony orchestra hundreds or even thousands of miles away.

How large is the concert audience today? I think it is fair to say that it's at least the audience that listens to the Sunday afternoon broadcasts of the New York Philharmonic-Symphony. That audience numbers about ten million in the United States, with another million or so in Canada. Ten million. That's about seven per cent of our total population. If Beethoven could have counted on being heard by seven per cent of the total population of Austria, he would have thought he was in Heaven.

Nor is it a barbarian audience. It is young, if you like—not in years but in listening experience. It is unsophisticated and, to a certain degree, ignorant. It certainly does enjoy a lot of bad music, but it also has a pretty keen ear for good music. It is partly to blame for the comparative neglect of American composers because it lacks confidence in its own taste; it is too timid, and, as yet, too inert, to make its wishes known. But all that will pass.

Nor do I quite agree that America has never produced anything better than third-rate musicians. It is true that we have not as yet produced a Bach, a Beethoven, a Wagner, or a Debussy. It is also true that even Europe produced only one of each. But our great composers are on the way. They are not going to sound like Bach or Beethoven or Wagner or Debussy. They are going to sound like themselves, and so listeners such as my correspondent won't recognize them for a while. But they are on the threshold, because they have, at last, the thing, the only thing, that in any country produces great composers. They have an audience.

INDEX

INDEX